Natural Attachments

Natural Attachments

The Domestication of American Environmentalism, 1920–1970

POLLYANNA RHEE

The University of Chicago Press
Chicago and London

The University of Chicago Press, Chicago 60637
The University of Chicago Press, Ltd., London
© 2025 by The University of Chicago
All rights reserved. No part of this book may be used or reproduced in any manner whatsoever without written permission, except in the case of brief quotations in critical articles and reviews. For more information, contact the University of Chicago Press, 1427 E. 60th St., Chicago, IL 60637.
Published 2025
Printed in the United States of America

34 33 32 31 30 29 28 27 26 25   1 2 3 4 5

ISBN-13: 978-0-226-84061-1 (cloth)
ISBN-13: 978-0-226-84063-5 (paper)
ISBN-13: 978-0-226-84062-8 (e-book)
DOI: https://doi.org/10.7208/chicago/9780226840628.001.0001

Library of Congress Cataloging-in-Publication Data
Names: Rhee, Pollyanna, author.
Title: Natural attachments : the domestication of American environmentalism, 1920–1970 / Pollyanna Rhee.
Description: Chicago : The University of Chicago Press, 2025. | Includes bibliographical references and index.
Identifiers: LCCN 2024049887 | ISBN 9780226840611 (cloth) | ISBN 9780226840635 (paperback) | ISBN 9780226840628 (ebook)
Subjects: LCSH: Environmentalism—California—Santa Barbara—History. | Home ownership—Environmental aspects—California—Santa Barbara. | Urban ecology (Sociology)—California—Santa Barbara. | Oil spills—California—Santa Barbara Channel. | Santa Barbara (Calif.)—Environmental conditions.
Classification: LCC GE198.C2 R54 2025 | DDC 304.209794/91—dc23/eng/20241227
LC record available at https://lccn.loc.gov/2024049887

♾ This paper meets the requirements of ANSI/NISO Z39.48-1992 (Permanence of Paper).

For my parents,
Joung-Kil and Yeon-Hee Rhee,
고맙고 사랑해요

Contents

Introduction: What Is It about Santa Barbara? 1
  1 A New Order of American 17
  2 Education, Not Legislation 43
  3 To Cultivate and Protect 76
  4 Boundary Problems 101
  5 The Worst Place 128
Conclusion: The Ends of Environmentalism 160

Acknowledgments 167
Notes 171
Index 207

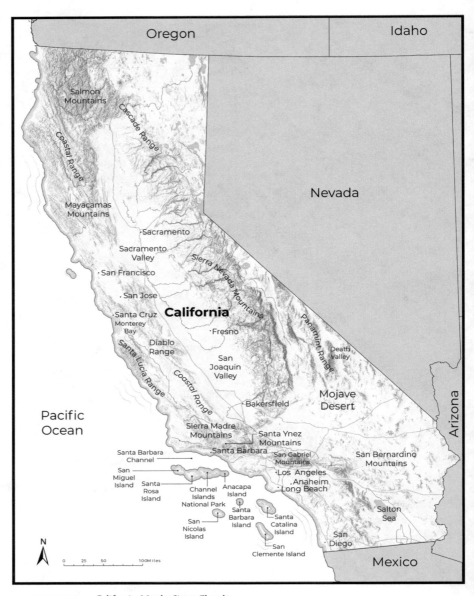

FIGURE I.1. California. Map by Sierra Chmela.

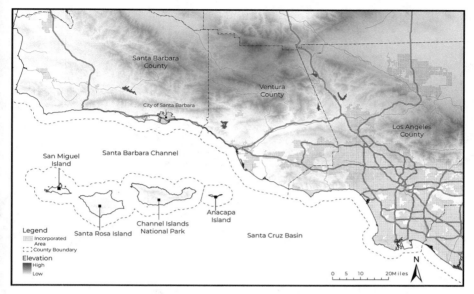

FIGURE 1.2. Santa Barbara County and the greater region. Map by Sierra Chmela.

INTRODUCTION

What Is It about Santa Barbara?

The cover of the *Sierra Club Bulletin*'s March 1969 issue contains two black-and-white photographs, one arranged above the other, against a white background (Figure I.3). The bottom photograph, a long rectangle, depicts a black shape of a bird against a grainy background. At a passing glance, one may simply register a flat silhouette, but a more sustained inspection reveals a lifeless three-dimensional figure with contours of wings and feathers against sandy ground. Above this image and offset from the cover's edge, a square photograph shows an offshore oil platform with water roiling on one side. Apart from the issue's title and date, the cover contains no text, and the photographs do not reveal any contextual information. Nevertheless, readers at the time would have had no trouble identifying the place and event.

Beyond the photographs' frame, horrified residents of Santa Barbara, Montecito, Goleta, and other nearby communities viewed the oil spill that began on January 28, 1969, three miles offshore and displayed wordlessly on the *Sierra Club Bulletin*, as an assault and betrayal of the life they made in this place famed for its natural beauty. Those sentiments and images spread far afield, bringing instant international attention to the region. The aftermath catalyzed environmental action. The Santa Barbara oil spill is often referenced in stories of the founding of the Environmental Protection Agency and the first Earth Day in 1970.[1] Widely circulated photographs of scenic beaches and wildlife drenched in oil contrasted sharply with the qualities and comforts local citizens assumed as one of the major benefits of making a home in the area. The newsworthiness of the event made the oil spill seem exceptional. In a certain light, it was. Until the Exxon Valdez disaster in Prince William Sound, Alaska, in March 1989, the blowout in the Santa Barbara Channel was the largest oil spill in US history. Yet oil spills occur regularly around the

FIGURE 1.3. Cover of the *Sierra Club Bulletin*, March 1969. Courtesy of the Sierra Club.

world.[2] Attention directed toward Santa Barbara had as much to do with its distinctive and desirable surroundings and affluent population as the blowout's scale. If a beautiful place with well-to-do inhabitants experienced that sort of disaster, what prevented similar occurrences in less remarkable locales? Or environmental disasters from happening again in the same place? The spill's recognizability testified to its resonance and the uncomfortable questions it raised. This disaster arrived too close to home.

How Santa Barbara came to attract enough horrified sympathy to usher in an international environmental reckoning is a story of a heralded location and its inhabitants' efforts to maintain and champion their surroundings. Over the course of the twentieth century, the city's residents constructed a version of paradise motored by an aspiration to create an urban built environment that aligned seamlessly with its remarkable natural surroundings. For several decades prior to the oil spill, Santa Barbara's interventions in the local landscape became a national template for an environmentalism centered on the desires of the propertied. In 1931, Pearl Chase, a prominent civic leader, made the goal explicit. Although she noted the city's work was "never finished," the proof of success was visible in the harmony between natural setting and man-made structures.[3] The ability to mold a place into an aesthetically pleasing form, perhaps most notably evidenced in the city's uniform Spanish Colonial Revival style architecture of its commercial and public structures, was more than an innocuous project of beautification. It underscores the degree to which a community of affluent homeowners wielded influence to serve their interests.[4] The results have drawn people, as residents and tourists, for over a century, lured by the "Mediterranean climate, beautiful beaches, scenic views and open space" that "make the coastal plateau a highly desirable place to live."[5] Sheltering these conditions took on considerable significance over time. Legal and perceived belonging and possession of land in and around Santa Barbara shaped expectations of a type of life recklessly violated by the oil spill. Ownership connoted improvement, investment, and worth. The propertied required protection.

This book argues that modern American environmentalism grew out of the political and social concerns of affluent citizens over the course of the twentieth century to make it a resonant and durable movement. The pages that follow examine how Santa Barbara served as a laboratory for negotiating and enhancing the relationship between the built and natural environments in the twentieth-century United States. This negotiation fundamentally shaped the direction of American environmentalism as well as its successes, limitations, and failures. The region's natural surroundings provided a convenient and powerful justification for the activities and standpoints of its affluent residents. This is an understandable concern. Who could lodge a serious complaint about placing the environment at the center of an urban design vision? By situating ideas about home and homeownership at the center, the book traces the origins of an environmentalism shaped by a political and social culture of homeownership.[6] Interventions through urban design, domestic architecture, and plant cultivation buttressed links between labor, cultural and economic investment, and land ownership. The work of transforming this exceptional natural space into a comfortable place of residence conferred privileges. What the book describes as ownership environmentalism acknowledges efforts to create this and similar settlements as especially deserving of protection. Ownership not only conferred title to possess land but also demarcated the boundaries of environmental concern to those with an acknowledged hand in contributing to its improvement. Features that register as typical to modern environmentalism, such as quality of life issues around open space and the rise of suburban sprawl, hold here and are expanded upon. Ownership environmentalism provided an ideological and material center—the home—and established a metric to evaluate who deserved access to environmental quality. After the work involved in creating ideal domestic conditions, appeals to environmental considerations served as crucial rhetorical weapons for homeowners in their arsenal of protection.

Focusing on Santa Barbara in the decades preceding the oil spill brings into relief the processes that elevated the home as a central influence on modern environmentalism. The interests of homeowners at once established and justified Santa Barbara's spatial organization and its social order. Property- and homeowners, business owners' voluntary organizations, and local political leaders endorsed the transformation of the urban landscape in apparent alignment with the region's natural surroundings. Economic and social incentives, including widespread publicity about Santa Barbara's aesthetic charms, attracted these individuals, and they assumed their interests spoke to those of the community. An interlocking set of commitments leaned on ideas of nature and natural beauty to rationalize interventions in the urban fabric and conveniently stepped aside questions about who made those claims and how their individual interests stood to gain.[7] The ability to fashion a place into an aesthetically pleasing form was more than an innocuous project of beautification. It underscores the degree to which a community of affluent homeowners stabilized community norms and established a collective identity that benefited their claims to agency and possession.[8] Santa Barbara's natural and built surroundings provided powerful justification for the activities and standpoints of its affluent residents.

In basic terms, environmentalism is a movement and an outlook that demands that humans place priority on the quality of the nonhuman world, including landscapes of all types, wildlife, other species, and bodies of water, when weighing their activities. Out of this general definition comes myriad qualifications, critiques, and competing interpretations. There are legal and regulatory explications; understandings based in social movements, biodiversity, and wilderness; and quotidian pledges that involve individual efforts to recycle, reduce waste, and use greener products.[9] Environmentalism very quickly becomes what writer and artist Jenny Price calls a "grab-bag" or even what historian Keith Woodhouse describes as a movement lacking a central idea.[10] This can be a source of the movement's power. Regardless, such a broad understanding risks diffusing environmentalism to the extent that if it is a catch-all for everything from protecting wilderness and buying sustainable products to reining in the excesses that come with economic growth and industrialization, it loses significance. There is another, more radical way of looking at environmentalism.[11] It is to declare that, ultimately, environmentalism's ambitions are not just a scattered set of interests regarding environmental quality or a movement placing a misguided priority on wilderness over human economic and social needs but an imperative to transform the world. Refusing to define human relationships with nature and other species by utility, domination, consumption, or entertainment takes seriously not just the survival of all but their flourishing.

This book concentrates on a more ambivalent, perhaps more widespread, and arguably less overtly combative environmentalism, one oriented to different objectives. Ownership environmentalism regards the environment not only as an end but as a means to fulfill social goals and claim authority. Nature might have independent value or seem prepolitical, but it can be weaponized to abet social exclusions and enforce community norms. Rather than historicizing environmental changes or interactions between humans and other species, examining the historical emergence of environmentalism requires looking squarely at human priorities and politics, ideas and actions. Beginning in the early twentieth century, individuals in Santa Barbara shaped environmentalism as a movement animated by conditions close to home as much as the conservation of natural resources and wilderness. This environmentalism helped maintain and regulate social stratifications. Instead of a challenge to property owners, environmentalism provided a bulwark against the encroachment of forces that would ruin one's immediate surroundings. As a result, homeowners formed one of environmentalism's major constituencies. Maintaining the economic value of single-family homes found a useful accomplice in appeals to environmental quality. The physical site of the home; ideas of localism, belonging, and domesticity; and a commitment to the environment provided an ideal cover to avoid scrutiny of resulting political attitudes and their consequences.

Taking the home, local environments, and ties to them seriously provide new intellectual and cultural interpretations of the rise of environmental awareness and action in an era when concerns about the environment, from pollution to suburbanization, became a common feature of everyday life. In a more general cultural register, ownership environmentalism lifts out the habits and priorities or even the "mental universe," to use Robert Darnton's phrase in his work on French peasants, of a local elite.[12] The home might seem a curious place to situate a narrative about the rise of American environmentalism. Nevertheless, within this ostensible modesty, described by historian Richard White as "so ubiquitous and seemingly so bland that it can vanish while in plain sight," is vast cultural power.[13] The sentiments attached to home created useful and ultimately illusory boundaries between the domestic realm and the workplace, commercial life, and foreign locales.[14] Literary scholar Amy Kaplan notes that though home is often set in opposition to the foreign, domesticity figures as part of a project of "conquering and taking the wild, the natural, and the alien."[15] Elevating domesticity as a value while separating the home from locations external to it allowed the former to register subtly, dissolve contradictions, and create tacit community norms. Exploring questions such as why constructing a particular image of place in the urban fabric took on such importance, how and why residents believed the resultant built environment reflected the character of its inhabitants, and why the effort expended on protecting the result took on existential stakes are central to elucidating the culture of ownership environmentalism.

This understanding of environmentalism became a central attribute of residents' conceptions of urban and social order, shaping expectations of place and society. Focusing on the home as an integral component of environmentalism's development is vital to understanding the larger dynamics of modern environmental politics.[16] Having a home provided legitimacy to claims on environmental quality. This emphasis means looking toward the formation of everyday political sensibilities and how, counterintuitively, the home came to connote a realm external to politics.[17] Yet advocates for homeownership in the 1920s linked the home to national power. "The greatest defense of any nation," contended Mrs. John D. Sherman, chair of applied education for the General Federation of Women's Clubs in 1925, "lies in the homes.... There was never a great land yet in any period of history or in any quarter of the world where its homes were not its chief strength."[18] Similarly, housing advocate John Ihlder argued the home represented "our present security and order and our hopes for the future."[19] The work of encouraging business owners to choose building facade designs that conformed to the surrounding architecture and residents to purchase or build single-family homes helped establish an environmentalism invested in maintaining a status quo for mostly middle- and upper-middle-class and educated white Americans. Figures that may seem minor in the history of environmentalism built constituencies that played a pivotal role in shaping the horizons of environmental politics. They achieved this through the ostensibly unobjectionable language of protecting community and the domestic realm. Individual freedoms associated with property ownership found comity with values associated with traditional community bonds. This political formation aimed at maintaining a status quo, protecting the realms, and taking seriously the grievances of the privileged.[20]

In lieu of providing an explicit definition of environmentalism, historians tend to narrative its origins.[21] This approach testifies in part to the diversity of values and interests attached to the term over time.[22] The general time line is familiar. Modern environmentalism's rise came about after 1945, "born of prosperity" and the consequences of atomic energy, chemical revolutions, ecological knowledge, industrial pollution, and the destruction of formerly wild lands to make way for burgeoning suburbs.[23] Created in cities and suburbs as much as in the wilderness, narratives of modern environmentalism's emergence have most often been portrayed by historians following Samuel Hays as rooted in "the vast social changes that took place in the United States after World War II."[24] While Hays acknowledges that some aspects of environmental concern began before the war, he argues that they became a "widely shared social phenomena" and the "forefront of public life" with the rapid growth of outdoor recreation, attempts to manage pollution, and recognition of the nuclear threat. Although he offers 1945 as "a convenient dividing line between the old and new values," Hays nonetheless sees such activity as "hardly extensive" before World War II. In contrast, after the war, the environment constituted "a major public concern." People witnessed the destruction of nature to make way for highways, infrastructure, and homes and experienced living in these ill-defined spaces between cities and wilderness. To be sure, after World War II, new ways of living featuring novel goods, services, and surroundings for a significant number of Americans prompted reflections of their conditions and potential consequences. Many Americans no longer had the willingness to accept pollution and spoiled land as the price for progress.[25] Nevertheless, scholars acknowledge the link between modern environmentalism and the earlier conservation movement but spend less time articulating the connections between them and the transition from one to another. Historians have pointed out that the rise of environmentalism distinguished itself from conservation through its deemphasis on the state and scientific experts, the rise in fears of pollution in relationship to maintaining existing green spaces and wilderness, and the widespread embrace of environmental quality.[26] Those same attributes are the source of continuities.[27]

Shifting the scale to the home clarifies what conservationism and environmentalism have in common. The move from conservation to environmentalism is evident in the changing emphasis from "efficient development and the use of material resources" including water, forests, and soils, which "gave way to environment after World War II amid a rising interest in the quality of life beyond efficiency in production." This rendering of environmentalism's rise, which historians have "long fallen back on," leaves the path from conservation to environmentalism untrodden.[28] In seeking to elucidate this process, this book begins with altering the chronology to start in the years after World War I rather than after 1945, not only to argue for the widespread support for environmental quality in that period but also to offer an explanation for the transition from conservation to modern environmentalism.[29] Additionally, modifying the time frame and perspective connects the emergence of environmentalism to national projects of territorial expansion, Indigenous displacement, and racial segregation. Providing this account means reading textual and visual sources on homeownership, do-it-yourself garden projects, and civic beautification schemes and bringing them into the same frame as standard sources in the history of environmental politics. The abundance of sources testifies to the measure of regard for these activities as they occurred. This material makes visible the architectural, cultural, and political context in which environmentalism was forged, contested, and eventually popularized. And much of the activity happened in the home.

Focusing on property and homeownership, both legal and perceived, provides a bridge between the chronological divide. Starting in the 1920s, civic organizations championed a corrective aesthetic uniformity across Santa Barbara as a means of delineating and policing community norms and spatial boundaries. Outwardly modest interventions such as beautification projects and encouraging homeownership worked as an unnoticed yet decisive means to reflect and reshape society and shrouded vast social ambitions. In a period when the state at local and national levels began to encourage widespread homeownership while private developers increasingly began creating neighborhoods covered by racially restrictive covenants, environmental language helped mask ethnic, racial, environmental, and class tensions and represented the built environment as rooted in immutable natural surroundings rather than the result of the deliberate choices of the powerful few.[30] As Santa Barbara embraced elements of the Spanish past in its civic and commercial architecture, Carey McWilliams observed in 1946 that the city's residents "firmly believe, of course, that the Spanish past is dead, extinct, vanished. In their thinking, the Mexicans living in Santa Barbara have no connection with this past. They just happen to be living in Santa Barbara."[31] Embracing and promoting the value of the environment as a neutral, "natural," and unchanging metric for urban development erased racial and social inequalities.

Telling the story of ownership environmentalism's rise requires attending to transformations in the built environment at multiple scales from domestic spaces and yards to wide swaths of Southern California beaches. Rather than centering the narrative in conservation organizations, federal government officials, or scientists, this book examines how private citizens shaped environmental sentiments and actions throughout the twentieth century chiefly through interventions in the built environment. Santa Barbara women, for example, mobilized traditional ideas about gender and homemaking to advance their agendas instead of advocating for broader political, economic, and social rights. By claiming the home as the first environment that needed care and attention, they facilitated the creation of small-scale social solidarities that ostensibly encouraged habits of associational life and community.[32] Home offered both material and psychic benefits and a core ideology. It reflected the character of its inhabitants.

While not jettisoning that narrative of the rise of affluence and suburbanization to explain environmentalism's rise, this book highlights environmentalism's imbrication with broader political and social developments. Critics commonly observe that environmental concerns seem distinct from seemingly more pressing economic or political issues. Environmentalism is a sort of shibboleth and only relevant once issues of greater relevance are resolved.[33] Yet others, following Santa Barbara resident and historian Roderick Nash, have argued that environmentalism is the "ethical extension of liberalism" and therefore necessary to grappling with the destructive impulses of modern society.[34] In the face of environmental ills, a segment of society with resources and power created boundaries to separate themselves from these ills while guarding their comforts, including a high-quality environment. Although a critique of modern society underlies environmentalism, responses to it can exacerbate rather than ameliorate existing conditions.

The ease of compatibility with the interests of the well-to-do explains why mainstream environmentalism has at times been regarded as a hinderance to or even an opponent of environmental justice efforts.[35] When treated as a commitment integral to broader developments in the twentieth century, environmentalism shows itself not merely as a supplementary concern but rather as central to the core of liberal society. Defending environmental quality became a powerful mechanism for enacting control over land and citizens while also safeguarding individualistic understandings of freedom attached to homeownership. Tracing the self-fashioning of an urban community as an exemplar of environmental ease and living in harmony with nature puts into relief the domestication central to environmentalism's wide acceptance as well as its contradictions, instrumentalizations, and diffuse obligations.[36]

The pages that follow inquire into the commitments of an environmentalism that operates within and therefore ultimately supports the advantages of homeownership and the liberal democratic state more generally. Exploring environmentalism's content to investigate who in the movement has cultural and political authority, how those with authority defined its boundaries of community, what virtues were praised, and what political choices were neutralized as natural helps explain its effectiveness. These questions show environmentalism to be a complex and at times contradictory movement with an underlying dedication to protecting a status quo, maintaining and replicating social hierarchies, or sidestepping politics altogether. Orientations toward the state here exhibit qualities of pragmatic opportunism or a relationship of convenience that summoned state powers to protect individual interests. Whether citizens reinforced or challenged the state's prerogatives hinged upon immediate circumstances. Organizations such as Better Homes in America stressed private initiative but worked alongside government officials to encourage homeownership in the 1920s. Neighborhood associations appealed to the state to enforce police powers but also protested local governments when they believed real estate developers threatened their access to open space and low density. In the aftermath of the 1969 oil spill, residents appealed to close contacts at high levels of government but often found themselves disappointed compared to the power of the oil industry. Calls for comprehensive federal environmental protections or transitioning away from fossil fuel consumption took less precedence than government responsiveness to their concerns. Placing the home and homeownership at the center clarifies the divisions and overlaps between private citizens and the state regarding environmental issues. Despite claims that their motivations were not political, residents' activities cut across typical understandings of the role of the state in the environmental movement.

Turning to Santa Barbara and its environs is a means to address a series of broader issues about environmentalism's social priorities. Moving away from common assumptions of environmentalism's assumed political affinities clears a path toward understanding the interests that motivated individuals, especially affluent whites, to embrace environmental quality as a recognizable good.[37] This testifies to the ability of environmental concerns to harmonize with the lives and existing commitments of a circumscribed group of residents. Despite understandable wariness toward this sort of environmentalism, framing the movement as simply a product of affluence betrays a narrow vision. Dismissing environmentalism out of hand ignores its wide general popularity and denies its potential for more forceful action across the globe. This is not to refute very real criticisms of what Indian historian Ramachandra Guha deems as "uniquely American" understandings of the environment.[38] Americans, Guha observes, "can simultaneously enjoy the material benefits of an expanding economy and the aesthetic benefits of unspoiled nature." This results in a contradictory situation where wilderness and civilization coexist in an "internally coherent whole." The convenient avoidance of any conflict between modernity and nature leads to Guha's quip that "it is no accident that Star Wars technology and deep ecology both find their fullest expression in that leading sector of Western civilization, California." But this environmentalism born of prosperity of postindustrial society arose in tandem with what literary scholar Rob Nixon calls the "environmentalism of the poor."[39] Those whom Nixon describes as "resource insurrectionists" assert their right to recognition and escaping the negative effects of resource extraction, pollution, and threats to human health. This environmentalism demonstrates that who makes demands matters as much as their content and reorients the movement away from a more parochial outlook.

Presented as a collection of shared expectations, reactions, and dispositions rather than demands for justice or an ongoing critique of the normative assumptions about a society, environmentalism can be a politically useful set of maxims and source of psychic comfort. Envisioning environmentalists' central interests as divorced from the affairs that occupy the average American has become a touchstone for those who believe caring for the environment means, at the very least, tacit dismissal of economic health and social justice. Even as Americans become increasingly aware and anxious about climate change, "the environment" retains vague connotations of wilderness and distance from pressing human matters. The term is open to charges about a lack of specificity in its aims.[40] Environmentalism can be shrugged off as an ancillary concern or a small component of the larger crisis of climate change. But that dismissal fails to acknowledge its fundamental importance of maintaining environmental quality to animate the politics of middle-class and affluent white Americans.[41] The absence of specific meaning becomes a source of power.

Distressing environmental events are increasingly unavoidable even in Santa Barbara. On December 4, 2017, in the foothills near Thomas Aquinas College in Santa Paula, about fifteen miles east of the coastal city of Ventura in Southern California, high winds caused two Southern California Edison power lines to slap together and ignited a fire.[42] The terrain marked with steep slopes and canyons covered with thick, dry brush made it difficult for firefighters to access the land. Abetted by the winds, the Thomas fire burned for over a month throughout Ventura and Santa Barbara Counties, becoming California's largest wildfire on record.[43] The fire burned 282,000 acres and destroyed more than three thousand structures. But the actual fire—which has slipped in rankings to be the tenth-largest fire in California as of 2024—formed only one part of the story.

Assisted by heavy rains, fire crews completely controlled the fire in early January. But in addition to bringing relief, the rain turned into a liability. In the early morning hours of January 8, a channel of tropical moisture dubbed the "Pineapple Express" poured half an inch of rain onto Santa Barbara County in five minutes. The burned landscape, devoid of vegetation and root systems that held soil in place, repelled rather than absorbed the rain, causing multiple debris flows in the hills above Montecito, a small, upscale community adjacent to Santa Barbara known for its celebrity inhabitants. A hydrologist with the US Geological Survey described the hills as consisting "almost exclusively" of large rocks or fine, sandy dirt. This combination created a "moving dam" during the heavy rains. Propelled by gravity, large boulders that were part of this dam allowed the water to increase in height and force instead of dispersing its energy. The mudslides added at least twenty-one casualties and destroyed more than one hundred homes.[44]

In the immediate aftermath, local officials decided to "delay and retool" their efforts to promote the region's tourism. After all, asked a *Los Angeles Times* reporter, "how do you encourage tourists to shop, relax in the sun and sip wine after a tragic disaster that killed twenty-one people and destroyed hundreds of homes?"[45] Responding to this question with sensitivity was no trivial task for a region with a $126 billion tourism industry. The owner of the Hitching Post II, a restaurant in Buellton forty-five miles from Santa Barbara that gained wide prominence by its inclusion in Alexander Payne's 2004 film, *Sideways*, quipped that "it's incredible how close you can be to a disaster and still have paradise." Another restaurant owner suggested that local celebrity residents, such as Oprah or Ellen DeGeneres, use their influence to publicize the region's outstanding features.

Before the Thomas fire reached its full force, Charles McCaleb, a resident of Montecito, told a reporter that he believed that the Tea fire a decade earlier, which destroyed 210 homes in Santa Barbara County, had presented a greater threat. Although he and his wife left their home during the voluntary evacuation period, he confessed that the effects from falling ash on their koi pond caused their greatest worries.[46] Despite the proximity to life-threatening hazards, blithe comments about koi ponds, mobilizing celebrity neighbors, and the uncomfortable proximity between paradise and disaster underscore these individuals' distinctive privileges even in the face of life-threatening risks. The convergence of disaster and paradise exposes two types of human-caused environmental change in their mutual creation: urban settlements, including the construction of paradisiacal homes and cities, and fossil fuel–driven climate change.

In 1969, homeowners demanded protection from the oil industry; now they wish to avoid the impacts of climate change while spending less time thinking about how their lives are made possible by the sources of anthropogenic climate change. The story presented in these pages asserts that residents of Santa Barbara should be seen less for their distinctions but rather for what they represent about the environmental, political, and cultural priorities of American society over the past century. Climate change's disruptive consequences reached their homes and affected their lives, yet the region's environmental features retain their attractions.

Acknowledged deadly threats looming in proximity had a counterweight in individual senses of security in coastal Southern California's lush environs. Today, California is the most populous and most ethnically diverse state in the nation. But widely known images of California over the past century of beaches, Spanish Colonial Revival architecture, counterculture groups, or Hollywood have emphasized homogeneous perceptions of the state. Santa Barbara was far from the only city that harnessed nostalgic visions to construct a modern landscape.[47] Shaping landscapes and homes as intrinsic or natural to a place testifies less to its inherent compatibility with nature than to the cultural power of a select group of residents who saw evidence of an ideal future in the past and in nature. Their activities and objectives should encourage individuals to look critically at environmentalism's contours and inquire into its social commitments.

Pointing out Santa Barbara's outsized influence in the history of modern environmentalism represents only one argument for looking closely at the city. Decades before the oil spill, Santa Barbara provided a home for numerous individuals prominent in environmental politics and social thought. The ecologist Frederic Clements, famed for his studies of the plains and prairies, made Santa Barbara his home and died in the city in 1945. Garrett Hardin, notorious for his views on the tragedy of the commons, resided in the city, as did the environmental historian and coauthor of the "Santa Barbara Declaration of Environmental Rights," Roderick Nash. Ordering an argument around a local case study of small city (Santa Barbara could be a version of Darnton's description of eighteenth-century Montpellier: "a fairly prosperous and progressive city of the second rank") may seem peculiar or even unpromising.[48] Local histories often encounter charges that they are unable to provide the sophisticated and substantive insights of national, transnational, or imperial analyses.[49] Yet to dismiss local concerns as parochial fundamentally misunderstands the capacity and influence they can have far outside its boundaries.

Rather than homing in on particularities of place to bolster familiar narratives, a more generative approach consists of putting into relief the work involved in producing those narratives. Instead of presenting a bounded history of region or attempting to account for a locale's intrinsic and unique character, this book highlights the material and conceptual effort required to shore up boundaries in order to present Santa Barbara as distinctive, exclusive, and timeless. Indeed, the popular image and character of Santa Barbara depended less on internal qualities than on ideas and events beyond the city's borders. The city, like all others, is less of an enclave than a result of continual maneuvers to selectively enfold and exclude. This follows geographer Doreen Massey's call to think about places as nets of social relations and localities as provisional and constantly in the process of being made and contested.[50] Santa Barbara, and cities like it, may seem peripheral to major events, but an examination at this scale can better clarify how external events order daily lives and expectations.

Situated one hundred miles northwest of Los Angeles, Santa Barbara had a long-standing reputation as a place insulated from the negative effects of sprawling urban settlements while retaining their cultural and social resources. As a city with a population today of around ninety thousand inhabitants, the allure and reputation of the city outpaces its size. The chapters that follow trace Santa Barbara's evolution from the 1920s, when local and national movements that privileged homeownership and civic beautification, through the post–World War II population explosion of California, culminating in the 1969 oil spill and its aftermath. Exploring these events offers a new way for understanding environmentalism's development.[51] The book is divided into two parts, focusing first on the creation of Santa Barbara as a locale that became an archetype for urban settlements that sought a balance between urban development and resources and natural idyll followed by undertakings to secure those conditions.

The first part of the book traces the mutually constitutive development of Santa Barbara's built environment and its residents' environmental awareness, showing how the seemingly apolitical domestic realm aligned with conceptions of the environment as another domain beyond politics and a neutral arbiter for delineating community norms.[52] The orientation that pursued the construction of an ideal environment for human settlements believed in a balance between humans and nature and coupled community values and environmental quality. This pursuit had both an environmental and nationalist temper. This book opens with a disaster several decades before the oil spill and focuses on the creation of the narrative of renewal and improvement. Chapter 1 begins with an earthquake in June 1925 that helped solidify plans for urban change that had been underway for some years prior. The earthquake provided a convenient origin for a narrative of the city's rebirth as a beacon and precedent for urban design and social cohesion. The event established a parable of a place that had betrayed its environmental gifts through the wrong type of urban development only to find its bearings again in the wake of disaster. This was made evident through the drive to regulate a cacophony of architectural styles simplified to those they saw as honoring the region's history and natural surroundings. This work created a racialized landscape neutralized in the language of nature. Chapter 2 turns attention to the single-family home and the private and state mechanisms that worked in tandem to abet its expansion. Homeownership provided pedagogical lessons in environmental discernment and the development of good character. These lessons were deliberately framed as external to state intervention and located within the private sphere of the home, shoring up boundaries between society and families. This is not to say that the boundaries did not have a measure of porosity. Chapter 3 examines the integration and domestication of various forms of plant life in California that offered vindication for assumptions regarding the mutual constitution of nature, the natural world, and the proper shape of society. Evidence could be seen in the lawns and gardens of private homes as well as trees planted along roads and botanic gardens. Plant life in this stretch of the Pacific coast validated the region as an ideal ecology for plant life globally. In addition to vindicating the environment, the process that brought plants to the region and nurtured their flourishing provided a natural development model of normal growth that could be transferred without qualification to human populations and settlements. The ideal order and form of cities and their inhabitants had a model in the natural surroundings. Plants ultimately informed ideas about human movements across continents and the necessary qualities for a thriving society. Nature in the form of earthquakes, plants, and the family offered insights into the proper form of cities.

The second part of the book looks to the aftermath of the construction of that urban order and efforts to protect the resulting city. Having created this place with a particular historical narrative and belief in its own exceptionalism, the emphasis shifted to protecting its status. Reacting against demographic, economic, and urban change in California after 1945, chapter 4 addresses how residents confronted the negative consequences of sprawl and the state's exploding population that creeped into their city by creating neighborhood associations. Protecting their work and environment, even if it required regulating the population through anti-growth land use policies, led to conflict with various local, state, and federal entities. The growth that marked the decades before 1945 shifted to activity against its continuation. Chapter 5 returns to the 1969 oil spill to grapple with the consequences of fossil fuel extraction, perhaps the most visible marker of modern life, and attempts to reconcile affluence with limits, including questions regarding who those limits would affect and who would be afforded protection from its consequences. Although Santa Barbara, like much of Southern California, in the mid-twentieth century was a bastion for the Republican Party, broad support and activism for environmental causes after the 1969 oil spill show how environmental concerns easily diverged from familiar partisan divisions. Creating boundaries for protection could only go so far and demonstrated the limits of an environmentalism oriented for the benefit of a limited population. Yet the hold on those limits showed their tenacity despite the well-publicized horrors of oil.

The ownership environmentalism described and developed here, centered on maintaining social hierarchies and protecting particular places, opts for protection rather than justice. The figures in this book may not have always identified themselves as environmentalists, but their activities laid the critical groundwork for popular understandings of it and the scope of its commitments. Focusing attention on their actions to protect and improve their surroundings imparted a sense of ownership and entitlement to maintain the environment they helped create. Although this book is primarily set in Santa Barbara, the influence and consequences of the events herein spread far beyond its boundaries and buttressed a widely palatable and far-reaching movement that worked within the boundaries of the normative political order of American society. Homeowners and their attempts to stymie increased housing and density remain potent and demonstrate how environmental concerns can easily, but not necessarily, be wielded toward social exclusion even, or maybe especially, in the most beautiful places.

1

A New Order of American

Around three in the morning on June 29, 1925, Herbert Nunn, Santa Barbara's city manager, awoke to a strong odor of crude oil. Since a refinery stood several miles away, he thought the wind had carried the smell to his house. Unable to fall back asleep, he ventured outside and discovered "no movement in the air whatever."[1] He then went back to bed. About three hours later, at 6:42 a.m., Nunn sat at the edge of his bed when a violent shock threw him back on it. Realizing he had felt an earthquake, Nunn began timing the vibrations while racing outside where his wife and gardener had already gathered. On his count, the first shock lasted eighteen seconds, followed by several six- to eight-second-long stirrings over the next twenty minutes. Nunn's house stood near a cliff edge on the ocean: he monitored the water for signs of a tidal wave but only saw two fishermen in rowboats seemingly unaware of the tribulations occurring on shore. One of the fishermen later told him that they had felt a "slight bump" and saw earth falling in masses from the face of the cliff.[2]

At 7:20 a.m., twenty minutes after he felt the last shock, Nunn took his car into downtown Santa Barbara and attempted to drive up State Street, the main commercial thoroughfare. Debris blocked his path. Undeterred, he steered the car along parallel streets to survey the damage and concluded that only two buildings in the city center, the San Marcos and the Arlington Hotels, needed heavy equipment for cleanup work. Upon reaching city hall, Nunn found that all heads of departments had already arrived and emergency crews with steam shovels, trucks, and cranes were at work clearing rubble.[3] Members of the American Legion organized themselves into a provisional police force to control traffic, prohibit looting, and generally maintain order. Despite the physical damage, Nunn noted admiringly that residents remained "cool and anxious to serve" with "good order and splendid morale."[4] Nunn's

FIGURE 1.1. Aerial view looking north of earthquake damage in downtown Santa Barbara on June 29, 1925. *Telephoto Book of Santa Barbara Earthquake*, published by American Autochrome Co., Chicago, 1925.

retroactive emphasis on order and tranquility contributed to a narrative that framed this natural disaster as something else entirely—a chance for improvement (Figure 1.1).

Sensational headlines about death and destruction in newspapers published across the country would not deter claims to the contrary. Although earthquakes remained unpredictable occurrences, Santa Barbara's example demonstrated that the right attitude would manage its effects or even turn the misfortune into an opportunity. The earthquake provided a clearing to transform a city that had yet to meet its potential. Four months earlier, Edward Lowry, a New York newspaper editor, announced that Santa Barbara, with its population of around twenty-five thousand, was "undoubtedly the most charming city" he had ever visited, a singular combination of commerce, civic pride, leisure, and aesthetic charm.[5] He praised its residents for their care in "architecture that is typical of the region and its history" and their preservation of "things traditionally associated with original Spanish communities." A writer for the *Boston Transcript* noted that the city's charms came from the fact that it lacked "the fever of trade, manufacture, or speculation."[6] Instead, the city had "an air of repose" due to its historic Franciscan mission and "most sightly situation between mountains and the sea." Others expressed an opposing view and found the city had a generic air. One visitor admitted that whenever he went up State Street, he "swore inwardly" to himself because it was no different from "a thousand Main Streets in a thousand American towns."[7] Regrettably, the city's architecture was unequal to its natural surroundings, which "few spots on the earth could match."

Although suggestions for improvement predated the earthquake, nature in the form of a geophysical rupture offered a rationale for narrowing the divide between the remarkable natural environs and unremarkable built environment. Reconstruction demanded rapid action. The famed natural setting bound by ocean and mountains contained inspiration and history to guide the path toward better urban conditions. Residents noted with approval that the earthquake accomplished in "a night what people might have taken fifty years to come to."[8] One well-known local civic leader, Pearl Chase, argued that the earthquake supplied the right circumstances, a blank slate, to enable inhabitants to take an active role in "mastering and shaping its own environment." The city, "justly famous for the treasures with which it has been showered by Nature's lavish hand," now had a chance for human-built renewal as a testament to the talents and social vision of its inhabitants.[9] Moreover, by arguing that the earthquake damaged parts of the city aesthetically incompatible with its surroundings, city leaders, property owners, and business owners found a way to align their economic and political interests in the urban fabric with aesthetic goals. Achieving this synthesis resulted from not only large-scale infrastructural projects or grandly monumental urban designs but also modestly scaled interventions.

Taking advantage of the opportunity provided a claim to possession by improvement. The earthquake contributed to a twofold and ongoing settler project of remaking the city, first as the territory of white Americans, then as an apotheosis of nature, history, and civilization. Tensions between interpretations of the past came to the foreground. The earthquake in June 1925 offered a tidy narrative reorientation to divide past and future. Yet it can also be understood as less of a split than a means of streamlining the arc of local and national development. The effort to define this architecture as genuinely Californian coincided with national anxieties about citizenship, race, and immigration. Throughout the 1920s, events such as the rise of the second Ku Klux Klan and the Johnson-Reed Immigration Act of 1924, which provided a legal basis for ethnic division based on race and set national quotas on immigration, meant that defining a regional architecture with foreign influences as American took on a new significance.[10] In a related policy, the Indian Citizenship Act of 1924 granted citizenship to Native Americans who had previously been exempt from the Fourteenth Amendment.[11] Questions regarding identity, tribal and territorial sovereignty, and assimilation engaged both Native and white individuals as the nation's enfranchised population grew.[12] By attributing the adeptness of Spanish Colonial Revival designs to American designers, critics and architects actively participated in shaping narratives about the roots of the style. Their work not only reinforced a seamless compatibility between the architecture and the environment but also presented the design's origins as distinctly the product of white Americans. Regional specificities marked by references to climatic distinctions and distance from the nation's population centers became integrated within dominant national histories.

Post-earthquake reconstruction as a concerted effort to make community identity visible follows Indigenous philosopher Kyle Powys Whyte's definition of settler colonial societies as those that "seek to permanently settle the territories of indigenous peoples instead of *only* exploiting resources in that territory."[13] These newly arrived societies seek to "inscribe their own homelands over indigenous homelands" to erase any presence of Indigenous peoples. A renewed city after the earthquake supported white Californians' objective to eliminate themselves as settlers and cast themselves as the rightfully indigenous inhabitants of the land. The earthquake provided a natural alibi to processes already in motion. With nature as a stimulus and template, an earthquake's risks and uncertainties turned into an opportunity for residents to demonstrate their cultural intelligence and environmental discernment. By putting past errors in construction into relief, the earthquake offered a necessary corrective while also revealing the essential character of the land and its inhabitants. When mobilized by Santa Barbara's civic leaders and property owners, understandings of environmental suitability rationalized cultural appropriation and territorial entitlement. The improved city validated the existing social order with its defined lines of racial belonging and demarcated the limits of the city's attention to environmental awareness.

The rhetorical and material remaking of Santa Barbara's past less than one hundred years after the takeover of California by the US military evacuated the violence of the eighteenth and nineteenth centuries by successive imperial forces from Spain, Russia, Mexico, and the United States and replaced it with a domesticated civic vision and benign historical memory.[14] This work paved over brutality of Franciscan missionaries, whose activities the writer Carey McWilliams compared to Nazi concentration camps in 1946 as well as relatively moderate actions by the Mexican government that gave legal rights to Indigenous Californians before undergoing erosion under the United States.[15] The Spanish founded the Santa Barbara Presidio, in the city's present-day downtown, in 1782. A mission followed in 1786, one node of a network of military and religious settlements stretching from San Diego to Sonoma built mostly from Indigenous labor.[16] Numbers testify to the bleak scale of extermination of Indigenous Californians in a period of just over a century. In 1769, approximately 310,000 Indians lived in California, yet the 1880 census recorded just 16,277.[17] In 1824, the Chumash, who lived on land in present-day Santa Barbara, rebelled against the Mexican colonists by burning buildings, killing non-Indians, and holding the La Purisma Mission in Lompoc, fifty-five miles from Santa Barbara, for a month.[18] It was this history, incompletely remembered, that became part of Santa Barbara's twentieth-century revival.[19]

Because California was distant and relatively unfamiliar to white Americans after statehood, writers described its enticements to raise its profile among Anglo-Americans from the East Coast and Midwest (Figure 1.2). Writing for *Harper's*, Charles Nordhoff depicted the state as a "New Italy" and extolled the virtues of its climate. Nordhoff's and others' writings set off a wave of tourism and real estate development through the last decades of the nineteenth century.[20] Even in the early years of California statehood, visitors reportedly lodged complaints about the shift to American control and the cultural changes that accompanied it.[21] By 1874, American practicality revealed itself through "broad streets at right angles" with the older fabric "bisected, torn down, and almost totally destroyed," even as some inhabitants protested the changes.[22] The idea of an "A Street or a First Street" in Santa Barbara seemed as "inconsistent as a mathematical computation done in verse" and would negatively transform the place into "Jonesville," leading to the departure of people with taste. Yet embracing generic designs was actually a strategy. Influential individuals assumed that visitors from the East Coast would be happiest if they found Santa Barbara exactly like the towns they had left behind—excepting the climate, consequently leaving "ugliness and utility" in command.[23]

At the turn of the century, observers continued to see the same mundane utility evident in Santa Barbara's urban fabric, but with a renewed appreciation for the past. This was coupled with a belief that California remained in an early stage of its development. In 1905, the architect Elmer Grey declared that when people arrived in California for the first time, they immediately saw the "newness of the country."[24] Settlements consisting solely of tents conjured a place suspended from the normal state of affairs. In California, an "able young clergyman" from the East would be found "applying for work at the packing house of a lemon exchange. A young architect who once had an enviable practice builds up his health as a hired hand on a ranch." Interspersed in these provisional landscapes were "monuments of rare beauty"—namely, the missions. These structures possessed a quality "peculiarly in harmony with

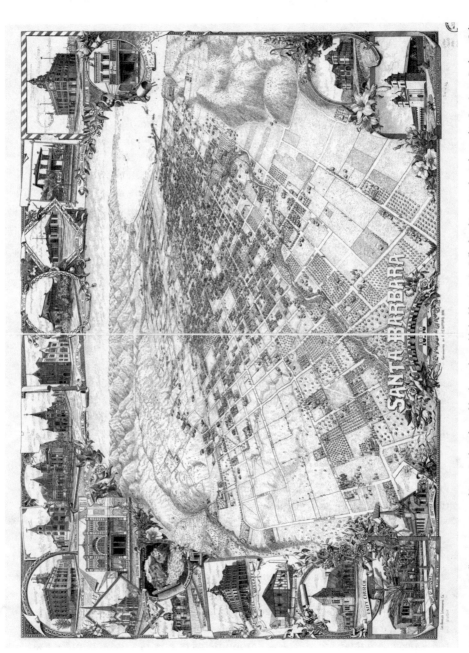

FIGURE 1.2. Bird's-eye-view map of Santa Barbara framed by the city's notable buildings. P. E. Gifford and Los Angeles Lithographic Co., *Santa Barbara, Cali-*

the Western landscape" as a result of their "broad, simple masses, plain wall surfaces, and of low-pitched roofs that do not compete with Nature's own mountain Architecture."[25] These buildings deviated from the norm. California of the early twentieth century was "rampant" with architecture that borrowed mission features, but "not its spirit," to create a "decidedly uninteresting class of buildings" without personality and "of questionable harmlessness."

This architecture's greatest fault was general and not necessarily specific to Southern California: it lacked simplicity and appropriateness. Architects seemed only to want to make their knowledge and education visible by applying architectural ornaments to "places where they do not belong." They disregarded the idea that architecture should align with its surroundings and neglected the benefits of a building assimilating with its surrounding landscape. Assimilation presented an underappreciated virtue. Indeed, culture came out of assimilation and integrated individuals into a "higher life" of a community. One explanation for the lack of absorption into the state's natural features was California's "extreme newness" and dearth of monumental architecture or other signs of an established culture in its buildings. Since "centuries of enlightened human effort" needed to precede the arts, California was still only at the beginning of the road toward artfulness.[26] Moving up the timeline of California's history made this narrative possible.

The image of the Pacific coast as a blank slate for Anglo intervention followed familiar tropes of America's virgin territories, the disappearance of native inhabitants, and a new beginning with the coming of white settlers.[27] In Grey's rendering, the "redskin in years past" emerged from the "brush on the shore of the Pacific to view the panorama of sea and mountain."[28] Instead of settling in that spot, he withdrew "to his inland wigwam," leaving "nothing which contributes to the interest or beauty of the landscape." Waves of European explorers and settlers began rectifying this inauspicious situation with seeds of "potent forces" spreading the word of the "utility and necessity of art in a finished civilization." While occupied with "subduing a continent, in pushing a frontier across the rivers and plains and over the mountains," men disregarded matters of taste and beauty as the province of women.[29] At the start of the twentieth century, Grey believed society stood on "the threshold of a new era in art . . . enriched by the heritage of the past" and bolstered by life of "an age advanced in mechanical development far beyond the wildest dreams of its predecessors." Santa Barbara had the promise to become a "new Riviera," but constructing in this natural "background of the rarest beauty" required sensitivity and learning.[30]

Santa Barbara's development subverted straightforward narratives of uninterrupted and advantageous progress. Cultural and economic development sometimes stood at cross purposes. Even supporters of American control of California could not help but see the city's architectural history as a promising one under the Spanish before descending into mediocrity after statehood in 1850. The Spanish city of Santa Barbara had been "a beautiful town" of only a few thousand with adobes and tree-lined courtyards set in masses of flowers on streets looking out onto the Pacific. But Americans precipitated an unwanted transformation. Brick business houses, "somewhat poisonous-colored tile," wooden structures with false fronts, and "raw and makeshift" streets replaced the simple yet picturesque adobes. This was supposed to be in the name of progress. "Ancient" adobes could not, in the eyes of rational business owners, have any value. They were replaced with "elaborate structures" of brick or "involved" wooden buildings with "Gothic towers and late Etruscan porte-cocheres . . . medieval doorways and James K. Polk piazzas."[31] Despite plans to reconstruct Santa Barbara's storied past before the earthquake, as seen in architect George Washington Smith's 1923 proposal for State Street or the construction of El Paseo by architects James Osborne Craig and Mary Craig that began construction in 1922, critics generally noted a betrayal of Southern California's environmental conditions.

Undergirding this attitude was a belief that each place had a commensurate style of building. Architecture, argued Henry Saylor, an editor at *Architectural Record*, should enliven a location's natural and national characteristics. Buildings provided straightforward visible evidence of how accurately inhabitants understood their relationship to the environment. Certain locations displayed suitable understanding. Saylor reasoned that Venice would not be Venice without canals and palaces; New England was not New England without the "white-painted homestead of shingles or clapboards" with green shutters. Other locations demonstrated an unfortunate lack of discernment. California at the beginning of the twentieth century was in fact an "architectural Babel."[32] If you should take, Saylor asked rhetorically, "a Frenchman, an Italian, a New England Yankee, a Mexican, an Englishman, a Dutchman, a Russian, and a Turk, each with his wife and drop them upon an uninhabited island, what do you suppose the community would look like after a year of building?" "Native-born" Californians, by which he meant Anglo-Americans, were only small children in the late nineteenth century and therefore could not contribute to the environment. So migrants from other parts of the country as well as Japan, China, and Mexico came in what he called a "deluge" to make Southern California their home. But two factors restricted their influence: first, "the string of old Mission buildings," and second, the climate "dictating a house that should provide for a less formal, more outdoor type of living than the settlers had practiced back home," whose buildings suggested the "strong architectural influence of the state of Iowa." Saylor's narrative fused these two factors to impart one fundamental lesson: a modern architecture suitable for California required attending to history and climate. The transformation that followed territorial conquest was part of what truly differentiated white settlers to California from their East Coast counterparts.[33]

For interested parties, the earthquake quickened the process of correcting the building mistakes that followed statehood. Earthquakes, resident Henry Pritchett argued, were not events but rather institutions that offered a framework for the future.[34] Records tracked regular earthquakes in the city and its region since at least 1812, but boosters and commercial interests took pains to emphasize that Santa Barbara—like San Francisco before it—was not actually in a seismic zone.[35] Those who experienced the earthquake on June 29, 1925, might have felt differently. Nevertheless, the earthquake's early morning hour resulted in a small number of deaths—about thirteen killed and several dozen injured—although the city sustained about $10 million in damages. A civil engineer at the University of California, Berkeley, who inspected the damage soon afterward believed the earthquake might have killed several thousand if it had occurred two or three hours later.[36] As news of the earthquake in Santa Barbara, "that glory-spot by the sea," spread, one newspaper claimed that "it seemed that the whole American national stopped to listen, and stopping, forgot trivial things to concentrate upon what could be done to aid those in distress."[37]

Photos of earthquake damage, especially of State Street, ran in newspapers across the United States transmitted by a Telepix system from Los Angeles (Figure 1.3).[38] The images displayed exposed rooms of the Hotel Californian after the wall collapsed and individuals removing debris from the San Marcos on State Street with the caption, "Santa Barbara Immediately Starts Work Removing Traces of Disaster It Suffered."

In contrast to a tranquil vision that Herbert Nunn described, other visitors and residents recounted unfortunate ordeals. The *New York Times* reported ten minutes after the quake that "thousands of persons" were in the streets clad in bathrobes, many refusing to go indoors for fear of collapsing buildings.[39] Pritchett, who was head of the Carnegie Foundation for the Advancement of Teaching and a former president of the Massachusetts Institute of Technology, recalled that his family "made haste" to clothe themselves and run into their back garden.[40] The London-based *Daily Express* reported "scenes of panic" with the shock followed by fire and a flood caused by damaged masonry on the Gibraltar Dam north of the city in the Santa Ynez Mountains, the destruction of the city's Sheffield Reservoir, and broken water

FIGURE 1.3. Earthquake damage on the corner of State Street and De La Guerra Street with the Legion of Honor building on the left and Rexall drugstore in the center. *Telephoto Book of Santa Barbara Earthquake* published by American Autochrome Co., Chicago, 1925.

mains.[41] A Mr. Hollister arrived in Ventura, some twenty-five miles away, and told journalists of the population's "hysterical condition" as women ran into the streets with their most treasured possessions. State Street, he added, was a mass of wreckage. Twenty people in the county jail escaped when the walls crumbled, but despite the swearing in of special police officers, there was no reported looting. The architect Julia Morgan happened to be in the city when the earthquake occurred.[42] She stood on State Street with a packet of drawings and saw white dust coming from a nearby building; this was followed by the tremor, which threw her to the ground. Unable to see through the dust, Morgan crawled on her knees until she felt streetcar tracks. From there, she worked her way to the front of an automobile showroom. After the dust cleared, Morgan returned to her bag and then spent hours among the buildings to see "materials working," describing it a "great practical experience." Ultimately, she claimed that the "greatest menace was from electric wires" and asserted that no matter the expense "all wires in public streets in California should be underground."

In the days afterward, lawn space became a premium commodity as residents shunned interior spaces, since the earthquake was "too recent and fresh in their minds" to risk sleeping under a roof.[43] A reporter found State Street a "ghastly avenue of ruin" with "cornices, walls, and fronts of practically all principal structures shattered."[44] A janitor at the *Santa Barbara Daily News*, Harry Alford, was downtown when the quake began and described that the "twisting of the earth was like a violent storm at sea." The manager of the Arlington Hotel noted that he had been through fifty earthquakes, but this one was unlike the others since it "just took the hotel that we considered strong as a fortress and shook it back and forth as if it were a rag." Incidentally, perhaps the most well-known figure to die in the quake was a guest at the Arlington, Mrs. Charles E. Perkins, the widow of the president of the Chicago, Burlington and Quincy Railroad.[45] Another man staying at the Hotel Californian said that the walls of his room shook "with the same motion as imparted to an accordion being played." As he raced downstairs, he passed a man with a small child, but the building collapsed just as they reached the door.[46] The guest, who had dived through a window to escape, later stood in a vacant lot occupied by other hotel patrons and found "many of the women were hysterical and the condition of the men was not much better."

Despite these panicked descriptions, others displayed a desire for a quick return to a normal state of affairs and optimism. Gertrude Hoffmann, a visitor and the sister-in-law of a well-known resident, Bernhard Hoffmann, noted that by the afternoon "people had adjusted themselves to the new situation as people always do."[47] The Red Cross served coffee and cooked in wash basins on an improvised brick stove on De La Guerra Plaza in downtown Santa Barbara. By the middle of the afternoon, telegraph companies had set up tables to send news. In addition to footage of men clearing rubble, a news reel showed a dentist at work on a patient outside and restaurant patrons dining in the open air. Despite the post-earthquake damage, Hoffmann claimed, "We already see a newer and a finer Santa Barbara rising Phoenix-like from the ruins of today." She accepted that "what man has created has perished," but "the Sea and Mountain still appear under the opening eyelids of the morn," inviting Santa Barbara's inhabitants to imagine a new city built as one harmonious whole of a "solidity and beauty hitherto unimagined." Renewal could come out of ruin.

Downplaying the earthquake as an isolated, local circumstance in addition to minimizing the extent of damage provided a convenient justification for critics of Santa Barbara's commercial architecture. Some, such as the British architect S. Hurst Seager, took a sanguine view of destruction in the city's downtown since the structures there were "of the usual heterogeneous character and had no particular interest." A month before the earthquake, Santa Barbara's city council passed its first building ordinance, which set standards for construction but provided little aesthetic direction.[48] This commercial area differed from the city's residential neighborhoods, which suffered relatively little damage and had a reputation as an aesthetic highlight of the city. A survey of 411 downtown buildings on and around State Street by engineers from Los Angeles and San Francisco found that about 60 buildings needed demolition, 72 were considered unsafe for use, and about 250 were labeled safe. The engineers concluded that the new building ordinance had not been stringent enough, but those buildings "which are scientifically designed and honestly constructed, of whatever material, may be proof against any shocks which are likely to occur."[49] Instead of a misfortune, the earthquake assisted, in the words of one journalist, a "well-executed leap at the throat of the dullness and commonplaceness and grime and turmoil that overwhelmed and tangled so much beauty, peace, and civic character in almost every city in America."[50] The event signaled a renewed recognition of nature as the measure of urban beauty. Rendered as "Nature's touch," the earthquake reminded "man of her fundamental law, sham, ignorance, and error." This was a difficult lesson to accept but opened the way to "a wonderful opportunity."

Acceptance of aesthetic quality as a value became more effective when tied to economic development. At a national level, the advertising executive Earnest Elmo Calkins advocated for beauty as a recognized business tool. Calkins presented a negative example in Henry Ford's indifference to "the cult of beauty" and a related inability to recognize women's purchasing power in his company's early automobiles as a cautionary tale.[51] Beauty's benefits extended beyond consumer objects to improve homes, shops, hospitals, offices, and cities as well as the experiences of those moving through those spaces. Calkins leaned on a teleological narrative to explain increasing acknowledgment of beauty's worth. Despite having passed from handwork to the "triumph of the machine" that allowed wealth, education, travel, and sophistication, cheap and ugly products remained due to insufficient acceptance of the benefits of aesthetic quality. Efficiency alone fell short. Machines did not satisfy the soul, so by necessity beauty took its rightful place next to utility. Although Calkins believed in economic gain as beauty's selling point, he averred that the world, including its cities and landscapes, would be more alluring as a result of thinking about appropriateness.

Advancing beauty as a value commensurate with economic imperatives pushed institutions and governments to formalize aesthetic standards through regulations. Merely repairing and replacing buildings haphazardly added little value to a city. Visions of urban reconstruction as a harmonious whole congruent with its natural surroundings required coordination and management. A report on the damage commissioned by Nunn proposed that any plans for

Santa Barbara be set before a committee of architects, City Planning Commission members, and real estate interests. Following this recommendation, the city council organized an Architectural Advisory Committee with forty-four members, which in turn created an Architectural Board of Review of three architects and two community members to approve plans for reconstruction. In its eight-month existence, the Architectural Board of Review examined almost two thousand sets of plans and, in its members' telling, by "tact and persuasion" convinced almost all local builders to construct in "good design and good taste" in the "California style of architecture."[52] From this perspective, the earthquake seemed less of a damaging event and more of a pretense for action beyond reconstruction and toward social control. As one man wrote to Bernhard Hoffmann, residents with influence over building design provided an "invaluable service" to ensure that buildings would not be "too rampantly individualistic."[53] A "glaring red front" might offer "momentary advertising advantage" but was actually "selfishly barbaric." These interests were more than simply aesthetic. The resulting benefits gave an individual a path to "rise above the material things" and live nobly with "his soul nourished by the beauty of his handiwork—beauty that will accord with that which Nature has so lavishly bestowed upon this blessed spot." In addition, the "right civic spirit, a little deference to those who know how, and a lot of careful thinking" promised to increase Santa Barbara's reputation around the world. Lofty prose conveyed higher principles of spiritual regeneration and civilizational advance, but the material objectives remained mundane and utilitarian.

Although improvements in engineering conveyed technological advancements, some architects concentrated on establishing workable solutions to avoid earthquake damage while fretting about the possible loss of cultural traditions. Less than two years before the Santa Barbara earthquake, the Kantō earthquake on September 1, 1923, and subsequent fires destroyed an estimated 75 percent of Tokyo's 483,000 buildings. Most buildings in Tokyo were constructed with wood, which had a good degree of flexibility and resilience against earthquakes but was defenseless against fire.[54] Hearing the news, the architect Louis Sullivan lamented over the destruction of traditional Japanese architecture. He expressed sorrow for its replacement by the "helplessness, the shabbiness, the ruthless debauchery of commercialized American architecture—which means death."[55] Modern Tokyo's six- to ten-story steel and concrete buildings inspired by foreign models that were "imposing to look on and equipped with all the complex apparatus of our urban civilization" became figurative, if not literal, "death traps." In contrast, Old Tokyo, "medieval in character," withstood earthquakes "without much harm being done."[56] By opposing the failure of a global, technologically advanced architecture with the resilience of traditional wooden structures, Sullivan criticized the tendency to ignore the specificities of one's immediate environment and the verities it provided in favor of a placeless and ultimately spurious modernity.

Rebuilding Tokyo with the right balance between a universalizing modernity with its technological acumen and local traditions exemplified in indigenous Japanese cultural products concerned numerous non-Japanese architects. Foreign observers worried about the loss of Japan's unique aesthetic characteristics by giving in to Western-style development, thus hastening the nation's cultural destruction.[57] One architecture writer noted that Yokohama, a major port just south of Tokyo, with its "modern docks and rows of dingy European structures . . . not unlike the water-fronts of London or Amsterdam . . . gives a feeling of disappointment to the visitor who on his first venture from shipboard is looking for the picturesque in Japan."[58] Another writer claimed that "no country, not even Greece, not even Italy," reached Japan's artistic achievement.[59] Unfortunately, upon exiting from Tokyo's main railroad station, "there is found wilderness of shapeless atrocities, the hasty output of speculative builders" educated in the United States. In an account with similarities to California, the story of Japan, up to the 1870s, was a "semi-barbarous country" with architecture and customs that had stayed the same for centuries. But the late nineteenth century brought "radical changes" to the point that Japan of 1923 was "barely distinguishable" from fifty years earlier. The wholesale adoption of technologies from the West resulted in a "serious loss of national characteristics in architecture." Architects held on to the hope that Japan would rise from its ruins, but not in such a modern way to "lose racial identity" and its artistic beauty while building with "proper regard for safety."

Ironically, one antidote to this decline was a piece of American architecture and the most well-known building to survive the earthquake: Frank Lloyd Wright's Imperial Hotel, which had its completion ceremony on the day of the tremors.[60] Located on a site adjacent to the Imperial Palace, this $3 million project—the largest in Wright's career to that point, with three hundred rooms—was meant to be a social center for Tokyo society, Japanese government officials, and international diplomats.[61] Wright repeated many assumptions about Japan and Westernization. Instead of yet another example of Western architecture transplanted to the nation, he conceived of the hotel as a "new ideal of art entering modern life."[62] This approach, he argued, returned "what was true in old Japan" while including "every approved feature of modern building construction." Similar to the American architects working in the Spanish Colonial Revival idiom and other foreign-influenced designs, Wright offered himself as an adept translator and steward of an external tradition to ensure its continuation in the modern world. His method was not specific to Japan, but portable. Wright credited the Imperial Hotel's survival on the engineering, but others regarded it as a symbol of cultural strength.

The inevitability of earthquakes meant that architects needed to embrace that responsibility and not invite destruction through hastily designed buildings in inappropriate settings. Unfortunately, Sullivan believed American values privileged the opposite view and tempted fate by diving into hasty development. This distinctly American credulity that included the "impulsive acceptance" of "go-gettism," "pep," "progress," and "enterprise" replaced serious thought and social responsibility. Nevertheless, he admired traditional Japanese builders with their "free will" in the face of successive "invasions" by Americans, Germans, and the English. These alien cultures built masonry structures on earthquake-prone lands and resulted in architecture that "groaned and buried their dead."[63] Although Wright emphasized that the Imperial Hotel was not a piece of Japanese architecture, he and others believed the hotel epitomized honesty and appropriateness for its particular setting and culture. The key to the right type of construction for earthquake-prone areas was not simply engineering but having an eye for recognizing the best innate aesthetic features of a place and the intrinsic characteristics of its land. That vision for revealing a locale's essential characteristics was portable and applicable for use in the modern United States as much as ostensibly traditional cultures undergoing the process of modernization.

The return to an image of a Spanish past in Santa Barbara was less of a natural emergence than an intended result of social coercion. Removing unattractive features and deliberately replacing them was a maneuver to metaphorically and materially possess property through improvement. The earthquake emboldened influential residents to consider the city as a whole their territory. Over the course of several months in 1925 and 1926, the Architectural Advisory Committee and Architectural Board of Review wielded considerable control over the aesthetic direction and defined the particular ways architecture and nature came together in Santa Barbara. The committee recognized that the influence of Mexican, Spanish, and Italian styles served more than aesthetic purposes and embraced issues concerning climate, sunlight, and nature. This influence provided a clear narrative of the region's history. Franciscan friars, despite their limited materials, built the missions and with it did "so much to stamp the Spanish-California or Mission Style of Architecture."[64] Afterward came Americans "and their Eastern ideas" with a grid imposed on the adobes "clustered along their irregular trails." These new settlers brought "provincial intolerance" for building in alignment with their actual surroundings. New tools, such as the planing mill and jigsaw, precipitated "an orgy of fretwork and decoration" with Queen Anne–style houses, including "turrets and restless decoration." In the name of speed and progress, "longer and higher" buildings crowded together while simple lines of the Franciscans were ignored with "evident contempt."

Although residents heralded their foresight in implementing regulatory controls on aesthetic features of their city's built environment, precedents from other cities strengthened the view that controlling architectural forms would mean that "no further careless ugliness is permitted." Like Santa Barbara, Washington, DC, had an Architects Advisory Council, a voluntary group with members of the American Institute of Architects. The council had no enforcement power but informed property owners when their plans were "inadequately or improperly designed." Forest Hills in Queens, the Country Club District in Kansas City, and Palos Verdes Estates and Rancho Santa Fe outside of Los Angeles adopted aesthetic regulations and zoning. But regulations merely constituted the first step. The state's legal hand required the discernment of individuals who accepted regulations as a cultural given. The eye, mind, and hand of an architect endowed with an ability to consider the "town picture" would elevate and complete the environment. The developer and planner Charles Cheney argued that without vision, "we neglect and generally lose altogether that subtle thing which is indicative of the soul of the community."[65] Going further, the Minnesota Supreme Court sustained the use of police power to protect residential districts to enhance individual security and community esteem.[66] Supporters argued that controlling the aesthetic features of a community would at the very least lead to higher property values and "produce a better type of citizen."

Convincing some businesses to embrace aesthetic uniformity required coercion. Lofty language regarding the benefits of community alignment alone remained unconvincing for some property owners. Bernhard Hoffmann lamented that appealing to the city's "spirit of cooperation" was insufficient for some businesses, but financial incentives helped adjust attitudes. The Richelieu Hotel on State Street requested support from a city-helping fund for reconstruction.[67] But Hoffmann objected to the new design that had a "most uninteresting and unfitting front" for a hotel located in a prominent place near the train station where "it would meet the eye of every through traveler." He convinced an executive financing construction to instruct the architect to make changes since the value of the surrounding real estate would be adversely affected by such a building. Hoffmann argued that since the hotel was a new building, the owners should "make a greater concession to the spirit of community quite aside from the importance of enhancing the section from the real estate point of view." Similarly, Pearl Chase wrote to officials at the Standard Oil Company of California after news that it was planning to construct a service station on the corner of Cañon Perdido and Anacapa Streets, one block east of State Street. She implored the company to "erect a building in California style of architecture" that would harmonize with "all the important structures" near that corner, including the Lobero Theatre by George Washington Smith, the Carleton Winslow-designed Anacapa wing of the De La Guerra Studios, and the US Post Office designed by Reginald Johnson.[68] She stressed that each of these architects had well-regarded reputations and expressed the hope that Standard Oil would modify its "originally modernistic" design to harmonize with the California style. "If you could arrange," she proposed, "to use a design along the lines of some of your other successful stations in and near our community, we feel that the corner will undoubtedly become known for one of the most attractive commercial group of buildings in the west."[69] They assented.[70]

Appeals to citizenship and community for architectural form were not merely aesthetic but provided visible evidence of belonging. Stressing beauty as a value commensurate with economic considerations culminated in the formation of institutions and regulations to formalize aesthetic standards across the city. Alongside the Architectural Board of Review, a Community Drafting Room staffed with architects helped demonstrate to "people that art is neither irrelevant nor necessarily costly" and that individual desires and the public good were actually "one and the same." Despite the claim, organizers believed that the aspirations of individuals could only be trusted to a limited extent, and not at all when it came to aesthetic matters, since trusting individual judgment led to "unfortunate results." Therefore, the drafting room was considered a "clever device" through which buildings that "might have become public eye sores" were transformed by the "simple application of intelligence." This raised the stature of architecture as a profession since one would consult a lawyer when making a will or a doctor when ill, but in building a house, one was sure that "he, a layman, is entirely competent to pass on all architectural or aesthetic considerations of his building." The gentle pressure of expertise not only pointed out defective designs but also reduced shortcomings in personal character. The greed and selfishness of those "making a livelihood from the sale of poor materials," "careless, irresponsible workmen," and "unprincipled, self-seeking, petty politicians" who "ridicule the efforts of any well-meaning group of men in order to advertise themselves" would halt once they encountered the benevolent knowledge of the forward-looking architect of sound disposition.

Though a combination of aesthetic and economic arguments buttressed rebuilding efforts, many of the remarks centered on recovering the beauty that had been lost long before the earthquake—but with a modern focus on economic outcomes. Simply repairing damage and replacing buildings in Santa Barbara would be a disservice to the "lovely amphitheater that lies between the mountains and the sea." Because loss of life was "apparently small," the most prominent damage was "material and aesthetic" and thus easily repaired by "American and California enterprise." Completely disentangling aesthetic and economic and private property considerations from one another would not be possible, but taking the logic of beauty on its own terms brought to light its role in measuring a city's status. Combining beauty with economic growth made it more palatable to business owners, but beauty had its own claims to apolitical and objective roots. Nature provided beauty's proponents with a basis for creating an alternative measure to dollars and cents. The argument followed an Edenic arc of an idyllic and unspoiled land tainted by human action. A man wrote a letter to the editor of the *Santa Barbara News-Press* and noted that his initial impressions of Santa Barbara years before the earthquake could be summed up in a quote from the Anglican bishop Reginald Heber: "Every prospect pleases and only man is vile."[71] While nature's contributions were "so insistently evident" and man's "neglect and indifference" apparent, there seemed little hope in rehabilitating a push toward physical improvement. Since man could not live by bread alone, the "combination of beauty and strength with the bread winning must make for prosperity both of mind and body." Calkins's declaration that "efficiency was not enough" pointed to an alternative consideration of nature and society. If efficiency's reign suffused economics and conservation, the addition of beauty offered an alternative consideration of natural and urban environments.[72]

Contrasting images of State Street before and after the earthquake provided evidence of the fruits of this effort to combine beauty and economic impact (Figure 1.4). Rather than eclecticism or "six different styles" on one street corner, downtown Santa Barbara after the earthquake had uniformity. Structures designed and constructed before the earthquake, such as the Scottish-born architect James Osborne Craig's "Street in Spain," also known as El Paseo, provided a model for "righteous building."[73] Moreover, this undertaking was conceived as a community effort to demonstrate that "when the people of an entire town are interested in building," the results would be something "worth investigating and reporting." Wise builders and town boosters taking stock of local public opinion and the existing urban fabric before building, and "fakers of false fronts" would "hesitate before they try to put something over on that town."

Collectively, public and private regulation "set up a barrier to stop the

SANTA BARBARA HAD THESE SIX DIFFERENT KINDS OF COMMERCIAL ARCHITECTURE BEFORE THE EARTHQUAKE IN JUNE, 1925

WHEN the people of an entire town are interested in the building which is going on there, we may be sure there will result something worth investigating and reporting.

Builders and promoters will, if they be wise, stop, look and listen before they begin to build; individuals will know what the town thinks of them; fakers of false fronts will hesitate before they try to put something over on that town.

It is just this which the Community Arts Association of Santa Barbara has accomplished for that California town through its unusual "Plans Committee," with whom arrangements have been made to publish in this leaflet photographs of work done.

FIGURE 1.4. Six different kinds of commercial architecture on display on State Street in Santa Barbara before the earthquake that ushered in a much preferred aesthetic uniformity through Spanish Colonial Revival–style architecture. *California Southland* (November 1926).

bad architecture" and brought an elite segment of the city's inhabitants together. One writer claimed that private enterprise allowed every resident to have the opportunity to do his part according to "his gifts and inclination."[74] In aggregate, those parts reverberated through the community. Whether all the city's inhabitants found this work convincing was unclear, especially if they were not among the city's white inhabitants. One presumably concerned white resident wrote to Bernhard Hoffmann that he believed the disaster, "if it might be called such," should help make a radical change in Chinatown, centered two blocks east of State Street on De La Guerra and Cañon Perdido Street. The neighborhood was "an asset in so far as it entertains tourists who seldom fail to visit that unique quarter." The writer suggested that it might be worth considering a reconstruction of Chinatown in the "realignment of Santa Barbara's building scheme" but "under Oriental lines" to retain its atmosphere and become "doubly interesting." He also acknowledged that the "Chinese are shrewd and doubtless will rebuff any attempt by speculators to secure their holdings."[75] The implication was that Santa Barbara's Asian population interrupted the convenient and appropriate arc of growth.

Embracing Spanish Colonial Revival architecture as the sanctioned style for the community resulted in notable social erasures. Chinese and Japanese residents clustered in close proximity, often with multiple families occupying the same addresses near State Street, especially on Cañon Perdido Street on the blocks east of State Street and on Salsipuedes Street, a north–south street on the city's east side (Figure 1.5 and 1.6). The archives of the Community Arts Associations reveals little about the attitudes of these residents in the earthquake's aftermath, but chronicler of Southern California Carey McWilliams described Santa Barbara's early Chinatown as a "collection of battered old frame and adobe buildings" that had been lifted from "squalor to romance" by "red papers, varnished ducks, rattan baskets, calico partitions, exotic smells, and a brooding, spiritual atmosphere in the Orient."[76] Often working as manual laborers, launderers, and agricultural workers, the presence of these residents countered the narrative of reconstruction offered by Santa Barbara's affluent white inhabitants, and they were made invisible.[77]

Like others, Bailey Willis, a seismologist and president of the Seismological Society of America, described Santa Barbara as a bucolic place during the years of Spanish control when the city had "stateliness, license, piety, and poetic romance." The transfer of power to the United States resulted in a cultural downfall. This earthquake put into relief the ways such an event could invert hierarchies that classified the primitive or civilized. Willis noted an irony by acknowledging the creative force of earthquakes in creating Santa Barbara in the first place. The Mesa fault raised the land, providing a shelter for the beach below. In addition, the Santa Ynez fault "conditioned the uplift" of the mountains defining the valley where Santa Barbara was located. "Are we wrong then," asked Willis, "in calling the earthquake force creative?"[78] In contrast to the "over-individualized American city," there was a wisdom in having unified rather than haphazard planning, and aesthetic expression succeeded because of what he called "earthquake love." The earthquake, for Willis, was not only an aesthetic but a civic and environmental contribution returning the values of tradition, romance, and civility that had been lost in the name of progress.

Two months after the earthquake, the *Los Angeles Times* announced that

FIGURE 1.5. Residential addresses of Santa Barbara's Asian population in 1920. The cluster of residences is on East Cañon Perdido Street. Data from US Census Bureau, 1920 US Federal Census. Map by Sierra Chmela.

FIGURE 1.6. Residential addresses of Santa Barbara's Asian population in 1930. The cluster of residences near downtown is on East Cañon Perdido Street. Residences outside the shaded map area are on the present-day Mesa. Data from US Census Bureau, 1930 US Federal Census. Map by Sierra Chmela.

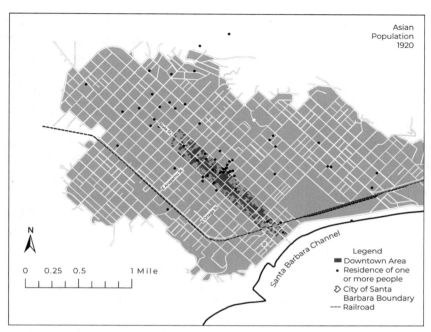
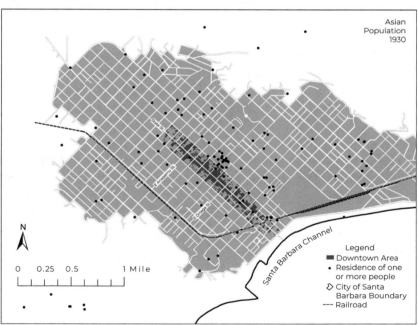

Santa Barbara's boosters for reconstruction adopted "Bigger and Better Than Ever" as their slogan.[79] The debris was swept away and "building activities are to be seen in almost every section of this picturesque coast city." The article posited that in a few months, no evidence of the earthquake would be seen in the city, which was, it quoted Willis, not supposed to experience another earthquake for "at least a century" since the "strain is off." Some advertised the city in 1926 as "earthquake proof" due to increased regulation of construction and the elimination of faulty building practices.[80] In the days after the earthquake, reports publicized the assertion that Santa Barbara was now "one of the safest places" and even nearly immune from another tremor.[81] Willis added that the Hotel Californian's walls had been fastened incorrectly and the San Marcos's construction of heavy, rather than reinforced, concrete and lack of bracing caused its destruction. Santa Barbara's superintendent of building, Oscar G. Knecht, argued that the damage could have been minimized if buildings had been properly built and further claimed that 80 percent of property loss could have been prevented if "good judgment, appropriate materials, and sane structural engineering practice had been used when structures affected were built."[82] A year later the mistakes of the past seemed to have disappeared with "almost every trace of damage" removed and records made in "building construction, money turned over and in real estate transactions."[83]

The Spanish Colonial Revival had a central role in another narrative, one regarding California's status in the United States. While some worried that the end of the frontier represented the declension of national territorial expansion, others argued that California was the culmination of American ascendancy and pointed to the state's architecture to make this case. Henry Saylor's words highlighted the seemingly contradictory impulses to embrace Spanish Colonial Revival architecture as a naturally occurring outgrowth of California's environment while simultaneously elevating Anglo-American architects as codifiers and perfecters of the forms. Emphasizing the work of twentieth-century white architects—many of whom were transplants to California—presented a revisionist account of this architecture's origins. By absorbing or denying Spanish, Mexican, and Indigenous sources as part of American architectural development, Spanish Colonial Revival architecture could be framed not just as intrinsically Californian but as intrinsically American.

Synthesizing the regional with the national required minimizing Spanish Colonial Revival architecture's racial and ethnic connotations. The formation of an alternate genealogy of buildings helped fulfill this task. The architect and writer Thomas Tallmadge believed it was "curious" that while "Anglo-

Saxons" built Georgian mansions and meetinghouses on the Atlantic Seaboard, Spaniards "on the shores of a still-mightier ocean" converted Indians and built other types of meetinghouses, with little knowledge of each other. Despite their synchronicity, an "abysmal gulf" did more than physically separate the two groups.[84] Serious differences in architecture, religion, government, customs, and "every social and cultural activity" distinguished the two coasts. Tallmadge added that one could never imagine Junipero Serra, priest and founder of some of California's earliest missions under the Spanish, doing that work in Salem, Massachusetts. Conversely, the idea of Jonathan Edwards reading John Calvin's commentaries to the friars and Indians was ridiculous. The "easy-going and, in mundane things, ignorant" monks and their "copper-colored and childlike neophytes" in their "Cytherean" climate could not compare with their "energetic" and "highly educated" Atlantic counterparts who "built not only for beauty, but for efficiency and protection from the elements." Tallmadge's distinctions not only created a hierarchy between America's Pacific and Atlantic coasts but also replicated widely held assumptions about southern ("ignorant") and northern ("highly educated") Europeans.[85]

Despite the discrepancy in intellectual capacities, Tallmadge acknowledged that both built in harmony with their environments. He even claimed that the California monks surpassed Atlantic Seaboard Americans in architectural charm and religious atmosphere—though this could be credited to the problems being simpler on the temperate western coast as opposed to the changeable conditions in the East. Nevertheless, he argued that Spanish and Georgian architecture were "cousins" originating in the "great family of the Renaissance."[86] After a "full century of neglect and ostracism," the architecture that lined the Pacific coast had been "received into the American family, has become part of us." In California, the crossing of the "old blood" with the Puritan tradition produced "perhaps the loveliest daughter of our architecture—a daughter with the vigorous constitutions of the north and the slumberous eyes and orchid coloring of old Mexico." Assimilating the roots of California's architecture would bring it into the right lineage and make its improvement inevitable.

The racial cast of Tallmadge's assimilation project provided space for some equity of skill, but others theorized a different lineage for California's architecture, one that more overtly masked the Spanish influence in favor of a more generalized European or English heritage. American art critic Sheldon Cheney downplayed the Spanish elements as only "very faintly" flavoring the architecture designed for "the purposes of today's mechanistic living."[87] Cheney argued that California's architecture attained a standard of achievement that stemmed from "rationalized" English cottage designs by Edwin Lutyens, George Gilbert Scott Jr., and C. F. A. Voysey. He positioned the English cottage and the California house as braided strands of modern architecture's development through a shared "fine simplicity" of its forms and massing. California's architects enhanced these traditional English designs. The architect Reginald D. Johnson, writing in *California Southland* in 1926, endorsed the bond with English designs. He argued that the previous four decades demonstrated a transition between the eclecticism of the "ginger-bread period" to a "most interesting architectural development and search for architectural styles which are truly Californian."[88] For Johnson, two central styles that comprised California were Mediterranean and English. He hoped that they could be "fused together" to create a new style that satisfied "those seeking the home atmosphere" of the English while maintaining the "romance of the Mediterranean." Differences in environmental conditions—namely, California's superior climate—meant that modern architecture could truly flourish in the state since it offered the possibility of arranging rooms around a garden courtyard for openness between inside and out, building flat roofs, and using easily available materials.

Some advocated for preserving a connection to Spanish Colonial Revival architecture's colonial roots since it was in that "portion of the United States which has much the same traditions and climate" as Mexico.[89] Others bristled against that connection, asserting that California had a style distinctive enough to warrant recognition beyond Spanish, Mediterranean, Mission, or Pueblo. In Los Angeles County, the Palos Verdes Art Jury, which set guidelines to maintain the architectural character of the community, excised the words "Spanish" and "mission" from descriptions of its architecture. Those words, they contended, caused "much confusion in the public mind" regarding a style of architecture that was "so general" in California.[90] Architecture "of a type peculiarly appropriate to California" had been developing for so many years that it needed to be designated as "California style" rather than "Mission style" or "Spanish style." Those latter terms were simply "unfortunate misnomers" for an art "which has progressed to a degree in which we may justly take pride." Spanish Colonial Revival architecture's aesthetic qualities were not up for debate—they were embraced as a contribution to urban beauty and unity. But the roots of this style would determine how far it could be considered a truly American architecture. Tracing or denying Spanish Colonial Revival architecture's genealogy was not a straightforward project. The process of assimilating this architecture testified to racial hierarchies and cultural assumptions that marked the United States as a whole. This revisionist lineage designated this architecture as indigenous to the environment and climate. More importantly, it defined the style as indigenous to the United States' white settlers, with all the racial assumptions attached to it.

A year after the earthquake, newspapers announced that Santa Barbara erased "all trace of tremblor" with new structures in "real California architecture."[91] With a photo captioned "Santa Barbara Puts on New Dress," an article proclaimed that the average visitor would not know that the city had even experienced an earthquake. The subsequent year resulted in permits for buildings totaling $6 million that included a new Biltmore Hotel but did not include municipal buildings such as a $110,000 beach pavilion. Two years after the earthquake, the writer Charles Lummis celebrated the changes he saw in the city. Short-sighted materialists "who would sell you (soul included) for the commission" failed in their task.[92] Despite the fact that Lummis lost a close friend in the earthquake and others' homes were destroyed, he felt that the earthquake was ultimately the "greatest good fortune that ever fell" to the city. Although one could not "legislate sense or taste or morality," Santa Barbara's architecture set an example and even skeptics would eventually learn that it does not "pay to be ugly or common place in handsome company. They will feel like a woman in her old suit, surrounded by the brilliance of her sisters in the 'up-to-the-minute' gowns." Ultimately, the city would be a more honest and true version of itself with no more jerry building nor "silly ambitions" for skyscrapers.

A decade and a half later, a local architect, Roy Cheesman, like many before him, acknowledged the earthquake as a "catastrophe of first magnitude." He followed this observation with praise for the city's residents who transformed the place from "just another small city drowsing in the California sunshine" to an aesthetically pleasing community of "a kind and quantity never before accomplished" in the United States.[93] The natural disaster revealed their "civic regard for the importance of the city's appearance and a program for preserving" the city's Spanish character. This regard went beyond merely evincing an aesthetic preference. The design choices signaled an allegiance to a set of community values and conceptions of civic belonging. The Santa Barbara that came out of the "ruins of the old" was more than a simple revival; it was a "distinct adaptation of the best of the past, designed to fit into a modern scene."

By arguing that nature's geophysical processes guided architects to those forms, city leaders translated the earthquake into a happy circumstance that allowed the location's intrinsic character and individuality to emerge fully. The destruction of "slavish copying" and eclecticism that marred other American cities and realization of "Southern California idealized" required both natural intervention and continual human action. Unfortunately, the effort to rebuild could be foiled through the acceptance of "discordant notes" in the urban fabric that if "unopposed will gradually accelerate and finally undo all the good accomplished in the years immediately following the earthquake." Presenting nature as the catalyst and regulator of urban form allowed affluent whites to offer themselves as the authentic custodians of their city and its future.[94] This custodial responsibility circumvented political processes and conflict by offering abstract and ostensibly timeless universalisms about art and nature as grounds for their work. Clearing away debris and panic prepared the groundwork for a more promising future. The landscape authorized the idealized history represented in the built environment as residents made the place their own.

2

Education, Not Legislation

> Americans of all ages, all stations in life, and all types of disposition are forever forming associations . . . Americans combine to give fetes, found seminaries, build churches, distribute books, and send missionaries to the antipodes . . . if they want to proclaim a truth or propagate some feeling by encouragement of a great example, they form an association. In every case at the head of any new undertaking, where in France you would find the government or in England some territorial magnate, in the United States you are sure to find an Association.[1]

In 1923, the California booster Charles Lummis offered a thundering account of the 1849 gold rush as the beginning of the "biggest, bravest, wildest Epic the sons of man ever scrawled across a continental wilderness—the most Homeric Adventure that people of English speech ever plunged into."[2] Events in the remote outpost of California transformed the money markets of the world. The modernizing hand of hard currency replaced the old romance of missions and adobes with Anglo prospectors spurred by mineral extraction and other roads to profit. Sanitizing an organized campaign of state and settler violence into a heroic epic, Lummis's enterprising Americans reordered California's environment by leveling mountains, "leading rivers by the nose," and overhauling a "hamlet into Los Angeles in thirty years." But this power had limits. Brains, brawn, and money alone could not construct a century-old adobe or Franciscan mission. The "cold utilitarian" from the modern United States lacked the tools and know-how to continue the tradition of romance in the land.

Despite the invigorating tale, California's transformation from a locale permeated by timeless romance into just another American place that prioritized economy and function disturbed Lummis. So he offered an alternative vision for the future that combined what he viewed as the best qualities of romance and utility, tradition and innovation. He recast the turbulence of nineteenth-century California as the birth pains of an emerging genteel civilization. By resuscitating California's romance while continuing to support economic and social development, Lummis's ideas evoked themes familiar to the then-burgeoning conservation movement marked by a negotiation between managing resources and revering nature.[3] On a visit to the Grand Canyon with Theodore Roosevelt, a proponent of conservation and settler colonialism, Lummis recalled that Roosevelt looked upon the scenery and proclaimed, "Here is your country. Do not let anyone take it or its glory away from you! Cherish these natural wonders, cherish the natural resources, cherish the History and the Romance as a sacred heritage."[4] Lummis declared Roosevelt's words contained a "two-fisted gospel" free of "Sissies and sentimentalism."[5] Modern romance did not represent a fuzzy weakness or overly feminine mawkishness. Instead, it projected national invigoration and renewal.

At the start of the twentieth century, few places in California remained that exhibited that distinct mixture of romance and practicality, but Santa Barbara was one such place. The climate and natural surroundings that attracted health seekers and the affluent from other parts of the nation in the nineteenth century also enchanted Lummis. Other American cities, he asserted, evinced an "unseemly eclecticism" due to buildings made from a "tiresome bolt of machine-pattern, stenciled, unimaginative and rather tardy American Calico." In contrast, Santa Barbara had the potential to be as "beautiful, as artistic, as well worth crossing the world to see as . . . any one of the 500 towns along the Mediterranean."[6] One major obstacle stood in the path. Despite the racial superiority of Anglo-Americans in other realms, they, unlike the Spanish and Mexicans, lacked an intuitive command of the "historically fit and artistically delightful" architecture intrinsic to California. Despite the absence of an ethnically based instinct held by "'Dagos' and other Latin races we have been taught to look down on," white settlers had "American wit." That wit indicated an intellectual capacity to integrate environmental particularities and heritage into architectural and urban development. Through "community intelligence" and "civic art feeling," a white population could learn not only to recognize but also to despise ugliness. This discernment required an almost surgical excision of eyesores since "as a chain is no stronger than its weakest link . . . one ridiculous building outfights fifty beauty spots."

Nature was simply better in California than the rest of the United States, but how would Americans respond to it? Lummis's words captured the opposing logics at play in California's Anglo-American development. Although his epic began with "Homeric Adventure," it ended with the domestic architecture of respectable Santa Barbarans. Making California a home for white settlers required less adventure and more of the mundane tasks of establishing conventions for everyday life. California's exceptional natural features, climate, and history gave that labor a distinct tenor. Territorial expansion may have reached the end of the continent, but errands related to internal civilizing remained. So the trajectory of development required a shift. It was not hard-charging men but rather women who often took charge in this phase of California's life. With large-scale matters of conquest and environmental transformation complete, the focus adjusted to an outwardly more modest but no less potent vision centered on the home. Rather than opposing domestic concerns to national interests, home constituted a vital component of the same project. This follows what literary scholar Amy Kaplan notes as the internal logic of domesticity which "relies on, abets, and reproduces the contradictions of nationalist expansion."[7] What began with two men looking rapturously upon the Grand Canyon terminated in the tidy homes and gardens of Santa Barbara. The extractive capitalists and conquerors that exemplified California in the past transformed during the twentieth century into refined characters advocating for civic improvement and beautification.

Education and private initiative characterized efforts toward domestic improvement. Instead of entrusting the state to guide settlement patterns, Santa Barbara's white inhabitants had clear directions from mostly private institutions (Figure 2.1). Starting in the early 1920s, national organizations including Better Homes in America (BHA), a program to encourage homeownership, and those local to Santa Barbara, especially the Community Arts Association (CAA), spearheaded many of the efforts that Lummis viewed with admiration. A voluntary organization with a membership dominated by the city's affluent residents, the CAA advanced the arts—ranging from music to urban design—as a primary channel for community improvement. The quotidian content of these pursuits, which included house-design competitions for professionals and school children, tours, and classes, belied their ambitions. This domesticating work was the culmination of settler colonial conquest and defined ownership and belonging.[8]

Casting the home as a microcosm of the community made all problems domestic issues and spread responsibility for urban conditions to every resident. The CAA made spirited claims for the significance of residential neighborhoods and homeownership as the basis of true community flourishing and renewal. Promoting homeownership and aesthetic standards for single-family residences encouraged women especially to consider their broader environments—namely, their neighborhoods and cities as extensions of the domestic realm. In observing the expansion of home as a microcosm of society, historians have argued that the "most effective ground of ideology" may not lie in the realm of high politics but in the places structured around everyday activities—the home, workplace, schools, and media.[9] Similarly, Kaplan observes that rhetoric around domesticity from the nineteenth century onward reveals the contingent boundary between foreign and domestic that "negotiates the borders of an increasingly expanding empire and a divided nation." Those borders reenact the "contradictions of empire through its own

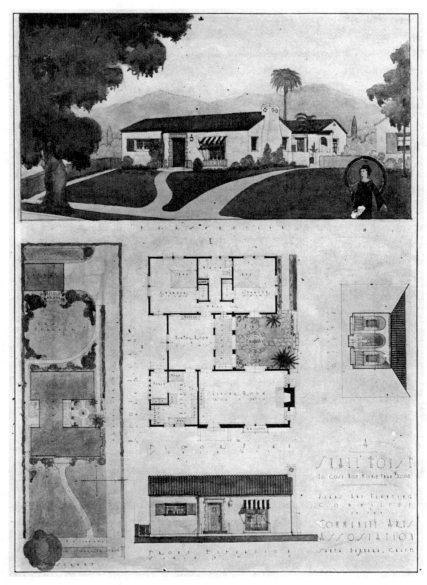

FIGURE 2.1. L. H. Kreinkamp, "A Small House to Cost Not More than $5,000." Although the jury had doubts that the house could be built for less than $5000, Kreinkamp's design was described as "particularly appropriate for southern climates. The lines of the building produce a pleasing and harmonious result." From *Small House Designs*, edited by Carleton Monroe Winslow and Edward Fisher Brown, 1924.

double movement to expand female influence while simultaneously contracting the women's sphere."[10] Centering the home as a primary root for environmental and social improvement cast their activities within the familiar scope of the private and privatized sphere distinct from the anonymous hand of the state.[11] This work had clear political goals while cast as anything but.

Despite this distinction, the state and the domestic sphere often shared objectives. The more modestly scaled reach of associations, clubs, and civic organizations could build support networks and a bridge between interested parties and the state. Undertaking community improvement provided individuals with opportunities to demonstrate their self-reliance, financial responsibility, and commitment to community. Homeownership offered the primary vehicle to realize these qualities at multiple registers and provided individuals a means to make claims on the conditions of their surroundings. Although the BHA and CAA denied the political content of their activities, their work illustrates how shared commitments and values among a group of citizens identifying as homeowners formed its own privatized politics, especially regarding environmental quality.[12] Improving domestic spaces and encouraging homeownership required thinking about the property values—in quantitative and qualitative terms—not just of one's own home but in neighborhoods and the city as a whole.[13] Home offered a counterweight of security and constancy in the face of large-scale economic transformations, immigration, and urbanization in the first quarter of the twentieth century. Framed as a community-based undertaking rather than a top-down exercise in urban control, civic improvement had a sheen of organic neutrality. Nevertheless, urban beautification represented more than aesthetic improvement; it authorized a project of naturalizing existing social orders that defined who belonged and who had marginal status.

This updated romance of place with its emphasis on domestic matters was invested in concealing its power. Mild suspicion of the state's impersonal hand followed, thus reinforcing a divide between public and private. Individuals bound by shared interests could encounter and recognize community bonds in their surroundings and personal relationships rather than through legal force or public regulations. Despite the nonpolitical veneer of these actions, they privileged a political and social consensus that enabled citizens in power to speak with one unified voice. Prioritizing consensus extended to nature as well. Instead of competing with the environment, the CAA's work, according to its members, brought the city's form in greater alignment with its natural surroundings. The exceptional climate and natural environment provided a useful gauge to assess the compatibility of Santa Barbara's homes and neighborhoods—and by extension, its residents with nature's charms.

Improving the conditions of the city's physical environment through the voluntary contributions of its citizens underpinned an environmental sensibility that placed community norms and social cohesion at the center. Owning a home conferred privileges, including full participation in society. The home was a microcosm of all other places and, significantly, the root of political commitments.

The tensions of urban growth that marked California's first few decades of statehood concerned the entire nation. The 1920 census declared the United States an urban nation, marking an explicit demographic and conceptual shift from the nation's agrarian origins. Americans worried that urbanization and immigration risked destroying the civic attachments that gave order to their lives, which would be replaced with alienation and vice. Centering the home as the wellspring of a functioning social order in the 1920s evoked images of the past as a period with a simpler temper of life. Political theorist and son of California chronicler Carey McWilliams, Wilson Carey McWilliams described the politics of the 1920s as "a vain struggle to reestablish the old equilibrium" and a futile quest for normalcy.[14] Suburbanization that ran alongside urbanization was one, arguably successful, part of that vain effort and was based on an illusion to "recapture the atmosphere of the small town within an urban economy," with "neighborliness" as the "new ethic and a general theme in the social thought of the time."[15] The spatial insularity of suburbs made it possible to believe that one could shut out "threatening reality." McWilliams observed that rather than removing threats, these places merely demonstrated a fervent commitment to maintaining outdated traditions to shore up social boundaries even as an unknown future came hurdling forward.

Although McWilliams found the idea of community objectionable and obsolete, the concept flourished in the 1920s. Defining and locating community occupied the attentions of researchers in response to its perceived loss and elusiveness. Familiar definitions such as a "group of company of people living fairly closely together . . . to act together in the chief concerns of life" led to questions about the types of settlements, social groupings, norms, localities, and demographics that constituted a community.[16] In its ideal form, community suggested face-to-face interactions, neighborliness, porous boundaries between public and private, and consensus without conflict. But criteria for membership into a community included exclusions that limited belonging.[17] Defining community and its qualities was not merely an academic project. Coming to a shared understanding paved the way for its renewal. Individuals across the political spectrum have seen community invoked as, in the words of political theorist Iris Marion Young, an "unequivocal good, an indicator of a high quality of life, a life of human understanding, caring, selflessness, belonging."[18] Radical theorists and activists often evoke community as an ideal and critique against liberal individualism.[19] In contrast, critic Raymond Williams observed that the idealization of community can also be lodged as "conservative critiques of changes in the given social hierarchy."[20] Those boundaries help enact a localized universalism and shared investment in a particular structure of social relations.[21] Investigating how individuals deployed conceptions of community and to what ends underscores that a term's definition can be less important than investigating its social effects. Historian Stuart Schrader points out that community is a "technology of social intervention and manipulation."[22] Community commonly reveals much more about those in power and the stabilization of norms than its actual features. Emphasizing consensus rather than disagreement or anonymous bureaucracy aided the removal of clear paths to challenge power. A consensus that ostensibly emerged from working out personal disagreements could naturalize a status quo to present it as intrinsic to a community rather than a deliberately engineered outcome.[23]

The impression of Santa Barbara as a distinct and even improved alternative to the reigning features of American urban development arose as much from its inhabitants as its enticing natural surroundings. Until 1880, Southern California's population rose steadily but slowly. Then in the 1880s and 1890s, California's population increased dramatically, though unevenly. Los Angeles County's population tripled from thirty-three thousand to over one hundred thousand inhabitants between 1880 and 1890. Santa Barbara's growth was much less pronounced but also notable. In 1890, the city had about thirty-six hundred residents; by 1900, it had about five thousand, many of whom—unlike those in Los Angeles—came from families of means with ties to the eastern United States.[24] The slower growth and influx of a more desirable type of immigrant presented Santa Barbara as an attractive alternative to Los Angeles—if one could afford it. One historian even characterizes these migrants from the East as a demonstration of "the intersection of Bostonian and Mexican culture."[25] Contemporary observers expressed similar views with a sinister cast that implied not only racial but also sectarian divisions in the aftermath of the Civil War. Charles Loring Brace, a philanthropist who founded the Children's Aid Society in New York, which sent children from the city to the West with often tragic results, believed, like many, that immigration to California by "Yankees could easily overcome many of the moral disadvantages which result from the 'Southern' and Spanish influences."[26] Another eastern traveler believed population growth from individuals with "the energy and business acumen of the keen Yankee, the smart Middle Westerner, and the sharp Northerner" would produce a new energy in the "stimulating climatic conditions," so that even in the heat one could feel a "healthful, vigorous, stirring quality in the atmosphere that provokes to labor."[27]

Or at least labor of a certain kind. Early twentieth-century visions of cities as overcrowded and dirty from industry signaled a type of labor best avoided, especially in a place like Santa Barbara. In an unrealized 1909 plan for the city, the urban planner Charles Mulford Robinson proclaimed Santa Barbara a place of "extraordinary beauty," as well as "one of the most interesting" since its economic prosperity depended on its natural beauty.[28] As a result, manufacturing or other industries posed little risk of enticing residents to sacrifice the city's aesthetic charm. In Robinson's eyes, the worst thing that could happen to Santa Barbara would be to "GET BIG" and transform "into a madhouse like Los Angeles."[29] A controlled urban development that foregrounded a complementary relationship with the surrounding environment was not only desirable but also practical and achievable. Framed in this straightforward manner, this understanding of place assumed that all who came within the city's borders would recognize this self-evident truth.

Maintaining an urban settlement that contrasted favorably with unattractive and overcrowded cities required the intervention of individuals who shared a common set of priorities. Those convinced of not only the aesthetic but also the social benefits of building with the values of the "keen Yankee" found a welcoming place in Santa Barbara. Bernhard Hoffmann was one such figure. The son of a man from the Habsburg Empire who left for the United States during political unrest in 1848, Hoffmann grew up in Stockbridge, Massachusetts, a major center of village improvement activity popular throughout New England inspired by the writings of Andrew Jackson Downing on "country life" and "rural improvement" during the second half of the nineteenth century.[30] In Stockbridge, Hoffmann's father, Ferdinand, involved himself in the region's historic preservation projects and even purchased a house once occupied by the eighteenth-century Calvinist revivalist minister and theologian Jonathan Edwards.[31] Soon after World War I, during which he had served as assistant director of the New York Federal Food Boards under Herbert Hoover, the younger Hoffmann moved with his family to Santa Barbara, in part to improve his daughter's health, and cofounded the CAA in 1920.

Transferring his interest in preservation to Santa Barbara, Hoffmann embraced the region's Spanish Colonial Revival style. He commissioned James Osborne Craig, an architect well-versed in the style, to design his family's home. In addition, he and his wife, Irene, purchased several adobes in downtown Santa Barbara, including the De La Guerra adobe and the Casa La Aguirre, and tasked Craig with their restoration.[32] Undertaking these preservation projects put Hoffmann in national company. After World War I, philanthropists and industrialists including the Rockefellers and Henry Ford underwrote the preservation of buildings in Williamsburg, Virginia, and Greenfield Village as historically significant for the nation.[33] The physical restoration of the past showed their place in the formation of the nation and reminded modern audiences of these formative contributions.

Hoffmann's undertakings in historic preservation had material benefits for the CAA, which had its headquarters in the De La Guerra adobe. Centrally located and just two blocks from State Street, the CAA profited from the active participation of the city's elite citizens with wide social networks and the ability to mobilize others. Working closely with Hoffmann was Pearl Chase, secretary of the CAA throughout the 1920s and chair of the Plans and Planting branch from 1922 until 1969. Like Hoffmann, Chase was born in Massachusetts, but to a family that traced its American origins to the Mayflower. Her family moved to Santa Barbara when she was young and her father started a real estate investment business.[34] After graduating from the University of California, Berkeley in 1909, Chase returned to her hometown to teach home economics. Finding the work dull, she soon quit to devote the rest of her life to local causes as a volunteer or "professional amateur."[35] Admitting that she was financially "free as few people are" due to a private income from her father's investments, she dedicated her life to projects centered on improving Santa Barbara's built and natural environments. Late in her life, Chase recalled returning to Santa Barbara during a break from Berkeley and realized how ashamed she was of "the dust and dirt and ugly buildings."[36] That embarrassment pushed her toward beautification and urban design projects. Through the Plans and Planting branch, she became known as "the de facto city planner of Santa Barbara."[37] Figures such as Hoffmann and Chase demonstrated how community-oriented groups such as the CAA wielded significant influence in shaping an environmental sensibility through alterations of physical spaces and used those changes to define the city's civic identity.

The home connoted timeless values, but its actual construction required attending to particularities of climate and geography. In California, home construction, especially after World War I, displayed the state's aspirations. Lummis and other writers saw the state at the beginning of its development. California coming out of "earthquake and fire, drought and labor," according to architecture writer Henry H. Saylor, risked squandering the "fine fabric of her civilization." Fortunately, those tribulations passed on and the state emerged "unbowed."[38] Saylor acknowledged an asymmetry in his focus on housing quality compared to the "titanic upheavals" of California's first years of statehood, describing the juxtaposition as perhaps a "big thick." Yet more than simply providing shelter from the elements, architecture's significance came from its status as the "really vital matter of recording in the history of civilization what manner of people this is." The home disclosed everything one needed to know: a society's conditions and the character of its inhabitants.

But who counted as a true Californian? For Saylor, the answer was a white person. Outsiders from Japan, China, and Mexico as well as the Midwest and East Coast arrived in the state to make it their own, while "native-born"—meaning white—Californians were just children. This heterogeneous mix of peoples settling in this unfamiliar climate resulted in a wide variety of homes that fell under the umbrella of "California bungalow," which he felt might be an outsize complement.[39] These homes were mostly "one-story wooden buildings of a nondescript character that suggested the strong architectural influence of the state of Iowa—that is to say, no architectural character whatever." Other builders adopted colonial types, flat roofs, Swiss chalets, or ranch homes, which together precipitated the construction of "the Babel of Southern California." The promise of retreating from this "jumble of incongruities" arrived in the 1920s since "native" Californians were now old enough to resist "their former imported provincialism" and shoddy construction to make "modern demands for better things." Similarly, Gustav Stickley, the furniture maker and proponent of the Arts and Crafts movement in the United States, explained that some of the disappointments in California's architecture stemmed from architects not following the "clear indications given by Nature" but instead pursuing the "precedents established in other parts of the country."[40] He declared that in California, "where English traditions are wanting, the Colonial style is false as a matter of art. It is also false in principle since it is illy adapted to the conditions of climate and scenery."[41] As designs suited to other locations started to fall from fashion, the particularities of California's climate came to the foreground as a regulating influence.

Assumptions about California's climate gained influence and encouraged the idea that the state's housing should be distinct from the rest of the nation, with the added requirement of reflecting California's "sincere and vigorous spirit" as well as the general "strength and straightforwardness that characterize Western life."[42] The climate served as a central regulating force. "Several basic facts" of house design for the climate included thick masonry walls to repel the summer sun, the use of stucco, and the absence of elaborate heating systems. The sunny climate made the patio "a logical provision for the shaded outdoor retreat" and "steadily" grew to be "more of a necessity than a luxury." These facts pointed to the Spanish Mission and the Colonial Revival as styles most logical to the climate. The question remained of how to integrate design features to "complex modern civilization." Despite these "basic facts," Saylor lamented that this type of environmentally sensitive California house remained in the "regrettable minority." The slowness of adoption was somewhat understandable since architectural progress moved slowly; and because other examples, such as half-timber and plaster houses of England or New England homesteads "did not spring up in a day," hope remained for California's eventual flourishing.

Homes did more than provide shelter. They represented one's character, living standards, customs, and place within a community. The features of good California homes told a story of the state's material progression from adobes to lumber to stucco. Moreover, vigilance over aesthetic conditions allowed cities, such as Santa Barbara, to claim a measure of immunity from the perils of industrial urbanism, even if their single-family homes did not follow Spanish Colonial Revival or Mission influences. Protecting these conditions required sustained maintenance and often occurred through private channels. This was a coercive form of private police power cast as a public good.[43] Yet the state was a useful ally. Bernhard Hoffmann, for example, had no qualms about using his personal relationships with public officials to encourage business owners with "a tactful line of suggestion" about the unsightliness of large and electric signs and pasteboards. He noted that his home state of Massachusetts had a "delightful law" that made posting pasteboards a misdemeanor and that "any Citizen may abate said nuisance."[44] Invoking community standards and aesthetic qualities put a concerned yet seemingly harmless temper on such actions.

Local skirmishes over urban development occurred in affluent areas throughout the country. Palos Verdes south of Los Angeles, the Country Club District in Kansas City, and Coral Gables, Florida, all presented their uniform built fabrics as spaces that required constant vigilance to maintain.[45] Surveying these cities, the editorial board of the *Santa Barbara News-Press* asserted that they showed a favorable contrast to unsightly neighborhoods that dotted the nation.[46] Defenses of aesthetic uniformity contended that a city's appearance was "as much a function of a community as supervision of traffic, of health, of morals—for what man BUILDS we must all LOOK AT." Ignoring community norms and building "without advice and without regard for his neighbor" risked foisting suffering upon "the whole community." While some individuals might have countered that building without regard for a neighbor was "the rule of the people," others saw "the ruin of the people" and a regrettable dismissal of community. Embracing a uniform spatial organization portended a bright future for Santa Barbara as a haven for homeowners, "progressiveness and unity in all Civic undertakings," and a path toward becoming the "Nation's greatest Recreation Center." Urban conditions set Santa Barbara apart, but not without effort.

Concern for aesthetic conditions of the city's housing only obliquely gestured toward existing social and spatial issues, especially regarding racial segregation. In 1920, the *Santa Barbara Morning Press* published a lengthy article on local housing conditions that began by noting the dominant understanding of the city as a place "without a slum."[47] Yet surveys undertaken by voluntary organizations and visiting nurses undermined that image. Just a few blocks east of downtown, observers found "deplorable conditions," "bad sanitary features," and living quarters where five to eight people shared one room. A racial logic informed remarks about the connection between housing and its inhabitants. The article explained that the city's poor were "for the most part Mexicans" who refused to sleep on porches, so they aggravated ventilation issues in their overcrowded domiciles, which risked exacerbating "immorality." Census data from 1920 and 1930 shows the city's Mexican and Black populations clustered east of downtown and south of the railroad (Figures 2.2 and 2.3). Correlations between race and housing gestured toward pathologizing the sources of crime. Anna McCaughey, the superintendent of the county detention home, claimed a "close link between juvenile delinquency and bad housing conditions." But families, "really trying hard to live cleanly," encountered difficulties in finding adequate affordable housing. Alleviating these problems required the construction of small houses to provide families the opportunity to "rise from their shack surroundings" and "constantly improve things." Pearl Chase argued that a "good building ordinance" with housing regulations to prevent windowless rooms and ensure proper ventilation was a good first step, but beyond that the issue was "largely one of education of the public." Chase's words clarified and obscured the social and racial presumptions attached to housing conditions and dissolved them through the language of education and voluntarism.

From the start of the twentieth century until US entry into World War I, voluntary organizations performed many of the functions now associated with state and local governments, including providing social services, po-

FIGURE 2.2. Residential addresses of Santa Barbara population from Mexico or Mexican descent in 1920. The concentrated cluster is on East Haley Street between Garden Street and Laguna Street. Data from US Census Bureau, 1920 US Federal Census. Map by Sierra Chmela.

FIGURE 2.3. Residential addresses of Santa Barbara's Black population in 1920. Individuals living north of Anapamu Street are generally live-in servants to white families. Data from US Census Bureau, 1920 US Federal Census. Map by Sierra Chmela.

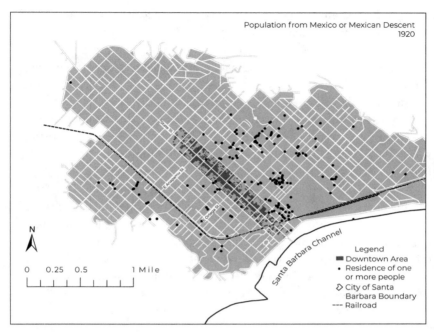

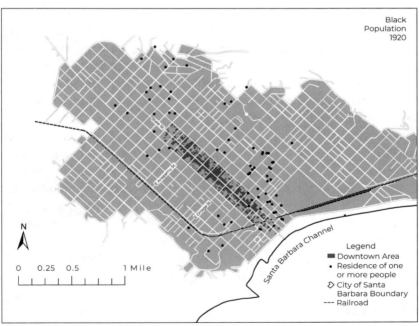

licing, and managing community norms. These organizations often folded the home and other ostensibly private spaces as central to the effectiveness of their public activities. With their formal structures and practical orientations, they offered Americans a place for carrying out significant community contributions and building up civic sensibilities and identity. Voluntary associations combined aspirational politics with quotidian social activities. Imparting republican values, more than government intervention, could provide assistance.[48] Large charitable and research institutions sponsored projects in small- and medium-sized cities to gauge reigning attitudes, support local cultural and social institutions, and investigate their benefits.[49]

As a voluntary organization with women constituting the majority of active members, the CAA's work operated outside of formal political channels while maintaining a connection to them. Standing outside traditional realms of politics and work, Chase, Hoffmann, and others advanced the pedagogical and social value of the arts as a path to strengthening community bonds. The organization's founding quickly became a minor myth in the city in no small part due to their efforts. Promotional materials claimed that the association had "never organized in the accepted sense." Instead, it was rather spontaneously born "in humble way" as "simply the expression of a community idea" before spending its first decade in the middle of an Arabian Nights tale.[50] Buttressed by a fifty-dollar loan to support an objective of meeting the "natural hunger of the human being for some form of artistic expression," what began as a local drama society expanded to include a string orchestra, art school, and, from 1922, the Plans and Planting branch.[51] The arts provided a creative outlet and a path toward augmenting community life. Although the CAA as an organization used the arts to promote interactions between community members in a recreational yet cultured atmosphere, the Plans and Planting branch had a self-proclaimed public role as a clearinghouse for Santa Barbara's architectural development. Leaders claimed this aspect represented the organization's "most tangible fruits" to the community and demonstrated their significance to the city's public life.[52] The emphasis on personal interactions in neighborhood meetings could have a nostalgic temper, such as when government reformer Mary Parker Follett observed in 1918 that the distinction between "party system and the genuine group system is the difference between the machine-made and man-made."[53]

Before national suffrage, women involved themselves in municipal improvement as a central means of entering politics—in an often voluntary and unpaid manner.[54] Municipal activities regarding sanitation and health were similar enough to domestic labor that women seemed naturally suited to the work. In 1915, the historian Mary Beard observed that women always set moral and aesthetic standards for a community since they had the ability to see the social issues at stake in the physical environment. This contrasted with men, who tended to reduce everything to economic values.[55] Developing an "actual community life" demanded more than waiting for organic connections to grow naturally. Maintaining an authentic democratic politics focused on the "homely relatives of the neighborhood meeting" differed from the platitudes of a national party. These "homely relatives" underscored the "creative power of democracy" centered on individual citizens rather than a political party.[56] Lectures, classes, clubs, and community arts—ostensibly mundane features of life—had a vital hand in this development. Efforts at beautification and civic design testified to the public role of private, voluntary labor for enacting social norms.

Modestly sized voluntary organizations in small- or medium-sized cities across the country had critics who depicted them as narrow-minded and provincial. But others found the seeds of social renewal within them. Small towns and community organizations might be insular, but cities were anonymous, dirty places populated by atomized, antisocial individuals driven only by a corrupt focus on capital accumulation and political power. Furthermore, a modestly sized settlement provided counterintuitive benefits. In a large city, one could feel pressure to wait for "ideal institutions" or "perfect men" before making decisions. But in a small town or city, an organization had to take advantage of "whatever creative forces are within a community" and build a future from those resources.[57] A neighborhood in a small community with its provincial residents offered something more interesting because "cosmopolitan people are all alike." In marked contrast to the variety of individuals one would meet in a small community, the best society in Petrograd, Paris, London, and New York were all the same.[58] The social world of a small community displayed the potential for decisive action through creative means while also suggesting its potential to constrain.

With benign intentions to "encourage in every way possible the development of good architecture" and "safe-guard and develop the natural beauty of both city and county," the CAA advocated for bringing the city in line with its natural surroundings by constructing the right type of buildings.[59] Rather than stressing mastery or stewardship over the environment, the CAA emphasized alignment with it. The CAA sponsored some larger-scale projects, such as the Lobero Theatre, which was designed by George Washington Smith with marked Spanish Colonial Revival features and stood on the site of a small adobe built by an Italian immigrant, José Lobero, in the 1870s. But for the most part, the group focused attention on its ability to "assist hundreds of individuals with their house and garden problems" and promote cooperation between local and state organizations with related interests.[60] In scale and substance, housing offered a means of wielding broad influence, while the CAA's philanthropic focus on improving conditions for families of modest means evaded scrutiny of the organization's social objectives. Despite its local priorities, the organization recognized the national or even international significance of its work. At first glance, the broad banner of the "arts" and activities such as home beautification projects might not seem the most auspicious path for social improvement and cohesion. Yet in aggregate and propagated throughout a community, these efforts resulted in notable transformations in urban space. Advancing uniformity in urban design did more than just control aesthetic features; it put elite priorities on display and normalized them as the community standard.[61] Appealing to community betterment as a justification for aesthetic values naturalized those standards as a matter of fact rather than taste.

Evoking the social role of art sheltered conservative and assimilationist objectives. The combination of local concerns and abstract ideals of human progress that governed the CAA's ambitions reflected national anxieties about modern life. Known for its financial support for libraries, large institutions, international peace, and the study of Americanization, in the early 1920s the Carnegie Corporation of New York began to direct its attention to arts organizations with "a hospitable attitude toward the development of cultural values of art."[62] Propelled by a desire to examine the long-term viability of community-based arts organizations, the Carnegie supported groups focused on the "diffusion and appreciation of art among all the people of the community" rather than sizable institutions or established artists.[63] Carnegie's staff argued that developing the "cultural values of art" for a wide audience provided a mollifying response to "the present hurried every-day life of the American people." In the face of unease over the assumed chaos of urban life, the arts provided an antidote to a life "keyed high" with the "whirl of modern machinery. . . . roar of the subway" and "the staccato rattle of turnstiles, like machine guns in action."[64] The arts not only augmented the "satisfaction and to the happiness of its people" but also fostered more practical habits of "steadfastness and self-control." This conception of art contrasted with avant-garde practices to emphasize a morally unambiguous art oriented toward mass appeal and cultural assimilation rather than an art that critiqued modern conditions.[65]

With its sights set on art for the common citizen, in 1924 the Carnegie Corporation agreed to provide $25,000 a year for five years (later extended to eight) to the CAA for its programs to aid, in its words, the "cultural improvement of the people and in the beautification of Santa Barbara."[66] The city offered "an exceptional location for testing the possibilities of such a community enterprise in the interests of art."[67] Around the same time, Carnegie supplied grants to two other arts organizations, the MacDowell Colony in New Hampshire and Philadelphia's Graphic Sketch Club. All three mobilized the arts as a path to improve American habits and culture through local interventions. Founded by Edward and Marian MacDowell in 1907, the MacDowell Colony's primary mission to provide studio space in rural New Hampshire to artists seemed an outlier from Carnegie objectives. But by offering "the seclusion essential for creative work," the MacDowell engaged in a different type of cultivation.[68] For Edward MacDowell, nature furnished individuals with ideal conditions for artistic creation, a remedy to the noise, pollution, and distractions of the city. The rural New Hampshire woods with their tucked-away calm equipped fledgling artists with "an inspirational boost up the discouragingly tall ladder" at a stage when "so many careers are blighted through lack of understanding and sane sympathy."[69] The chance for privacy, creative exchange, and fellowship with others striving to cultivate their artistic capacities while surrounded by nature may have suggested an eccentric or nonconformist strain of artists, but supporters stressed that the colony was in "no sense Bohemian" or "exotic."[70] Some admitted that the word *colony* brought to mind an ominous feeling or the belief that it served as a "summer resort for incurable amateurs, or an experiment in misapplied aesthetics," but the emphasis was on productive and accessible creative work by demonstrated though relatively unknown artistic talents.[71]

In addition to sustaining artists by providing a respite from urban life, the Carnegie Corporation supported programs that used art to flatten distinctions between disparate groups. For the Graphic Sketch Club, located in an area of Philadelphia inhabited by "Italians, Poles, Russians, Germans," art was not the "end in itself" but the key to establishing shared cultural foundations across distinct ethnic backgrounds.[72] This version of sociability liberated from hierarchical stratifications imposed by modern life, be they ethnic, economic, or political, harkened back, according to a journalist from the *New York Times Magazine*, to the Middle Ages and the mood of the "craftsman rather than the mood of the trader."[73] For the Carnegie Corporation, both the Graphic Sketch Club and the CAA met the challenge of finding a proper approach for assimilating disparate groups together through the arts. Henry S. Pritchett, the president of the Carnegie Foundation for the Advancement of Teaching and later a resident of Santa Barbara, saw some promise in universities, but he believed that Americans thought of them primarily as mortuaries. Pritchett also looked to medieval guilds for a spirit of cooperation and common interest in beauty and skill. In his mind, communities in the Middle Ages had almost no differentiation of social status but were drawn together "without reference to class prejudice or social distinction." The absence of political, theological, and class lines, he claimed, shaped a distinct type of knowledge of beauty and skill in the arts. This conception of the arts, he contended, was not sectarian but "essentially democratic."[74] While acknowledging that the Carnegie Corporation's decision to award funds to the CAA or any community art project might have seemed an odd choice, Pritchett surmised that a "widely diffused knowledge and appreciation of Art in American life" had the potential to seep through and improve multiple levels of American society.[75] He specifically pointed to the CAA's School of the Arts as an effective avenue toward cultural assimilation, since the school attracted "all classes of the population," with the most promise shown in the children of Mexican parents who had "become American as a consequence of the transfer of California from Mexico to the United States."[76]

Its financial resources allowed Carnegie to pursue two avenues for democratizing art: art education and expanding the scope of art's definition. Reflecting on the CAA and its mission, Pritchett concluded there was no reason that the organization's approach could not be generally applied in "any other association of human beings." Despite admitting that he had very little knowledge of the arts, Pritchett viewed Art and Nature (with a capital A and capital N) as the two general fields of human interest that brought about a remarkable combination of value—through an appreciation for form, beauty, and color—and technical skill. That combination operated in communities as a means for inhabitants to recognize beauty not simply in high works of art but also "in their homes, their gardens, their streets and public buildings." On their face, these claims "to promote life, love, and laughter" through art seemed innocent enough.[77] Looking to the public library, art gallery, or symphony orchestra as public social goods rather than profit-making enterprises required "the support of public-spirited citizens" and avoiding compromising on their ideals. Such endeavors highlighted the investment of philanthropic organizations in making localized changes rather than structural interventions. This expanded into a strategy for addressing national transformations. Limiting the definition of art's social value to its usefulness for localized improvement made it a tool for maintaining order. But that limited outlook raised the possibility that art transcended political strife. When associations used resources to support "the cultivation of the sense of beauty" by training individuals in the arts, they would not "run against the ordinary barriers of political, social and religious antagonism that tends so often to separate men into classes." Appreciating beauty suggested something innate about human character. Tapping into this intrinsic trait through arts programs and classes had an immediate effect. But "more notable than the direct work" was how these programs held "an unusual value as an agent for the social integration of a community." By consolidating and unifying rather than differentiating and dividing, the arts enacted a civic politics without conflict. In Santa Barbara, the vision of community harmony came through in music and drawing classes but was most visible in the city fabric. Ultimately, CAA members presented their solutions as a natural phenomenon, as if through their work Santa Barbara would reveal its essential self. Revealing this objective truth of California's environment encouraged an aspiration that it could benefit the character of its citizens as well.

Settling on the home as the chosen location for inspiring social uplift and improvement encouraged individuals to think about their domestic arrangements as a template for society. This perspective elevated homeownership as a form of civic duty and marker of good citizenship. Economic investment in the land expressed more than a financial act. The home was only the beginning. How one maintained domestic spaces sent messages that spread beyond its immediate environs. Ideas of home improvement informed efforts to restrict billboards, clean vacant lots, and intervene against other potential "eyesores." Developing the city's natural beauty demanded entering "with great vigor" into the heart of the city's building industry.[78] Supporters of Santa Barbara's efforts couched the economic benefits of these projects in terms of virtue and visual grace. This attention separated the city from other urban areas with their tendency to erect "cheap buildings to catch the demand for offices" and homes "built to sell and satisfy the moment." Unfortunately, these places lacked "both in architectural beauty and in actual utility."[79] Working through public and private channels, the CAA viewed the suitable development of the city's urban fabric as one of its primary responsibilities and an essential contribution.

Embedding moral purpose through architectural standards in house construction lent the task a high-minded temper, but advocating for aesthetic uniformity and quality also reaped financial benefits. An aesthetic purist, one journalist observed, might be shocked over the question whether beauty pays since it was "its own justification" without need for any "conventional financial balance sheet."[80] Santa Barbara, however, provided a counterexample as a place where beauty paid handsomely (Figure 2.4). Upholding the city's reputation as an affluent haven required encouraging home maintenance and ownership to those on modest budgets. Therefore, the CAA worked to demonstrate that a "meager purse is a bar to a beautiful effect" for homes.

How a Community Arts Association Is Raising Architectural Standards

By Edward Sajous

THE rapidly growing city of Santa Barbara, Calif., has a live Community Arts Association, with a Drama Branch, an Orchestra Branch, and a Plans and Planting Committee.

In such a period of hurried construction, which has accompanied the growth of many cities, the tendency has been to erect cheap

THE ROGERS BUILDING BEFORE REMODELING

buildings to catch the demand for offices and to put up homes which are built to sell and satisfy for the moment, but which are lacking both in architectural beauty and in actual utility. In Santa Barbara, however, the Plans and Planting Committee of the Community Arts Association has entered with great vigor into the very heart of the building industry. Its aims are to encourage the building of good houses; to maintain high architectural standards; to arouse interest in beautiful gardens and in the planting of empty spaces with flowers; and to advocate municipal legislation controlling vacant lots.

Recently, a prize was offered by the committee to the local business house which, in altering its building, would conform most closely to high architectural and esthetic principles. Among the buildings altered during the past season was that of Rogers & Son, a furniture company. An effort was made to make the building front beautiful, and after inspection of several buildings, the committee, composed of well-known architects, awarded the prize and the right to set a plaque in the side of the doorway, to the Rogers firm.

THE BUILDING AS IT NOW APPEARS

Lectures by architects and designers are frequently held under the auspices of the Plans and Planting Committee. The Spanish motif, though it is not forced, is encouraged in Santa Barbara as that most suitable for the climate and topography. The committee is willing at any time to confer with home builders and to give advice on their problems. Recently the new Santa Barbara City Hall, soon to be built, was the subject of the committee's advice and help.

FIGURE 2.4. Edward Sajous, "How a Community Arts Association Is Raising Architectural Standards," from *The American City* (July 1926).

To prove the point, in one of its earliest programs, the Plans and Planting branch established the Small House Planning Service and recruited local architects to participate in house-design competitions.[81] Encouraging interest in the "art side of the project" and homeownership contributed, the organization hoped, to community building. As individuals realized that every member of a family, including children, could take part in improvements in and around the house, they would also conclude that the home was a microcosm of their neighborhood and city. Supporters hoped that growing awareness of the link between the quality of the home and the quality of the city would result in more families who regarded domestic spaces as a contribution to the "community mosaic."[82]

Nondescript, tidy, and modest houses formed the backbone of an environmental understanding that prioritized community alignment and quality of life. The Plans and Planting branch held its first house-design competition in 1923 with a brief that asked for a house suitable for California of not more than five rooms and a garage for one car on a lot 50 feet wide on the street line and 150 feet long with a cost of no more than $5,000.[83] In order to verify the cost limit, entrants needed to provide estimates from builders validating the amount required to cover the cost of construction, painting, and decorating, though not plantings or gardens. That year, architects from across the United States submitted ninety-two designs, though the majority came from California. The judges, who included a former employee of Bertram Goodhue, Carleton Winslow, and Mary Smith, the widow of a well-known Santa Barbara architect, George Washington Smith, awarded $1,000 in prizes.

Submissions included one from Paul R. Williams, a Black architect who had just started an independent practice and who would later gain prominence for his designs for numerous public buildings in Los Angeles as well as residences for celebrities (Figure 2.5). He received a special mention for his submission of a two-bedroom house with a "straightforward, simple, and economical" Spanish-California-designed exterior with a porte cochere with entry into the living room.[84] His accompanying exterior drawing set the house in front of an outline of mountains, and palm trees stood on both sides of the porte cochere. A typical non-California style house, such as one of an "English Rural Stucco Type" designed by Emmet G. Martin, an architect from Los Angeles, included two bedrooms, a large living room with a fireplace, a dining room, a kitchen, one bathroom, and a laundry porch with a detached garage. Oak floors covered most of the house, and Martin included details for decorative bookcases lining the wall separating the common areas from the bedrooms. In addition to the competition, the winning projects and other selected entrants were exhibited at the Paseo de la Guerra, a Spanish

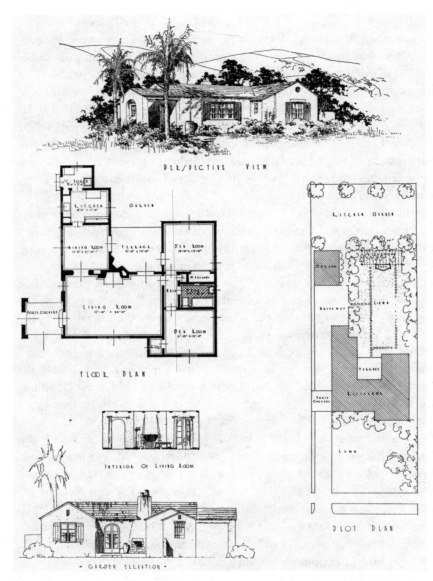

FIGURE 2.5. Paul R. Williams, "Competition for a 5000.00 Dollar Residence." This plan, the jury noted, "recommends itself at a glance" with a "splendidly handled" exterior in its straightforward simplicity. From *Small House Designs* edited by Carleton Monroe Winslow and Edward Fisher Brown, 1924.

Colonial-style space designed by James Osborne Craig, in downtown Santa Barbara in September 1923. Together these house designs showed that private individuals supported the view that "homes and garden can and should be developed which take every advantage of climate, location, skilled architects and workmen."[85]

Based on the popularity of the exhibition, the branch collected sixty-two entries, including those by Williams and Martin, into a book titled *Small House Designs*.[86] The book arranged the houses by type, such as Spanish-California, English Rural Stucco, English Stucco, and Wood Exterior, and included comments on each design, as well as hints and guidelines for builders. The CAA envisioned *Small House Designs* as a contrast to numerous popular "Bungalow Books" that merely sold collections of plans without commenting on quality or the desirable and undesirable features of rooms and spatial arrangements (Figure 2.6). *Small House Designs* stated that bedrooms should not open into the dining room and the toilet should not be in "too prominent a location when viewed from the door." In other contexts, the CAA foregrounded the economic benefits of urban uniformity, but here it stressed that this project had "no motive of profit," but that it wished only to make "data available which would enhance the aesthetic building effects in California communities."[87] Additionally, the branch arranged for a smaller group of architects to sell working drawings of the designs at a moderate fee based on the belief that individuals with only $5,000 to spend on a house would not be able to consult an architect.[88] Those who purchased plans had to agree that no major modifications, especially of the house's exterior, would be made without the organization's consent. The regulations over the plans came from the idea that only "the most creditable designs" would be released, with the strong points emphasized and the "weak points guarded against."

Codifying and regulating tastes in designs for houses in the name of encouraging homeownership occupied many others outside Southern California. Architects, contractors, real estate professionals, and members of the building trades had vested interests in home building and ownership to "high community standards." But so did media outlets, local governments, and chambers of commerce. Yet the influence of this local focus went far beyond Santa Barbara's borders. Requests for copies of *Small House Designs* came from forty-five states and Canada, the Panama Canal Zone, Hawaii, the Philippines, Puerto Rico, Cuba, five European countries, Australia, Africa, South America, and China; additionally, fifteen hundred copies were sold within California.[89] One man from New York wrote to say that he had visited California over the summer and was impressed by Santa Barbara's building program and motivated to form a similar group in his own town so those

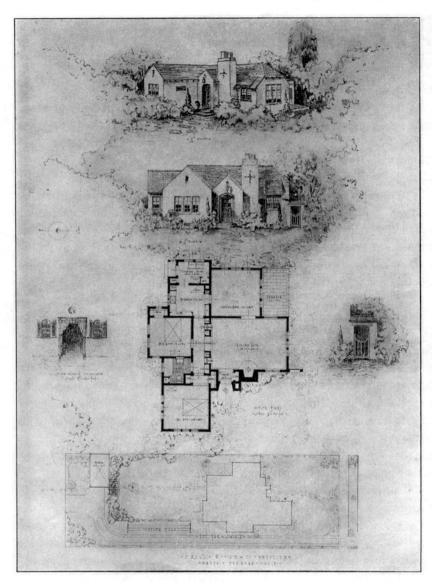

FIGURE 2.6. Emmet G. Martin, "Small House Competition," described as "an interesting house, though not Californian," that would be "charming in the right setting." From *Small House Designs* edited by Carleton Monroe Winslow and Edward Fisher Brown, 1924.

constructing new structures would "conform to a general plan of architectural development."[90] A resident of Westmoreland, Jamaica, inspired by the idea of "controlling the architectural features of your city and . . . making a success of it," asked for photos of houses that provided modern comforts for a tropical climate. The writer hoped to convince his neighbors to embrace uniformity through features typical of American cities.[91] People who ordered the book included organizations such as the American Building Association and White Motor Trucks of Havana, Cuba, the Canadian Department of Agriculture, building manufacturers, public libraries, banks, and architects.[92] Helen Spotts, a resident of Los Angeles and head of a branch of the public library, wrote to declare the book a "great joy," stating that "its influence will surely be felt in Southern California." She noted that the book was in constant circulation.[93] The organization became a more general source of counsel. Some requests included comments on the perceived suitability of the designs for certain climates, and others hoped to use Santa Barbara's community-based achievements as a model for civic improvement activities in other parts of the United States and its overseas territories. Pearl Chase received correspondence from a Mrs. W. P. Gaddis, who was married to the captain of the yard of the US naval station in Cavite, the Philippines, that included newsletter clippings regarding local housing conditions and expressions of concern that suggested to Chase that poor conditions negatively affected both the servicemen and natives.[94] In the spirit of voluntarism, Chase proposed a Clean-Up Week and promised to bring the matter to officials in the US Navy.

If Santa Barbara had realized its distinctive character through the voluntary efforts of individuals, then other places could follow its example. Developing house plans and collecting them into a widely available and popular book brought national attention and praise as "pioneering work" for the Plans and Planting branch in local urban development.[95] As an educational project to foster appreciation for the types of architecture "fitting in this region for climatic reasons and because of architectural traditions," the branch promoted the economic and social benefits of uniform domestic architecture.[96] Deploying the language of art and beauty made the city into a "veritable laboratory of California art . . . the art of building its more personal and humanly significant aspects; of the character which is at the core of a truly popular style of architecture."[97] Any visitor to Santa Barbara, supporters claimed, would find that the Plans and Planting branch's influence infused this "unusual city" with a working "community leaven" and an "art spirit" that had taken "permanent roots."[98] The popularity of the designs and accompanying national and international accolades fortified the conviction within the CAA that its work was exceptional yet portable.

National media and political leaders sought to enshrine homeownership as a symbol of social investment. This lent further currency to the CAA's work. In 1924, the Plans and Planting branch began taking part in the BHA program and gained access to a national platform for disseminating its small house designs. Initiated in 1922 as a proposal in *The Delineator*, a women's magazine published by the Butterick Publishing Company with a circulation of more than one million, by its editor Marie Meloney, the BHA advocated homeownership and a modern approach to housekeeping for women.[99] The program grew quickly and by 1930 had over seven thousand local chapters.[100] In 1923, the first year of the national campaign for Better Homes Week, held annually during the last week of April, at least fifty-seven cities across the United States built seventy-eight demonstration homes and held home tours. The organization's growth testified not only to a broad interest in single-family housing and the benefits of homeownership but also to the mechanisms and publicity that produced this interest.

The United States' entry into World War I curtailed efforts by real estate interests to encourage homeownership in the early twentieth century. After the war's conclusion and spurred by evidence recorded in the 1920 census that revealed fewer than half of Americans owned their homes, efforts to advance homeownership started again in earnest.[101] The BHA, like the CAA, presented itself as a voluntary organization, but one with a much more overt economic and political agenda. For BHA leaders, social problems in the United States could be "solved through specific instruction in the construction, organization, and supervision" of homes rather than state intervention.[102] Despite support from government and private organizations such as the US Departments of Agriculture, Commerce, Interior, and Labor; the US Public Health Service; the American Home Economics Association; the Architects Small House Service Bureau; and the US Chamber of Commerce, the BHA claimed first to be an educational movement supported by public gifts rather than commercial backing and therefore upheld community ideals that emphasized individual initiative.

The BHA's expressed presentation as an educational voluntary movement focused on improving housing quality implied a modesty to the organization's objectives. Yet the organization received enthusiastic public support from prominent officials and brought together myriad interests invested in increased private home building and ownership. Alongside this endorsement, the organization worked against municipal or state housing programs.[103] Soon after the BHA's inception, support arrived from President Warren Harding and governors of twenty-eight states. Its national advisory council included Vice President Calvin Coolidge, Secretary of Treasury Herbert Hoover, and officers of the General Federation of Women's Clubs. Despite the overwhelming number of men in BHA's national leadership, the organization's success depended on the work and moral example of women who were a "force for a better America."[104] The organization's goals of raising the standard of living and stimulating interest in the "development of more attractive, enduring, and better homes" was vital to all citizens, but perhaps especially to "young wives and foreign-born mothers" who needed to learn the "fundamentals of American home-making tendencies and find inspiration for new endeavors in their own homes." As "one of the most fundamental of our human institutions," the single-family home provided the "happiest and most wholesome" life for a family with children. Such a house was "the American ideal" and ideally accessible to all families.[105] Homeownership improved housing conditions, benefited a population's stability, and elevated "the standard of citizenship and self-respect."[106] The valorization of the modest single-family home, rather than a large public building, conveyed a civic vision based on private ownership and received endorsements from the highest levels of the state.

For the volunteers, staff, and supporters involved in BHA, homeownership functioned as a barometer of the nation's cultural and social conditions. The United States, proclaimed the 1926 Better Homes guidebook, "has justly been called a home-loving nation." Normalizing ideals of the home set the tone for a promising future vision of the country. Calvin Coolidge asserted that the American home was "the foundation of our national and individual well-being."[107] The organization's executive director and professor of social ethics at Harvard, James Ford, believed that the home's significance was evident in the "effects of environment upon human character and activities" and compared raising children to plant cultivation.[108] Revealing himself as a supporter of environmental determinism, Ford reasoned that if the environment did not matter in the life of vegetables, then "all such seeds when planted would result in plants of high quality." But a trained horticulturist knew that unfavorable environmental factors hindered the germination of even the best seeds. Children underwent a similar experience, and that fact required a strong consideration of the home environment. Disadvantageous circumstances of upbringing prevented "children of the best heredity or of the best native environment" from a high level of development. As homes were the central location of children's lives and experiences, their improvement became the "primary means to the development of individual character." The ultimate result of environmental improvement, according to Mrs. Thomas G. Winter, president of the General Federation of Women's Clubs, was "better children and better families ... better citizenship."[109] The path to an improved nation flowed through the home and private initiative. Homeownership offered a primary vehicle toward national improvement.

The CAA encouraged participation in its Better Homes Weeks to address changing conditions of urbanization, housing shortages, and population growth. In 1924, the first year the Plans and Planting branch participated in Better Homes Week, Santa Barbara tied for first prize with Atlanta, Georgia, in the demonstration home competition, with four homes opened for tours and one built specifically for Better Homes Week. Demonstration homes included one at 108 West Yanonali Street near downtown Santa Barbara on a lot purchased for $2,000. Architect John Frederic Murphy drew plans based on one from the first Small House competition, and landscape architect Lockwood de Forest directed the landscape and gardens. This "House that Budget Built" had six rooms, including two bedrooms, and the plantings included a lawn, flowers, and "decorative vegetables" such as artichokes, rhubarb, parsley, and herbs that were to be sold.[110] The example homes needed to inspire visitors to make their own domiciles "more convenient, attractive and wholesome," however modest they might be.[111] Within each house, volunteers chose color schemes and furnishings to highlight the beauty of simple designs. The national BHA organization added to the message, noting that local groups should convey that "simplicity and dignity in its architecture are essential" and offering advice on how to furnish the homes, including toys for nurseries.[112]

Despite encouraging aesthetic uniformity, members of the Plans and Planting branch could not completely jettison individual preferences. Some of the demonstration homes received public criticism, such as the unfurnished House B at 821 West Valerio Street designed in a Spanish Colonial Revival style.[113] While some visitors enjoyed the aesthetic details ("I like the front door—it looks so quaint and Spanish"), others wondered why the house lacked a dining room or even felt "furious that they had us waste our time to come away out here to see this pile of junk." Another home, the 1926 Demonstration House 1 at 1432 San Andres Street, called "La Recuerda" or "Remembrance," was considered a successful use of Spanish style for a modest and unpretentious home; it was designed from a plan drawn by the wife of the lot's owner, with suitable use of color from its tile roof and orange trim alongside a "typically Spanish" garden.[114]

At a national level, BHA presumed its primary audience was white and that others required specialized programs. If a community had "a large population of immigrants or of negros" who "because of limited education have not yet learned the ways of securing the best living conditions which are within their reach," a demonstration house might be "of particular value to such groups in the population through the work of special subcommittees."[115] Ignorance of a better way to live was assumed. While the Plans and Planting branch focused on encouraging Santa Barbara's white residents into home-ownership, it had some opportunities to work with Santa Barbara's Black and Latino communities with mixed success. Programs advocating for orderly, modest houses, neat gardens, and proper homemaking were developed with the hopes that those efforts could connect an entire community. But that connection had distinct boundaries and standards. Investigations in 1919 by volunteers found that it was in the "homes of these non-English speaking people that the worst conditions were generally found, conditions of dirt and filth, and over-crowding."[116] The ideals of community needed a supplemental "through-going extensive program of education for the foreigners," including night classes since these individuals, in most cases, had been "interested and quite amendable to suggestions, realizing that the end in view was their own good." Focusing attention on the domestic customs of non-Anglo residents promoted the assumption that it was "education, rather than legislation" or otherwise confronting structural economic or racial conditions that would pave the way to reform.

Organizers of the 1925 Better Homes Week hoped to have a separate set of programs exclusively for Santa Barbara's Mexican community, including exhibits on proper sanitation, fly control, and garbage disposal; talks on child care; and demonstrations on affordable appliances and furniture "within the reach of Mexican families," but a smallpox outbreak prevented its deployment.[117] In 1926, Better Homes Week featured a demonstration house at 209 Gray Avenue that was constructed after the 1925 earthquake and was owned by Charles Harris, a Black minister, and his family.[118] Better Homes officials claimed that Harris wanted the house to serve as an example for Santa Barbara's Black residents to reveal what they could accomplish "at little cost" to better their own living conditions. Though Harris was unable to pay for his own furnishings, reports claimed that he knew through "his great faith" that a "way would be provided for him." After construction, Harris had little money left to furnish the house with secondhand pieces, so the Santa Barbara Women's Club took charge of the furnishings while the Plans and Planting branch completed the grounds he had planted with vegetables. It was coined the "Good-Will House" for Better Homes Week, and its opening included a choir singing "America" and saying a prayer of blessing and thanks for the Better Homes Committee. Approaches to Black Americans differed regionally. The South had a dedicated Negro Better Homes program created in 1924 because national leaders refused to confront local segregationists.[119] This turned into a universalizing standard for uplift and created lines of and restrictions to belonging (Figures 2.7 and 2.8).

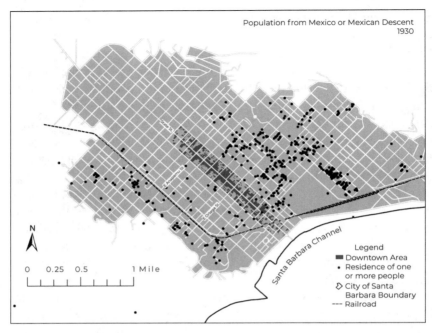
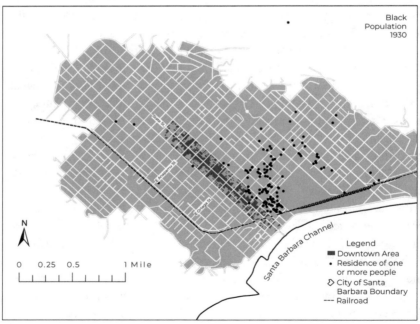

Having his house as part of Demonstration Week became an opportunity for Harris to finish his house completely while also providing a practical model for Santa Barbara's Black population who lived under de facto segregation. These individuals mainly worked as domestic servants, cooks, and day laborers. The city's Black residents' spatial concentration increased throughout the 1920s. Approximately two-thirds of the population lived in an area bounded by Haley Street on the east, Montecito Street to the south, State Street on the west, and Garden Street to the north.[120] Segregation in Santa Barbara came in more formal ways. In Hope Ranch, a beachside community west of downtown, a covenant written in 1924 affirmed that no stores, groceries, or mercantile businesses could be situated in the neighborhood. Moreover, no property, except streets, parks, and open spaces, could be used for "any other purpose other than residence" and no building could be built except for a private residence of no more than two stories.[121] In addition to building restrictions, Hope Ranch prohibited anyone of "African, Japanese, Chinese, or of any Mongolian descent" to purchase, own, lease, or occupy property in the area. There was an exception for live-in servants.

The 1926 BHA guidebook encouraged community participation in Better Homes Weeks as a strategy for thinking through race alongside new problems of urbanization. Harris's Good-Will House was only one such example. One "notable fact" about Atlanta, the cowinner alongside Santa Barbara for Better Homes Weeks in 1926, was that its local committee took "special care" to prepare programs for whites, Blacks, and immigrants "whose knowledge of American standards of housing and home life is slight and who may experience difficulty in adjusting themselves to American conditions." One of Atlanta's demonstration houses was designed specifically for a Black family with a subcommittee from the Black community in charge. There was also a demonstration home that represented "Americanization."[122] In the Territory of Hawaii, a local BHA committee designed "The Little House on Wheels" in Honolulu as a traveling educational exhibit and claimed that it "excited the greatest interest" among native Hawaiians, Chinese, and Japanese families.[123] These examples emphasized a view that Black Americans, Asians, and immi-

FIGURE 2.7. Residential addresses of Santa Barbara's population from Mexico or Mexican descent in 1930. The concentration of residences in the southeastern part of the city near the railroad is on or around North Quarantina Street. Data from US Census Bureau, 1930 US Federal Census. Map by Sierra Chmela.
FIGURE 2.8. Residential addresses of Santa Barbara's Black population in 1930. Many of the residences near present-day Gray Avenue just east of State Street were destroyed as part of the expansion of Highway 101 that began with the National Industrial Recovery Act of 1933. Data from US Census Bureau, 1930 US Federal Census. Map by Sierra Chmela.

grants required active instruction in the values of white Americans through homeownership and housekeeping.

Throughout the 1920s, the program registered signs of success. The single-family home comprised 60 percent of family units constructed in the country, a figure that rose to 90 percent in the 1930s.[124] Into the 1930s, the BHA program advanced design standards and the social benefits of homeownership to working- and middle-class Americans. In the local context, Santa Barbara's continued national success with the program validated the objectives of the CAA. This project supported by men in power and disseminated through the pages of a national women's magazine created structures for understanding the proper order of the nation with the home at the center. Couched as both a unique accomplishment and a portable campaign for civic improvement, the CAA, BHA, and related projects brought to light the priorities of the city's social elites. By channeling this work through voluntary organizations, residents created an alternative to government institutions, policy, and law. Moreover, improvements to the city's built landscape at the scale of the single-family home centered individual responsibility over municipal interventions. Together, these activities shored up the boundaries of community by making visible the appropriate types of homes—and by extension the appropriate types of people. In the absence of state regulations, community norms prevailed.

Ultimately, the emphasis on individualism through private homeownership imbued the home with outsized political and social importance. Refracting politics through the home rendered it less detectable as politics and potentially more insidious. Restrictions on design helped indicate desirable company or a distinctive and exceptional community. Aesthetic cohesion in domestic landscape connoted social tranquility and shared values. Though not all tactics met with success, the CAA's approach established a method that could be widely applied in other communities. By framing its work as educational, calls to reform domestic habits and care for civic beauty offered a useful replacement for politics. Rather than laws and ordinances, a "program of education in culture on a basis of extreme simplicity" easily reached the understanding of the average person.[125] Although not every person could cultivate great knowledge about art or architecture, almost all could unlock their instinct for enjoyment. The CAA advocated for a view that the "enjoyment and spiritual exaltation which comes from participation in [the arts] is not reserved for those with advantages of super education, but is native to the whole population."[126] Everyday activities rather than large-scale public transformations placed agency, responsibility, and obligation for democratic self-government in the hands of local citizens—at least to a limited extent. Ultimately, this work coalesced around a vision of community aligned with the values of well-to-do Americans. The arts and concern for aesthetic standards in a community stood as an ostensibly non-coercive means of enacting the norms of the well-to-do. Yet this community spirit centered on homeownership foreclosed pursuing alternative ways of making a home.

3

To Cultivate and Protect

"The United States was the only country in the world that began with perfection and aspired to progress."[1]

In 1877, a transplant from Australia arrived in Santa Barbara and began to flourish. Almost eighty years later, it remained on the corner of Chapala and Montecito Streets near a prominent entry point into the city, the Southern Pacific Train Depot. Rumored to be one of the most photographed trees in the country, the transplant was a type of banyan tree, a Moreton Bay fig (*Ficus macrophylla*) planted by a Miss Adeline Crabb.[2] By 1955, media reported that the tree had branches spanning 135 feet and shade spread over 13,000 square feet at noon so ten thousand people could stand covered by its shadow (Figure 3.1). An object of fascination on its own and one of several of the city's lauded trees, the species enjoyed wide popularity in its native Australia as one of the "finest avenue trees." Arriving in California as an ornamental, it thrived from a combination of "mild climate, rich soil, and enthusiastic gardeners."[3] Francesco Franceschi, an immigrant to Santa Barbara from Italy who introduced numerous plant species into Southern California, declared that the Moreton Bay fig was an "indispensable inmate" of every local garden.[4]

Trees conveyed historic and civic symbolism, colorful lore, and novelty of varying significance. Many of Santa Barbara's significant trees arrived from other parts of the world. A Norfolk Island Pine (*Araucaria excelsa*), native to Australia's eastern coast, stood in front of the YMCA building on the corner of Carrillo and Chapala Streets, and residents adorned it with lights at Christmas.[5] In Alameda Park, one of the oldest in the city, on land reportedly set aside by the Spanish stood a Montezuma cypress from Mexico, a Hawaiian loa tree, cone pines from New Zealand, and a wine palm from Central America. The king and queen of Belgium planted three redwoods in the city as a memorial of their stay there.[6] The "Ellwood Queen," a lemon-scented gum or eucalyptus and purportedly the tallest tree in Santa Barbara County

FIGURE 3.1. "Santa Barbara's Most Important Tree," a Moreton Bay fig planted in 1877, can reportedly provide shade for 10,450 people at noon. From *Santa Cruz Sentinel* (June 28, 1955). Courtesy of the *Santa Cruz Sentinel*.

at 130 feet tall, was named in honor of Ellwood Cooper, a resident credited with introducing eucalyptus varieties to the United States who served for two decades as president of the state board of agriculture.[7] Camphor trees, walnut trees, palms, and grapevines received similar notice, and some "famous tree citizens" even conjured glimpses into the city's darker past.[8] One "majestic" two-hundred-year-old oak tree, known as the Horse Thief Tree, stood at 422 West De La Guerra Street, the property of one H. L. Brandes.[9] When a cavity—reportedly ten feet high and three feet wide—threatened the tree's survival, Brandes arranged for what was said to be the largest tree surgery at the time. Locals believed the tree received its name because settlers used it to hang Native American horse thieves, thus condemning it to eternal haunting. The Brandes family countered that they had never observed ghosts of departed horse thieves from its limbs. However, the tree surgeon found several flattened bullets in the trunk, and residents attributed their presence either to Spanish riddling hanging bodies with bullets or a previous tenant who tested his guns from a target hanging from the tree.[10]

Stories about trees, innocuous and less so, structured and bolstered ambitions for national and regional progress. Farm and horticulture journals, forestry reports, gardening books, lifestyle magazines, and newspapers carried messages of plant life's significance to American culture and character.[11] Early pioneers, so the tales went, cut paths through untouched American wilderness and recognized forests as "essential to civilized man's welfare."[12] The abundance of trees in North America contrasted with Europe and its centuries of deforestation due to their usefulness as an energy source and in shipbuilding.[13] That trees anchored notions of plenty and national momentum was expected since, according to one US Department of Agriculture publication, the nation "has been quite literally nurtured in a wooden cradle."[14] The Moreton Bay fig's journey from the Australian coast to Santa Barbara illustrated a voyage made by countless specimens of plants across oceans and continents.[15] Its successful entry and establishment offered one consequential narrative about botanical exchange and buttressed lore about California's hospitable environment. The congenial atmosphere that aided the tree's flourishing provided the region with a convenient tale of both botanical and human flourishing—at least with the right sort of control. That certain plants arrived in California, easily thrived, and ultimately assimilated into the environs raised questions of which human beings could do the same and what that absence of difficult transition suggested about those who could not.

Plant life figured as a critical component of political and social projects that assumed observation, experimentation, and improvement of the environment conferred privileges and ownership over a territory. In California, plants and trees animated and justified assumptions about the state's climate and environmental quality. Botanical specimens from around the world encountering the state's rich soil and equable climate easily increased and multiplied. As a result, plants conferred a stable and natural authority compared to the whims of human culture. Human beings who flourished and those who did not given all of California's endowments revealed their own innate characteristics. The cultivation of plants compared to the cultivation of humans provided a basis of critiquing the latter. In the face of this singular environment, human activities and communities posed a potential threat. The work of bringing and establishing plant life from one location to another, or acclimatization, shaped into ideas of foreign and domestic, public and private, and scientific and vernacular knowledge, not as dichotomies but as interacting forces, linking daily life, such as tending a home garden, to imperial activities of territorial control.

In addition to the transfer of plant life, related activities such as gardening and landscaping connected discrete locales to wider geographical terrains and populations. Private gardens, botanic gardens, acclimatization societies, and garden clubs offered edification for the public and reinforced cultural assumptions with scientific and civic authority. The diverse audiences of these outlets meant that they had considerable variation in content and pedagogical objectives. Words used for horticultural purposes, such as *cultivation*, *heredity*, and *adaptation*, were smoothly transferred to human activities and thus connected botanical specimens and human beings rhetorically and practically. Individuals learned not just from observing plants but from maintaining them. Growing, cultivating, and caring for them imparted values of productivity and domestic order.

In its most sinister cast, linking social values to the natural world allowed individuals to avoid reckoning with questions of eugenic, racial, and economic associations while shoring up nature's normative influence. Plant life strengthened essentialist ideas about the proper order of society through a combination of science and domesticity and elite and popular preferences to shape narratives of human development one home and one garden at a time.[16] Connecting engineering principles with both plant life and the domestic sphere through centering economy, efficiency, convenience, and hygiene acted as one route to bring home, office, and garden together.[17] Those who extended domestic responsibilities to spaces outside the home in the late nineteenth and early twentieth centuries became known as "nature's housekeepers," spreading values of cleanliness and order to municipal services. These individuals created an urban analog to the conservation movement as well as a link to the roots of modern environmental thought.[18] Making oneself at home in new surroundings—or acclimatizing—was an essential part of this work. The inability to assimilate reflected the individual rather than the situation or circumstances.

Of the seven hundred species of eucalyptus, almost all are native to Australia. But since at least the eighteenth century, the tree has had a peripatetic history. Like the Moreton Bay fig, the eucalyptus had a celebrated transit from Australia. It traveled to England with Joseph Banks as part of James Cook's first voyage and to the Sahara by the French, who believed the tree could be used to prevent desertification.[19] The tree arrived in South Africa, Brazil, Palestine, India, and Chile, as well as other parts of the United States.[20] Reaching California in the mid-nineteenth century mostly by way of Europe, much of what was planted in the state was the blue gum tree (*Eucalyptus globulus*), lauded as one of the tallest trees in nature and believed to be highly suited for naval construction. Abbot Kinney, chair of the California Board of Forestry and developer of Venice, California, penned a volume on the eucalyptus in 1895 and wrote that the trees had anti-miasmatic properties and absorbed excessive humidity in soil (Figure 3.2).[21] The agriculturist Alfred McClatchie of Throop Polytechnic Institute, the precursor to the California Institute of Technology, hyperbolically surmised that the species had "probably served more aesthetic and utilitarian purposes than any other forest trees that have been planted on this continent."[22]

Europeans and Americans viewed the results of such journeys as clear evidence of their own scientific and technical capabilities. As a result, plants often had an easier time gaining acceptance in a new environment than people. The process of acclimatization, sometimes called "seasoning," was central to that acceptance. The word *acclimatization* first appeared in the eighteenth century and was associated with bringing exotic plants and animals, such as merino sheep, to new environments in the hopes that productive and useful species could adapt.[23] At its core, acclimatization intervened in the existing order of plants and animals by changing the geography and distribution of living beings. Acclimatization had its height in the late nineteenth century but continued to reverberate and influence ideas of race and belonging. The process assumed that it was up to European and later American interventions to realize previously unmet potentials of new and unfamiliar surroundings.[24] The migration of plants, animals, and people between climates worked in tandem with European political and military activities in service of colonization. Acclimatization societies created in the nineteenth century used plants as participants in imperial objectives by encouraging the introduction of non-native species into new locations.[25] This work informed "the anxious process of colonists transplanting themselves in new soil," and it helped distinguish between tropical and temperate regions. Whether for plants or people, adapting to a new climate and geography often ran "counter to rigid theories of geographic racial differentiation" as much as they affirmed them.[26] These activities sought to extend the boundaries of the home country and demonstrate their power to create flourishing places.[27] Acclimatization occurred at a considerable scale. In 1942, a survey found that California had some 570 imported varieties and species of trees and 260 types of vines.[28]

The tropics represented a place of fascination and fear to Europeans and Americans who generally occupied the world's temperate zones.[29] Contemporary scholarly accounts provided legitimacy to popular assumptions about the relationship between climate and racial hierarchies. As a locale, they often connoted less of a bounded climatic area than an imaginative space, almost Eden-like and filled with rich botanic life. On the other hand, they conjured images of a place rife with disease and populated with slug-

FIGURE 3.2. *Eucalyptus citriodora* at Cooper Ranch, near Santa Barbara. From Alfred James McClatchie, "Eucalypts Cultivated in the States," USDA Bureau of Forestry Bulletin, No. 35, Washington: Government Printing Office, 1902.

gish, unproductive people. Tropical regions posed a potentially grave threat to white bodies, habits, and societies, while they were simultaneously marketed as "an elixir of horticultural fertility" and youthfulness.[30] Writing in 1898, sociologist Benjamin Kidd believed that any attempt to acclimatize a white man in the tropics was a "blunder of the first magnitude."[31] He believed that good government was beyond the zone's native inhabitants, the earliest developed, he conjectured, of the human races, since their conditions of life were easiest. In contrast, white men could be "neither physically, morally, nor politically" acclimatized in the tropics, and this was a good thing since the people "among whom he lives are often separated from him by thousands of years" of development.[32] Warm climates yielded dark-skinned, overly emotional people predisposed to laziness, but white people risked becoming weak when exposed to the same conditions.[33] Plants, on the other hand, demonstrated an alternative and beneficial vision. Like climate, plants conveyed stability compared to the whims of human culture. Yet they also modified discourses on climatic differentiation across vast geographic distances. European and American interventions in plant life realized previously unmet potentials of tropical climates.[34] Motivated by ideas of improving land and transforming landscapes in new territories to make them similar to common spaces at home, the British in Australia and New Zealand and the French in Algeria and Polynesia transferred flora and fauna with enthusiasm between their old and new worlds and in so doing proved their superior intellect and skills.[35]

California appeared to provide an ideal testing ground for a variety of flora from across the globe. Positive publicity influenced this reputation and shaped assumptions about the state's environmental gifts.[36] Southern California, according to nineteenth-century writer Charles Nordhoff, was the first tropical land that white people had "mastered and made itself at home in."[37] Unlike both tropical and temperate regions, Southern California offered what Charles Dudley Warner, an essayist and novelist, popularized as a semitropical climate—or "our Italy"—providing the best qualities of both.[38] Oranges, eucalyptus trees, and palms eventually obtained citizenship, in the terminology of one prominent horticulturist, in California after emigrating from some other locale. California was a peripheral place in the nineteenth century, and advocates promoted its superb soil quality and equable climate in order to bring the state to national attention—outside the possibility of gold. The ability for plants from all over the world to flourish in California testified to the quality of its land and capacities for economic development through agriculture. Despite its location on the nation's geographic and social margins, boosters pushed the view that the state was the world's most promising location for a garden.

Of all the states, proclaimed British writer Ernest "Chinese" Wilson in 1930, California was "most favored as a garden region." No other place had the coast, mountains, and climate that offered such unlimited possibilities for planting. In Southern California, tropical plants flourished, while in the north, plants of cool, temperate regions were "perfectly at home."[39] Unfortunately for Wilson, it seemed as if few Californians took advantage of the opportunity offered to introduce new plants from Japan ("California's nearest neighbor"), China, South Africa, New Zealand, and Australia. Yet California's reputation as a globally exceptional place, even a microcosm of the whole earth, prospered. This was particularly vital in the 1930s and 1940s when California faced challenges of a rapidly increasing population and attendant land and resource use. Propelled by the Depression and Dust Bowl, migrants to the state gave rise to fears that California's essential qualities would be lost through an influx of careless inhabitants. Justifications for their negative attitudes against these newcomers as a matter of maintaining California's ostensibly natural characteristics coalesced into a political outlook abetted by the state's plant life. Social values that came from plants and trees testified to nature's ability to provide intrinsic lessons. Learning how to judge and improve their surroundings, especially their lawns, gardens, and streets, instilled environmental lessons. Concentrating on the maintenance of one's own lawn or garden placed responsibility on individuals.

Unlike many human migrants to California, plants often had an easy time gaining acceptance in new conditions. Eucalyptus species extended to the point of becoming nearly native to their adopted home.[40] Palms obtained "citizenship" in Santa Barbara, flowering and bearing as much fruit as in their native countries.[41] The transplantation worked in reverse as well. Australians welcomed the Monterey pine as warmly as Californians embraced the eucalyptus. Writing in *House and Garden* in 1929, Lester Rowntree looked to the example of an Englishman, David Douglas, who traveled to the state in 1825 and brought back "Californian loot" to Europeans.[42] Rowntree noted counterintuitively that Europeans accepted California's flowers for their own gardens before Americans living on the East Coast did. She surmised that the "roundabout way" those flowers arrived on the Atlantic coast meant that few realized these flowers actually came from America since the general belief was that California's flora were beautiful, though "unpractical and unattainable."

Not all of California provided the same botanical benefits, Santa Barbara residents in particular noted. The Italian immigrant and founder of the

Southern California Acclimatization Association Franceschi believed the city possessed unique and enviable qualities for cultivation. Compared even to other cities in Southern California, Santa Barbara held "the largest number of settlers . . . with intense love for plants and for flowers and to possess in her gardens the most remarkable and older specimens of trees from foreign countries."[43] Few would be able to find a similar hospitable environment for plants from throughout the globe to thrive. Other temperate and privileged locations, such as the French Riviera, Naples, the Canary Islands, the Azores, and New Zealand, could not match the success in this stretch of Southern California. He hoped to introduce new and desirable plants in the region to test their "fitness for economic or decorative purposes" since the climate provided the freedom to plant almost anything.[44] Franceschi's ambitions for Santa Barbara went beyond merely transplanting trees and plants. Prefiguring later civic improvers, he imagined a dramatic increase in palms to impart an "attractive and aesthetic character" in the city, with whole streets lined with palm trees following the example "of Hyeres, of Algiers, or Rio de Janeiro" that could be equaled, if not surpassed, in Santa Barbara.

Franceschi's dedication to Santa Barbara's ladies in his pamphlet indicated an awareness of the importance of bringing this information to a broad public. Laypersons translated and used the ideas of horticulturalists while adding an explicitly social register. Guidebooks to local trees and flowers in Santa Barbara offered Latin names, origins, and general descriptions as well as suggestions for planting, aesthetic characteristics and connotations, and the location of particularly well-known or fine specimens throughout the region.[45] These guides connected scientific information with practical applications for home gardens and in doing so influenced the reception of plant life in society.[46] Acclimatization as a process provided a framework for thinking about how to manage California's new growth and urbanization, especially concerning strategies for protecting and preserving the state's natural resources.[47] Ideas central to acclimatization found allies in the conservation movement. Conservationists argued that "no state has more to preserve," develop, and enjoy than California. The question was how to teach and practice it. Civic leaders, such as Pearl Chase, noted that the term was broad and "hundreds of activities are carried on in its name."[48] Individuals as well as governments held a stake in problems regarding protecting natural resources. Educational programs aimed to bring people together in a shared project of preserving land, water, plants, and wildlife, most especially to overcome the "great number of selfish individuals and corporations and the thousands of ignorant and thoughtless people . . . to whom natural beauty apparently means little or nothing." More significant than the individual satisfactions of increasing knowledge and appreciation for natural beauty was encouraging hostility to those who failed to see nature's benefits.

The pedagogical functions of plant life extended to botanic gardens, where they took a more organized and categorized form. Viewed as a "living laboratory," early botanic gardens in Europe and its colonies combined scientific, ornamental, and educational uses while serving expansionist, nation-building, or imperial projects.[49] Kew Gardens, one of the largest and most celebrated, opened in 1759 in London as a "showplace of exotic flora, an instrument of imperial botanizing, and the centerpiece of growing network of colonial botanical gardens." In addition, the garden served an instrumental role for meeting the economic imperatives of the British empire. The French, Dutch, Germans, and others followed developing botanical gardens to collect and array biota. Early botanic gardens in the United States displayed the products of a nation in its ascendancy as a place of beauty and refinement.[50] Nature was not just a neutral measure of sophistication as a nation but instructive. Moreover, in the United States, foreign plants were "exhibited as proof of the flexibility of the American environment and the skill of American gardeners in naturalizing them."[51] The control and categorization of natural resources signaled a mature nation, explained texts such as Thomas Jefferson's *Notes on the State of Virginia*. Botanic gardens were essential for civic improvement, science, and conservation, as well as "the display of superiority and economic independence." These sites not only disseminated information about plants and botany but also institutionalized and demarcated practices and categories for plant life.[52] Gardens transformed plants into political and scientific objects that indexed national boundaries.[53]

Plant life's moral lessons added rhetoric of civilizing influence and references to the United States' agrarian past to the project of territorial expansion. Territorial conquest was only part of the project. Cultivating this land, making it not only productive but also beautiful, required individuals familiar with domestic comforts.[54] Horticulturalist Liberty Hyde Bailey, writing in 1898, believed a garden was "the most personal part of an estate, that area which is most intimately associated with the private life of the home."[55] This work ameliorated the land as well as people. A garden's success, he argued, depended on a person's temper rather than money spent, region, or rarity of plants.[56] After developing a love of plants and nature, one could "cultivate that happy peace of mind which is satisfied with little." Gardening taught refinement and self-sufficiency. This activity contrasted with harmful qualities such as child delinquency, sloth, profligacy, greed, and a general lack of etiquette. Ernest Wilson believed that trees "entwined the heart of man since he became a sentient being."[57] This entanglement differed across time and space. Wilson conjectured that "the more simple the people," the closer they were to nature because "as nations become civilized they one and all by fire and axe . . . destroyed the friendly trees." White men ranked "head and shoulders above all others" in contributing to this destruction, laying waste to the "tree wealth" of lands in "an effort, often vain to make a blade of corn grow where two trees grew before." Modern, industrialized men replaced nature with something else entirely, leaving much to be desired. While reproaching modern trends, his statements erased Indigenous inhabitants and recast settlers as the land's original cultivators.[58] This work of environmental improvement through agriculture provided the warrant for domestication and ownership even if those improvements came with unintended consequences. Wilson's observations analogizing plant life and cultural development extended a long-standing practice of melding the idiom of science with social assumptions.

A similar melding of the definition and introduction of ecology to English-language audiences puts into relief the term's functional and conceptual ties to domesticity and home. Environmental historian Donald Worster notes that at its inception, *ecology* seemed "nothing more than an unusual coupling of Greek roots," before assuming a "complicated burden" of "flexible and inclusive meaning."[59] The word *oecologia* first appeared in the work of Ernest Haeckel, a German zoologist, in 1866 to specify a branch of biology. It derived from the Greek word *oikos*, referring to the household and economy, and Haeckel endeavored to define a single branch of knowledge concerned with the economy, lifestyle, and relations of organisms with one another. Like a family, earth's living beings formed a single economic unit dwelling in intimate relation together.[60] Day-to-day maintenance of this relationship sat at the heart of ecology.

Facilitating ecology's journey from German to English was Ellen Swallow Richards. Although Richards goes unmentioned in Worster's account, her understanding of the term displays the "complicated burden" he describes. The first woman admitted to the Massachusetts Institute of Technology and a founder of modern home economics, Richards viewed ecology broadly to encompass the home and the "proper care of the human machine" alongside scientific contexts.[61] Embracing popular ideas about climatic effects on human habits, she believed that people needed to avoid heat and direct sunlight. She admonished women to not make their homes a "tropical jungle" since such an atmosphere was conducive neither to work nor health. After all, she contended that "all great nations have lived in a temperate climate where physical and mental activity was possible for many hours a day."[62] A productive citizenry—in her definition, people who thought of working fourteen hours a day as a source of pleasure rather than a physical drain—depended on hospitable conditions. The goal of improving productivity linked home, office, and public environments. Home economics paved the way for transforming the kitchen into a modern workplace for women.[63] Transferring the language of efficiency and engineering to the home set a modernizing process in motion. Work, whether in the home or office, provided meaning and direction.

Despite Richards's expansive definition, ecology's general usage narrowed to scientific contexts. To recapture the comprehensive definition, Richards found an alternative in "euthenics." Centered on enhancing one's immediate, domestic surroundings to instigate beneficial changes in individuals and, by extension, society, euthenics as a term signaled a new route toward civic improvement through education. Adherents of euthenics aimed to teach individuals to make qualitative judgments about their homes, dress, neighborhoods, and environment. "Would you rather," asked one euthenics educator, "live in a community where all houses are exactly alike in design and surroundings than in a residential section where architects and landscape designers (that is, artists) have developed a unified and diversified plan giving variety and interest and pleasing character to the community?"[64] Home meant more than the discrete physical domicile; it encompassed one's town and development. For Richards, development was social, local, and material. She believed that capitalists should concern themselves more in developing new communities to diminish the suffering in crowded cities than a gold mine in "some distant land." A plot of land, such as an open field or slum, could create a new type of garden city. Originally devised and designed in the late nineteenth century by English men who considered themselves social reformers as much as architects and urban designers, garden cities were meant to represent an ideal balance between the benefits of both town and country.[65] Their very form critiqued the pollution and ugliness that resulted from industrialization.[66] Notably, Richards departed from aims to transform society through urban design in order to present a novel opportunity for capitalist investment.

With its objective of environmental improvement through education, home economics, and sanitary science, euthenics positioned itself as a complement and precursor to eugenics. Increased recognition of Richards's work in home economics as an early proponent of ecology in the United States often fails to note euthenics' tie to eugenics.[67] One of Richards's followers made the link explicit in defining euthenics as the science of "improving the human race by external influence, apart from consideration of heredity," or "having to do with the betterment of living conditions to secure more efficient human beings."[68] After Richards's death in 1911, euthenics continued to influence home economics scholars and experienced a small revival in the early 1930s due to the "growing restless and maladjustment" of the decade. Instead of ascribing those responses to social and economic conditions, proponents of euthenics placed blame on people looking to external factors for pleasure rather than their individual resources.[69] In 1941, the psychologist Carl Seashore argued that euthenics needed to again expand into a more capacious understanding of an art and science of well-being working in tandem with eugenics, which he benignly described as a "happy term" denoting the science of being well born.[70] Eugenics alone would not lead to improvement. Euthenics provided a way of right living because it centered on continual adjustment and improvement, and therefore had a "leading role in race betterment."[71] This was especially the case in the 1920s and 1930s, the "high-water mark" for eugenics.[72] Enshrined in laws, eugenics' popularity spread quickly throughout the United States. Thirty-six states passed eugenic sterilization statutes, mainly in the 1920s.[73] Legal codes and popular social activities offered rhetorical and practical bulwarks against threats from immigration and urbanization. Whether of plants or people, pursuing intentional improvement through the selection of positive characteristics and banishing unfavorable traits underscores an easy affinity between botany and eugenics. California was a center of the American embrace of eugenics in the early twentieth century.[74]

Francis Galton, a statistician and cousin of Charles Darwin, coined *eugenics* in 1853 and defined it as "the science which deals with all influences that improve the inborn qualities of a race."[75] For those sympathetic to Galton's so-called science, nature provided ample evidence for its adoption. Gifford Pinchot, conservationist and the first head of the US Forest Service, offered similar ideas about human fitness using forestry.[76] In his narration of the life of a forest written in 1899, the story was one of "help and harm" in which every tree was "engaged in a relentless struggle against its neighbors for light, water, and food." But it was not always a struggle since, like humans, trees constantly worked with "all [their] neighbors even those which stand at some distance."[77] Like human neighbors, trees depended on one another for food and safety, but significant differences between trees and people existed. He argued each citizen had a special calling in "which he works for the service of the commonwealth." At the same time, "vigorous strife for the good things of life" that could occur in a village also happened in the forest. Pinchot's conception of human communities in which every person had a clear role in society precluded the possibility of recognizing the value of those who might have lacked a requisite useful characteristic.

Pinchot cast the struggle between trees for light and space as a battle with victors and vanquished, a tale that had clear lessons for humans. Those that

FIGURE 3.3. "White pines helping and hindering each other. Dubois, Pennsylvania." In Pinchot's words, a forest "without young growth is like a family without children. It will speedily die out." From Gifford Pinchot, *A Primer on Forestry*, 1902.

emerged victorious did so because of inherent qualities coupled with environmental factors. Some trees grew faster than others because of better soil or lack of insects, but others had an "inborn tendency" to grow faster, "just as one son in a family is often taller than the brothers with whom he was brought up."[78] "Dominant" trees eclipsed "surviving laggards" while "enormous numbers of seedlings and small saplings are suppressed and killed during the early youth of the forest." Even establishing dominance over other trees did not complete the clash. Competition continued among superior specimens. Those that persevered over the first years of "deadly struggle" became more similar as time passed. All flourishing specimens in this final stage stood surrounded by "hundreds" of vanquished seedlings and proved to "be the best adapted to their surroundings."[79] Natural selection provided a clear trajectory and obvious preferences (Figure 3.3).

Those outside formal government and scientific institutions embraced the intertwined coupling of environmental conservation and management and eugenics. One such person was Charles Goethe. Goethe was born into wealth in Sacramento, and his enthusiasms led him to a life of activism over causes to shut down California's brothels, promote the expansion of the national park system with John Muir, acquire and donate lands with California redwood trees through the Save the Redwoods League, and contribute to laws on outdoor recreation.[80] After his death in 1966, the National Audubon Society held a moment of silence in his honor at its national convention.[81] In addition to environmental causes, eugenics comprised his major preoccupation. He founded and edited a series on eugenics, *Eugenics Pamphlets*, and wrote every word of its eighty-nine issues until 1955. The audience for *Eugenics Pamphlets* was popular enough that institutions, including the American Museum of Natural History, and scientific journals, such as *Nature*, happily allowed reprints of their work.[82]

Goethe was hardly an exception in his enthusiasms to meld eugenics and environmental conservation into one rhetorical package. The language of survival, dominance, and laggards could be transferred rather straightforwardly from trees and plants to human beings. For those who endorsed eugenics, its definition could be as benign as a concern for "the social direction of human evolution."[83] Like Ellen Swallow Richards before him, Goethe regarded garden cities as an attractive representation of his views, but he avoided discussion of those with overt socialist overtones. Instead, he praised Ungemach, "the world's first eugenic city," near Strasbourg, France.[84] Despite his wish to avoid hints of excessive state intervention, the Strasbourg city government supported Ungemach and several other developments.[85] One common narrative of Ungemach's origins is that the town's first administrator was inspired to build this community based on English garden city principles after reading *Applied Eugenics* by Paul Popenoe and Roswell Hill Johnson, first published in 1918. By 1923, construction began on Ungemach, with the first, carefully chosen, families moving in two years later.[86] Goethe visited Ungemach and happily relayed that inhabitants were selected for "eugenic fitness" and were encouraged to have at least four children.[87] Families were also expected to depart once their reproductive years ended, but many found life in the town so pleasant that they lingered for years, unwilling to leave.

Transferring this model to the United States seemed necessary to Goethe so that a "sufficient supply of brains" could continue the nation's military, economic, and spiritual progress. His concerns about the low birthrates of American "high-powers" were exacerbated by fears of an exploding birthrate of "the hillbilly, the Sicilian of the slums, the 'plantation negro'"—as contrasted with the "house negro"—all of whom "breed like rabbits." Population planning needed quality, not quantity. Utilizing the fear of mass immigration to the United States from Mexico, Goethe noted that in the mid-1940s, "old American stock" encountered difficulties in educating a family of more than three children. But "the last decade's Mexican trek over the Border" showed that "peon families" averaged over ten children. If all survived and procreated, then in three generations the "old American stock" would have 27 great-grandchildren as opposed to 728 from the "peon family."[88] Based on those numbers, he advocated for restricting immigration by performing background checks for deficiencies on at least twenty family members of anyone who wished to move to the United States. The strategy for humans, Goethe wrote to the future founder of Friends of the Earth, David Brower, "should be eternal watchfulness."[89] If selection, he concluded, was the rule in plant breeding, then one "wonders when we will apply the same laws to humans."[90] The one place he saw the effectiveness of selection was immigration control.

Goethe's interests led him across the world to investigate original conditions of plants, which he extrapolated into conclusions about eugenics' benefits. In attempting to catalyze high-quality population growth through fear and botanical analogies of "weeds and seeds," he singled out what he viewed as the uses of eugenic principles in horticulture. Crops such as tomatoes, potatoes, and corn offered a model for human cultivation. Natural selection only performed part of the task. Artificial selection—that is, human intervention—played a major role, just as "the power of mountain waterfalls had been so used to turn factory machinery." Those involved in plant breeding incorporated the language of improvement and superiority. A writer for *Scientific American* described the horticulturist molding "superior heritage" in crops as a contribution to the masses of John Publics who reaped the "real harvest in the form of better living and lower costs."[91] A superior plant was not just a matter of chance; it was made through technological meddling. A "streamlined" potato, unlike an unimproved potato, not only held more aesthetic appeal but also lacked the deep eyes that created waste and hampered peeling. Similarly, "short, chubby" carrots of the past had been replaced by "long slim beauties." Human technical intervention meant that modern vegetables had as little in common with their predecessors as a "modern streamlined car with a pre-war gas buggy." The continuation of favorable traits and the elimination of the negative brought plants and people together in a thoroughly current fashion. In contrast to his unfavorable view of immigration, Goethe regarded plant migration as a positive showcase of California's exceptional environment.

California's growth and prosperity provided ample testimony of the correctness of white Americans' interventions in the landscape. Large-scale agricultural production provided most of the evidence for California's fertile land, but gardens, roads lined with eucalyptus trees, and neat front yards also reflected the state's inherent gifts and tied nature and personal character together. Whether within a garden's boundaries or in an open field, plants offered insights into nature's processes, structure, and classification. Known for his work on the Great Plains, the botanist Frederic Clements arrived in Santa Barbara in 1925 with a mission. Alongside his belief in the dynamism of ecological succession, Clements maintained that natural landscapes eventually reached a climax stage. Nature's course was not an "aimless wandering to and fro" but rather a progressive, predictable, and competitive march. Climate determined the boundaries of this advance. White men upturned this progression with their activities and advanced culture. While midwestern grasslands exemplified a dynamic ecology, Clements came to Santa Barbara convinced that it was another model environment. Part of this conviction derived from his understanding of dynamic ecology that included human beings within the ecological community. The Pacific coast, and Santa Barbara in particular, offered a place where both a climax state of vegetation and highly developed human culture could occupy the same space. Nevertheless, urbanization and increased automobile usage threatened the region's "exceptional richness" of flora and fauna.

Santa Barbara's multiple habitats, "from strand to mountain," meant the region itself was a botanic laboratory. The introduction and improvement of exotic plants from around the world in addition to native species would drive further knowledge of their development and ideal conditions. To promote this research, Clements proposed the establishment of a botanic garden. Public and private botanic and demonstration gardens, he believed, served dual purposes by preserving plant life and edifying the public, especially if they came to the realization that "no genuine flower lover picks wild flowers."[92] Local leaders had discussed the idea several years before Clements's arrival, but with grander ambitions. Santa Barbara would simply be the central node in a two-thousand-mile-long World Botanic Garden that stretched along the Pacific coast lined with native trees and plants from Mexico to Canada.[93] With the Pacific Coast Highway nearing completion, the boulevard was envisioned as a series of regional gardens displaying plant life "indigenous to California" alongside those specimens with the "most economic value, artistic worth and scientific interest from all parts of the world."[94] Santa Barbara held a special position in this plan because "it has already been proven that a greater number of species of plants and trees of the world could be grown successfully." No other place in the world, boosters argued—even rival botanic gardens in Jamaica and Indonesia—supported "so varied a plant life" and had "the climatic condition centered to perfection." The proof was in the plant life.

Alongside climate and topography, the region's history factored into its prosperity. California had not started as a productive landscape in the eyes of white settlers. One *Los Angeles Times* writer in 1925 admitted that in its beginnings in the eighteenth century, "California of ours was a total loss to start with."[95] The padres "found barren land inhabited by sullen savages who'd never even tried to farm." Instead, the Indigenous inhabitants "just managed to rustle wild seeds and roots and grasshoppers enough to keep from starving." Undeterred by the inhospitable conditions, the Spanish priests, with "a lot of quite human optimism," planted a chain of "self-sustaining mission settlements up and down such an inhospitable coast." Those encountering this "sunny mesa" with the backs to the sea "dubiously" compared it to their homeland. For this development, California could "never repay its agricultural debt to those who proved its soils in the first place." But it was not until after statehood that California's inhabitants "awoke to the delight of living in our climate was the waiting paradise really wrested from the desert and made the test plot for everything that grows." Such assertions echoed common refrains regarding the inevitable extinction of Indigenous populations and their landscapes by the progress of European civilization. Nature could become perfect in California, but at the cost of the obliteration of past inhabitants.

Clements emphasized botanic gardens' ability to teach and argued that few institutions touched urban life with as much variety as a botanic garden.[96] Listed in documents as the first director of Santa Barbara's then-named Blaksley Botanic Garden, Clements created an initial master plan in 1926 for thirteen acres of land donated by Anna Blaksley Bliss, an heiress who lived between New York City and Montecito. Clements described the land located in the northern part of the city on Mission Canyon in the foothills of the Santa Ynez Range as "warm and frost-free" with a canyon and perennial stream occupied by oaks and bunchgrass prairie. He hoped the eventual garden would include numerous examples of California plant and tree life including redwoods, succulents, and sagebrush; experimental gardens to study adaptations; and climatic gardens. Clements's formal involvement with the botanic garden ended soon afterward, but the institution continued to develop. In 1937, landscape architects Beatrix Farrand, known for her work at Dumbarton Oaks in Washington, DC, established by Blaksley Bliss's stepson, and Lockwood de Forest began work on a new design for the renamed Santa Barbara Botanic Garden.[97] Despite his absence, Clements's ideas persisted not just at the botanic garden but in the larger community. He understood there to be a "correlation of the activities of the garden with the needs and interests of the entire community ... one that might well transcend the limits of city or county" and influence schools, park systems, and even highways.[98] The values that individuals ascribed to trees and plants, as well as gardening and related activities of cultivating land, homed in on the individual as the primary motor of social improvement.[99] In aggregate, these discrete activities formed a connective tissue linking the community in a common project of improving both nature and society. The claim that under the right conditions, which California in general and Santa Barbara specifically offered in abundance, any plant could flourish produced benefits but also risks—most especially the risk of losing that abundance. Protecting those conditions required social and environmental vigilance.

Emphasizing public opinion and developing popular approval regarding designed landscapes required more than merely "passing laws to protect and preserve." Laws, according to one of Santa Barbara's voluntary conservation organizations, were insufficient for fully discharging "our duty or responsibility as citizens."[100] Their shortcomings included that they were administered from anonymous institutions, they were difficult to enforce, and they did nothing to protect nature without the backing of "strong public sentiment." Individuals needed to publicize the value of natural resources and the importance of protecting those resources to their neighbors. Shaping public opinion to popularize studying and appreciating nature could counteract and control those who "respect no law, nature's or man's." Those who insisted on destroying nature needed to be forced to stand at the receiving end of the "weapon" of public opinion. Dispensing shame through publicity would expose those residents "known to be guilty of the destruction of plant and animal life, and who show their lack of civic and personal pride by leaving refuse about places where they picnic or dumping rubbish beside the roads."[101] Careless people and their improper behavior brought "appalling loss" each year, and despite dissemination of "vivid accounts of the ruthless destruction . . . wastefulness goes on and on."

Transmitting this message and leading by example to raise awareness furnished local leaders with opportunities to enact voluntary programs and soft regulations. Santa Barbara had regular "Everyone in Overalls" days with cleanup squads that urged property owners to clean and beautify their lots. Residents reported their own gardening accomplishments while noting unsightly areas around town that needed cleanup lest the city "slip back" in quality. Members of the Santa Barbara Garden Club mailed letters to local property owners that it had "been reported" that their lots had rubbish on them, which "may be a fire hazard, a shelter for insects and rodents, or a bit of ugliness in the neighborhood."[102] In normalizing informal rules for a neat and orderly home, residents could view their accomplishments and opportunities for improvement in terms of gardens planted, rubbish removed, roofs repaired, and mice killed.[103] Identifying these conditions helped develop a "critical eye" toward one's familiar surroundings. Noticing "rubbish dumps, ancient autos, signs on fences"; planting hedges and screens to hide ugly shacks; putting in lawns and ground cover; eliminating dumps along highways; and other activities were individual responsibilities with communal repercussions. "Be critical," a flyer proclaimed, "focus all eyes to see trash, disorder and ugliness."[104] A proposal to clean up the city's vacant lots to raise property values recommended planting poppies, daisies, primroses, and purple Chinese houses instead of native wildflowers because of their "inability to withstand the competition of obnoxious weeds which have been introduced by various means from other countries."[105] Overall, planting vacant lots demonstrated that with "a little effort," citizens could make the city, one of "nature's beauty spots," even more compelling.[106] Ultimately, these activities made Santa Barbara's properties "more attractive, more valuable, and more salable."[107]

Improvements through gardening, as in the embrace of Spanish Colonial Revival architecture, recalled a lost past. "In the beginning," wrote Margaret L. Dearing, a member of the Santa Barbara Garden Club, "all people studied nature."[108] It was in "their very existence" since rocks provided shelter, tools, and weapons; trees provided food; stars offered a clock and compass. Nature gave people "a glimpse of majesty and sublimity, developed their imaginations, and were their first storybooks." But since then "cement, steel, machines, automobiles, books, cellophane, cities and milk bottles make us feel very far from nature and quite independent of them." Most Americans now lived in cities, bought ready-made clothes, got their food from grocery stores, and hardly knew that the stars existed. Dearing lamented the obliteration of nature's laws as the ruler of human activities but believed they were coming back into focus since "we must know and obey her laws or we perish."

Accompanying the sense of loss precipitated by urban life was a belief that children offered the seeds of renewal. Educating children about nature, Dearing argued, was one of "the most delightful tasks, for every child is a young Indian at heart." The elision of the sensibilities of white children and Native Americans further accentuated the divide between the intrinsic character of the natural world and artificial manner of the urban one. Expanding discernment and observation in nature created a greater appreciation of beauty but also provided a barrier against "fear and superstition." Knowledge of nature provided multiple types of enlightenment but also a changed emotional register. Rather than receiving nature education from walks to country schools or the fields and woods around the farm, children had to learn in a less authentic and more manufactured way through institutions such as summer camps and scouts. Dearing wondered how "many of us pity the blind and the deaf, yet we ourselves are so bound in our narrow round of living that we never see the majesty of the stars nor hear the songs of linnet or meadowlark." Going back to nature's lessons developed a "sense of justice" and desire to protect other creatures from "the most ruthless of earth's animals—man."

Although Dearing implied that gardens presented an ersatz nature and a diminished educational experience, others considered their presence as an augmentation of nature. John D. Wright, a member of the Garden Club of Santa Barbara and Montecito, proclaimed that the city already occupied a "very unusual place" in the minds of people throughout the world. Wright said he had met people across Europe, Asia, Australia, and "even in Java and the Malay Peninsula" who knew about the city's delights in nature, culture, and society.[109] Those delights together turned vacationers into permanent residents and, importantly, taxpayers. Plants and climate alone did not cause this transformation but benefited from the presence of "good schools, good churches, good music, good theaters, and attractive home conditions." Nevertheless, being surrounded by beauty cultivated the intellect and taste: "If we see fine and suitable things around us we become accustomed to them and our taste unconsciously improves. If, on the contrary, we live amid ugly and unsuitable things we likewise become accustomed to them and they cease to affect us unpleasantly." Sordid surroundings made sordid people, but in orderly environments "our natures develop along the highest and best lines." The technical skill and eye for beauty and respectability that arranging flowers required was not just a matter of intuition. Designing a garden could be both an art—that is, something with a history, schools, and styles—and a skill, with hard principles regarding harmony and color.[110] At any rate, this activity required training. A writer for a publication released by the Massachusetts branch of Better Homes in America remarked that some individuals had a strong aversion to wildflowers, considering them quite inferior. The writer mused that those who felt such a dislike needed to first think about so-called cultivated plants. "All of them are wild somewhere," so the peony, much admired in the United States, was considered a "bad weed in the Balkan meadows because the cows don't eat it," narcissus covered the slopes around Lake Geneva and spoiled hay, and foxglove grew everywhere in the Belgian wood.[111] Every plant was "wild in its native habitat," so "why look disdainfully at our wild flowers?" The landscape architect Charles Eliot considered gardening as "essentially a fine art" with a function to "create and preserve beauty in the surroundings of human habitations and in the broader natural scenery of the country."[112] Those who designed these spaces accomplished their work by unifying and integrating features of the landscape. A well-thought-out approach, consideration of the surrounding countryside, and suggestions of the occupants were required of those who desired to modify their land.[113] Human intervention in a landscape ameliorated its natural beauty.

Planting afforded the chance for individual renewal in the face of modern threats. Those with little access to "rural views" had an urgent need for their "hurrying workaday lives refreshed and calmed by the beautiful and reposeful sights and sounds of high nature." Ideas of propriety and correctness colored views of gardens. Charles Goethe recalled that his own interests in gardens and gardening came out of he and his wife's volunteer efforts with orphans in Sacramento. They then transferred that work to "China, Japan, the Philippines, Java, and Hindustan, and Europe."[114] Igniting the "natural urge" to garden spread values and good manners while providing a "backfire" against juvenile delinquency and other "social maladjustments." Some saw environmental threats in transformations in population and leisure time. Frederick Law Olmsted Jr., like his father, a landscape architect, fretted about the "enormous increase in the proportion of people" who had enough leisure time to enjoy the outdoors "after earning the bare necessities of existence."[115] California's abundance of natural beauty was a resource "distinguished from things which are valued only because they can be exchanged for something one really wants." Unfortunately, that very abundance meant that "careless, hasty, shortsightedly selfish methods of exploiting the natural assets of scenic values are rapidly killing the geese that lay the golden eggs." Every year a pleasant site would be destroyed by a residential or pleasure resort development that would rapidly transform into a "rural slum." Teaching "the great mass of well-intentioned people" how to enjoy the landscape without "the slightest conflict" between public enjoyment and private economic uses of the land presented a quandary. Championing natural beauty's value as something beyond the merely monetary produced a rise in visitors among the "pleasure-seeking public." New infrastructures and services catering to those new visitors had a parasitic effect and tended to destroy the qualities that the public sought out in the first place.

New arrivals to Southern California in the 1920s and afterward, "excited at finding themselves living in a land of no snow . . . believed they were actually dwelling in the tropics and grasp at everything that would make their gardens suggestive of the more torrid zones."[116] As a result, the "average gardener" proceeded with "little real understanding" of the climate and "little or no conception" of the proper arrangement or selection of plants and flowers. In contrast to those modest homes and gardens, estates around Santa Barbara and Montecito occupied by industrial "hill barons" who made their fortunes during World War I had become "veritable fairy palaces" with gardens that were "gems of delight to be found only in the fabulous tales of ancient times."[117] That condition, according to one writer, was impermanent. Without directly referencing the Depression or migrants from the Dust Bowl, Victoria Padilla, writing in 1961, noted that "a change had taken place during the 1930s."[118] The transformation had been "so imperceptible" that those residing in Southern California "for years were unaware of it." Although the region continued to be advertised as "one of the great garden spots" and a "land of unrivaled opportunity for the agriculturist and home owner," Padilla argued that just a few years after the end of World War II it had lost "much of the charm" that had made it so attractive. Increased population and an "accelerated pace of living" transformed the character and values of inhabitants while also raising the cost of real estate and reducing room for gardens. Losing its former uniqueness through absorption of "much of the spirit that characterized the Midwest and the East," "California del Sur" became "a different kind of country" with an attendant apathy toward gardening.

The cause of maintaining a certain quality of life cloaked in the language of beauty and centered on outdoor activities papered over potential sources of conflict. Garden clubs could bring certain communities in line with desired norms. The adult education department of Santa Barbara City Schools organized a Mexican garden club with a Mrs. Minerva Gomez and Mrs. Dominga Salla as heads in part to encourage Americanization.[119] Other efforts focused on a smaller scale the challenges encountered resulting from the "alien character" of juxtaposed pieces of property. On one block a family might have a Spanish-style garden but have neighbors partial to English or American Colonial design. This situation thus required a designer to "exclude the surrounding landscape instead of attempting to harmonize his composition with it." The solution to this mixture of styles was to have each house be an isolated and enclosed unit, with property owners possessing the ability to shape their own spaces without consideration for external conditions. Despite the stark boundary between a house and its neighbors, the "inseparable relationship" between a house and its garden would compensate for it by demonstrating the "reconciliation of that which is organic, structural, man-composed." While landscape could not always mediate social relationships, it could connect architecture and nature by "stepping into the breach to show where rigid architecture" could be softened and designed in "such a noble way" as to "properly companion Nature." Familiar language of conquest and control extended to domestic settings, so that landscaped nature could "fit into man's everyday living."

The years immediately after World War II heralded the coming of a new but not necessarily better Southern California. So much of the past had been cast off, due to an increase in people coming "by the millions" attracted "primarily by the famed subtropical climate."[120] The region's renowned temperature inversion, a reversal of the normal situation where atmospheric layers decrease in temperature with altitude, insulated cool air in the basin and maintained a narrow and pleasant range of temperature of an "eternal springtime" risked being lost. The "roof" once provided by the temperature inversion was now a "ceiling" clamping down over a crowded area of five million people and half as many cars and hundreds of factories that "belch out smoke and fumes with which to pollute the air." Sparse settlement with its "fragrance of the orange blossoms from the groves sweetened the entire countryside" far from urban pollution took on a new romance. In the face of this newly unpleasant and overcrowded climate, signs of a return to order began to emerge by looking inward. Architects and landscape designers started to work following the end of World War II by bringing the outdoors inside through glass walls and picture windows so that more attention was paid to "pleasing shrubs, trees, and flowers." Those with no previous interest in plants and flowers learned their value as "a background for gracious living."[121]

The drive toward continuous innovation and growth had a countermovement with its own attendant social baggage. The continuous rush of migrants from other parts of the country—especially in the 1960s, when "five hundred a day . . . come to southern California in search of a new home"—brought "new ideas, new industry, new roads, new subdivisions, a new outlook on life" that shifted a century of California's heritage and transformed the landscape.[122] While front lawns turned into parking spaces, a businessman with no garden of his own because he lived in an apartment found "his kinship to nature in the plantings" around his factory or office to satisfy his inherent love of nature. A new profession arose out of this condition: the interior landscape architect, who designed and maintained indoor plants "without which the contemporary bank or office or store would be a barren place."

The effort to beautify despite inhospitable new landscapes underscored the importance of individual undertakings toward civic beautification in the face of indifferent public officials. In Los Angeles, the lack of tree-lined streets was rectified by business owners who considered it "expedient" to beautify their buildings with "luxuriant plantings so that prospective customers will not be discouraged by the grime of the city streets."[123] Such plantings were meant to create a visible dividing line between publicly and privately owned spaces. Public indifference and squalor contrasted with private attentiveness. Freeways, a "distressing symbol of the speed characteristic of the age," became beautiful in some places, such as Santa Barbara, where "the motorist is fully aware he is entering a city long celebrated for its gardens." Public values emphasized speed rather than beauty, and private citizens needed to maintain principles through interventions in the landscape.

Rights to wildflowers extended toward admiring them on hills and meadows, but a person picking them, according to Santa Barbara civic leader Herbert Green, "automatically removes them from public into private ownership and by his thoughtless selfishness prevents all other people from having a pleasure rightfully theirs."[124] Green further recounted his horror by news that an observer saw eleven cars parked on San Marco Pass with all passengers picking flowers in the meadow and some children even selling them. This type of response, much like letters complaining about unsightly lots or proposed boycotts of businesses that refused to adhere to the desires of community organizations, revealed that for some the primary offense was in breaching community values rather than the letter of the law. Grand landscapes and botanic gardens for public edification gave way to an inward vision that attempted to seal itself off from the outside world.

4

Boundary Problems

> Conservation and community are the two sides of the environmental coin. For the crisis of the environment is also the crisis of cities and of the man-made world.[1]

In 1973, at a luncheon honoring Santa Barbara's Man and Woman of the Year, Frank Kelly, a longtime employee at the Center for the Study of Democratic Institutions (CSDI), recalled when he had first heard of the city, in the late 1950s. The words came from the mouth of Robert Maynard Hutchins, the head of the CSDI and former president of the University of Chicago. Kelly recalled his shock and skepticism at Hutchins's use of superlatives, speaking "almost as lovingly about Santa Barbara as he did about his wife."[2] Nevertheless, in 1958, Kelly, his wife, and their two sons spent several weeks in the city to consider a permanent move. Over that time, the city passed every major test. It was "strikingly beautiful," the ocean "sparkled," the air was pure, the mountains "rose majestically against a blue sky, and the people possessed intelligence and good natures." Based on this experience, Kelly supported Hutchins's suggestion that the then-named Fund for the Republic, a think tank established with the support of the Ford Foundation, should relocate from New York to Santa Barbara.

The following decade and a half confirmed the flawlessness of this decision for their organization, their own lives, and even the state of California in the middle of a period that historian Kevin Starr describes as the "age of abundance."[3] Ambassadors, scholars, and leaders in numerous fields participated in CSDI conferences and marveled at the ocean view from the organization's hillside offices in an estate called Solana designed by a hobbyist architect, Francis Underhill, for a local businessman and philanthropist named Frederick Peabody in 1917 (one of Solana's recent owners is Eric Schmidt, former CEO of Google, and the house appeared on an episode in the final season of HBO's *Succession*). On a personal note, Kelly divulged that his visiting mother-in-law asked him, "What did you ever do to deserve this?" But

Kelly admitted to anxieties that blunted the paradisical surroundings. How long would the city's charms last? Could the place be "damaged and distorted by expansion in all directions?" Or was there a possible alternative that had once been evident in the "wide vision and calm courage" of an earlier generation of "farsighted Santa Barbarans who have made this such an exceptional community?"

The combination of environmental conditions and the conscientious population that fostered Santa Barbara's urban development from the 1920s faced rapidly moving hazards five decades later. Difficult conditions that seized other cities threatened to endanger this "temporary paradise." Although Kelly believed maintaining Santa Barbara's superlative environment took precedence, he acknowledged other residents believed otherwise. This was more than a simple disagreement over local concerns; it was a perilous crucible. How Santa Barbara confronted this "state of emergency" had national reverberations. At its center, Kelly identified the major conflict as one between environmentalists and others. But his point of view led to a surprising conclusion. Instead of acknowledging that his beliefs aligned closely with environmentalists, Kelly inveighed against them, disagreeing with their outlook and tactics. Environmentalists, he argued, were people dominated by their emotions who wanted to stop time. Rather than focusing on the substance of the disagreement, Kelly believed in changing its tone. The decline of civility, distrust of authority, and marked increase in pessimism risked impeding any sort of political solution or even compromise over Santa Barbara's—and by extension, the nation's—urban future.

Framing the issues at stake as matters of civility allowed Kelly to avoid grappling with uncomfortable questions about the causes of urban growth and unrest not just in Santa Barbara but throughout the nation. This move's effectiveness stemmed not from its rejection of environmentalism but in its reframing. Anti-growth sentiments and environmentalist leanings had a veneer of radicalism, but in Santa Barbara such attitudes took a contrasting orientation. Although residents acknowledged that their concerns affected numerous locales in the United States, their primary response consisted of shoring up boundaries between themselves and others, even within their own neighborhoods. Raising conceptual and spatial divides allowed the city's inhabitants to avoid acknowledging that their activities contributed to ongoing urban problems and social inequalities, evident, for example, in the city's shortage of affordable housing. Foregrounding environmental conditions as a major component in Santa Barbara's quality of life allowed property owners to wield nature, vaguely defined and depoliticized, to protect their interests. Through neighborhood associations, individuals argued for tighter zoning controls to safeguard open space and reduce multifamily housing developments as necessities for maintaining the city's attractive character. In their minds, these were simple matters of common sense and within reasonable expectations of protection. Expressing their concerns in the language of environmental quality rendered the exclusionary aspects of their views benign. Frank Kelly, Robert Maynard Hutchins, and many other residents saw Santa Barbara as exceptional, yet similar attitudes prevailed in affluent areas throughout the country.[4]

Owners of single-family detached houses developed a set of ideological commitments that regularly confounded traditional political fault lines and gained political force through neighborhood and homeowners associations.[5] Their influence rose to a degree that prompted urban critic Mike Davis to assert that the most powerful social movement in Southern California was "affluent homeowners, organized by notional community designations or tract names, engaged in the defense of home values and neighborhood exclusivity."[6] The alliances forged in Santa Barbara within these enclaves hinged on a set of general interests in open space, limited density, community character, and—most significantly—property value protection. Although they have considerable overlaps, the organizations discussed here mainly fall into the category of neighborhood associations rather than homeowners associations and their legal authority and expectation of social provisions. With their voluntary character, neighborhood associations serve as advocates for residents' concerns, especially regarding quality of life issues in relationship to the cities where they reside.[7] Scholars such as Lily Geismer have argued that the emphasis on so-called quality of life issues—for instance, good schools and environmental amenities—are part of a reorientation of Democratic Party priorities away from blue-collar and working-class commitments and toward white-collar interests in the 1960s and 1970s.[8] Yet partisan identification can offer only a partial explanation. Much of Southern California in the middle of the twentieth century tended toward support for the Republican Party.[9] Homeownership formed a shallow but broadly appealing coalition with a constituency that cut across tensions between conservative and liberal. The local scope of homeowners associations allowed a substantial degree of responsiveness to immediate events and therefore provided a hospitable base for political action. Rather than creating bonds of solidarity, homeowners associations connected families only insofar as to secure their boundaries. Historian Robert Self argues that the interplay between public and private resources in these communities "set the stage for the transformation of the physical American landscape and the terrain of national politics."[10] When focused on the interests of the affluent, this type of grassroots organization raises questions about the breadth of environmental protections and who ultimately benefits from them.

Environmentalism, so often aligned with liberal transformations and broader changes in the nation's political landscape, could excuse or even exacerbate inequalities. Conflicts over new housing construction or even the specter of it or any type of commercial or recreational building underscore how effectively the environment was brandished as a shield against development. Normative values attached to homeownership profoundly shaped social outlooks that limited the scope of acceptable changes to the physical landscape. Encroaching suburbanization, the specter of multifamily housing and the types of people it would bring, and the loss of open, if not quite wild, lands were some of the threats to be kept at bay. Santa Barbara's urban fabric reflected not only the "wide vision and calm courage" of residents but also how their forceful opinions defined local order, conceptions of the urban future, and boundaries of community. Situating Santa Barbara within national evaluations of urban conditions clarifies the stakes that shaped this homeowners' ideology and the belief in a zero-sum competition for environmental quality.

Critiques of growth as understood by affluent homeowners moved in directions that justified individual preferences under a rhetoric of environmental concern. Focusing on environmental quality and land use controls ostensibly offered a moderate alternative to radical and even anti-humanist strains of environmentalism.[11] At the same time, more radical proposals, such as population control, bubbled up in more moderate form. A major proponent of population control, Garrett Hardin, lived in Santa Barbara and worked as a professor of human ecology at the city's University of California campus. Impending limits of natural resources, Hardin argued, required active efforts to halt population growth. Despite overt and implicit racist and imperial attitudes attached to ideas in his well-known essays such as "The Tragedy of the Commons" and "Lifeboat Ethics," Hardin's controversial ideas inspired numerous environmentalists.[12] Homeowners' stances may have seemed exceptionally temperate compared to Hardin's envisioned population controls, but they had their own strain of antisocial politics and highly constrained ideas of the public good. Santa Barbara's desirable qualities—its natural beauty, its engaged residents, its temperate climate, and its amenities—made it clear to inhabitants that the place needed protecting, but at what and whose cost?

For those who benefited, the massive expansion of American suburbs after World War II heralded a new era of domestic and global prosperity.[13] This multidimensional transformation stemmed from material changes through new building and land technologies adapted from military uses during the war and new financial instruments that helped facilitate home mortgages.[14] These innovations instigated an enormous national project of social and landscape engineering on the outskirts of cities and formerly rural locations. From a certain perspective, circumstances required this scale of change. Between the 1930s and 1945, housing units constructed each year numbered fewer than five hundred thousand, resulting in overcrowding and shortages. Beginning in 1946, the number doubled to one million and reached two million in the early 1970s. Single-family homes built on subdivided lots of a size ranging from one-seventh to one-quarter of an acre comprised 80 percent of those units.[15] The conversion of land from agricultural to suburban shifted populations across the country.[16] Eleven of the twelve largest cities in the United States lost population while suburbs expanded.[17] Even cities that continued to gain population did so at a much slower rate than their suburbs. For example, between 1940 and 1950, the population of St. Louis's suburbs grew by 48 percent while the city itself only added 6 percent.

Federal, state, and local government interventions made these transformations possible.[18] The shift from cities to suburbs engendered a developmental narrative that the latter provided necessary relief from "the stricken American city."[19] Rather than accepting these changes as a naturally occurring phenomenon, the overdevelopment of suburbs and the underdevelopment of cities were one of the nation's "most significant political, economic, and spatial transformations."[20] Facilitated by interstate highway construction, suburbs grew further from city centers, and in lieu of adequate infrastructure and expenditures on public mass transit, owning a car became necessary for work and accomplishing daily tasks.[21] Expanding numbers of individuals tied to a sizable financial investment in the form of a single-family home encouraged a fixation on property values. This market-based attention resulted in a "defensiveness of suburban municipalities" and justified exclusionary policies against people of color and low-income individuals.[22] Suburban settlements defined by separation from cities and neighbors marked a reorientation of the family as the center of social life and "a bulwark against the outside world."[23]

California experienced a significant share of these changes and became a representative case. In 1962, the state overtook New York as the most populous in the nation. In October of that year, *Life* magazine devoted an entire issue to California, including an advice column for readers considering a move to the West.[24] Between 1950 and 1970, California's population almost doubled, from just over ten million to twenty million inhabitants. One real estate bulletin from 1963 described these arrivals as "the greatest migration in the history of the world."[25] This incoming population wave included young people, migrants from Mexico, and—especially after the 1965 Immigration

Act—Asians looking for economic and social opportunities.[26] Even internal migration in Southern California was such that one writer quipped, "Old maids change address almost as often as call girls do."[27]

Despite celebratory portrayals, policies around suburban development supported racial divides spatially, legally, and ideologically. The democratization of homeownership throughout the middle of the twentieth century coincided with increased racial segregation through federally sponsored redlining and other discriminatory practices.[28] In November 1964, the state's voters overwhelmingly approved Proposition 14, a constitutional amendment authored by the California Real Estate Association to repeal the Rumford Act of 1963, also known as the California Fair Housing Act.[29] The amendment exempted the real estate industry, apartment owners, and individual homeowners from almost all antidiscrimination legislation. Its reach was expansive and prohibited the state from addressing patterns of racial discrimination and segregation in housing. Support for the amendment came from across the political spectrum. Members of the real estate industry even argued that the amendment had nothing to do with endorsing racial discrimination. Rather, they claimed the change protected the right of Californians to rent and sell property without government interference. Despite the call of freedom, in 1967 the US Supreme Court struck down the amendment for violating the Fourteenth Amendment. Despite the ultimate result, scholar of race Daniel HoSang argues that in the aftermath, grassroots fair-housing activists became less confrontational and suburban homeowners associations augmented their authority and power.[30]

Statistics about the population belied Santa Barbara's affluent image. As in many other California cities after 1945, the city lacked adequate affordable housing. Some city officials hoped to implement policies to mitigate the problem. A study in the mid-1960s found that one-fifth of families in Santa Barbara lived under the poverty line, and in some neighborhoods, particularly east of downtown, that proportion rose to over one-third.[31] Average rent in the city was $93 a month, or 26 percent higher than the national average. The 1960 federal census found that 284 units, mostly in the east side, were classified as "dilapidated" and a further two thousand were in a state of deterioration. Housing construction, or lack thereof, had been a problem for decades. In 1948, the city's mayor, Norris Montgomery, began a program to address housing needs in the city in the face of increased population due to rising tourism, the expansion of Santa Barbara College that became part of the University of California system in 1944, and the postwar defense industry. Just after the war, about three-quarters of the population could not afford to pay more than $63 a month in rent or $7,500 to buy a home. Yet over eighty-five days in 1948, out of 124 permits for new residential construction, only 27 percent were for homes under $10,000. As for multifamily homes, there were permits for six duplexes for twelve families and five apartment buildings for twenty-two families.[32] A similar study in 1938 that found multiple families living in one- or two-bedroom homes or structures originally built for livestock and poultry resulted in a call by then-mayor Patrick Maher to create a local housing authority, but voters rejected this proposal in 1940. The 1948 report ended with a statement that people would be "appalled and astonished" by the quantity of overcrowding and unaffordability "anywhere in America, let alone in Santa Barbara." Recognizing that the city faced a housing crisis was akin to "understand[ing] something as basic as two and two making four." But the report's authors feared that "reasonably-priced houses slipped into history with the end of the war." The ongoing shortage of political will to address housing conditions indicated a deliberate strategy to deny the existence of the problem in the first place. Affordable housing presented an easily ignored burden to communities rather than an enhancement.

Despite a popular image of the state as representative of midcentury prosperity, California simultaneously exemplified the negative consequences of the nation's suburban condition. Scientists, planners, and concerned citizens seemed unable to refrain from commenting on the deteriorating environment and its lamentable effects on American life. Urban conditions instigated voluminous observations decrying the unsightly monotony of suburbs and construction oriented toward automobiles. Authors of these withering critiques contended that the conflation of growth, development, and progress was untenable. California symbolized what happened when one had too much of a good thing. Books with titles such as *The Destruction of California*, *California Going, Going . . .* , *Eden in Jeopardy*, or *How to Kill a Golden State* offered pessimistic outlooks on the human habits that threatened not just California but the planet. The double-page title spread of William Bronson's *How to Kill a Golden State* showed two photographs of roadsides outside two small cities—Orinda and San Lorenzo—cluttered by signs, wires, and chain-link fences, far from California's famed natural beauty. Photographs of squalid urban and rural landscapes regularly accompanied the texts as visible evidence of the state as a cautionary tale. Images of traffic-filled roads cluttered with billboards, vacant lots, and the starkly bland houses associated with waves of suburban development reinforced the perception that American landscapes were undergoing a profound decline in a time of supposed expanding prosperity. Bronson attributed the ruination of California to the rapid increase in population after 1945.[33] Moral indignation over the state of affairs fused with grand yet indistinct prescriptions. The state was a dismal portent. California's explosion, as demonstrated in photographic evidence, showed there was "no hallowed ground" anywhere.[34]

Two supposedly contrasting images of California emerged. One was the state as the epitome of unrestrained sprawl and unsightly urban forms. The other presented California as a cultural vanguard leading the world into an era commonly referred to as the age of mass affluence. Yet these diverging portrayals shared expanding wealth and their intended and unintended consequences as a root. Bronson even articulated a causal link by arguing that "man's infinite capacity to befoul and destroy" came from "the quest for an ever-higher standard of living."[35] The single-minded focus on economic growth as the primary societal objective threatened to ruin what little pristine space remained in the American environment. Richard Lillard, author of *Eden in Jeopardy*, considered California under two "mighty symbols": the bulldozer and the word *progress*.[36] The idea of progress imbued people with the sense that California was "young, exceptional, and has its own rules." Change was good in and of itself, the past was wasteful because it was unprofitable, and everything could be improved from "the banks of Coyote Creek to the sex life of married couples."[37]

Critics found California's experiences compelling as a window opening out onto a generalized vision of the national future. The state's geographic features, "isolated by desert and ocean," offered the "controls of laboratory study."[38] Given the exceptional natural surroundings, some concluded that whatever "has been allowed to happen in such a special region as Southern California may well happen anywhere." At a 1965 conference on the future environments of North America, prominent scholars and critics such as the geographer Clarence Glacken decried this "bulldozer mentality." Mayors and those with "practical utilitarian points of view" liked to see towns grow because "growth is progress and progress is undefined."[39] Proposed solutions to uncontrolled growth included drastically limiting access to resources and places. Raymond Dasmann, author of *The Destruction of California*, published in 1965, saw new generations of Americans growing up at an intolerable distance from wild lands. In his home state, he saw the burgeoning population threatening a way of life marked by a closeness to nature for those who had long inhabited California. Dasmann argued that the state was beset by a growing population that it could not accommodate. Each month, fifty thousand new arrivals demanded jobs, housing, education, and highways. Not satisfied with those basics, they also insisted on access to "hunt or fish, use the beaches, play in the state and national parks, ski on mountains slopes and wander in undisturbed mountain wilderness."

Dasmann's animus toward newly arrived residents offered the presumption that tenancy conferred legitimacy and authority to white Californians of appropriately long standing. The fact that newcomers wanted everything that Californians of the past enjoyed without the territorial ties added to the indignity. While surprised that the state had survived the initial population onslaught, he feared more acute changes. The destruction of farmland to build suburban housing tracts, which Dasmann derisively referred to as "slurbs," led residents to behave as though they were in a "desperate war for survival." These developments highlighted the need for a radical redirection. Adapting human living to "the shape of our environment" required curbing population by restricting in-migration. While avoiding the extreme conclusions of population control advocates, he acknowledged that his plan included an "uncomfortable" infringement in freedom of movement. Nevertheless, these discomforts needed to be measured against the fact that California no longer had the resources to accommodate new residents. Instead of implementing hard restrictions, Dasmann suggested that the state could strategize to discourage industry and the expansion of economic opportunity. Despite the veneer of anti-growth sympathies, he stressed that he advocated those limitations only in places where "our segment of the expanding economy will not be affected."[40]

To long-established residents, newcomers constituted a formless or even unsightly mass. Newfound affluence and pathways to homeownership clearly improved the lives of a wider swath of Americans, but others simply perceived its harmful consequences for their own situation. Gestures toward anti-growth attitudes showed how easily ostensibly progressive or even radical ideas could accommodate exclusionary political outlooks. Individuals not just in California but throughout the nation embraced similar positions to express their discontent with changes in their immediate surroundings. Environmental determinism gave a focus to this dismay. The generalized fear of "slurbs" and other types of unwanted developments along with the accompanying people expressed a belief that physical conditions in the landscape influenced human behavior. When channeled through the primary concerns of homeowners, environmentalist ideas shifted from those "dismissed contemptuously" as "pansy pluckers" or "bugs and bunny people" to understandable anxieties about protecting land from hasty development and protecting property values. Longer-standing homeowners prioritized safeguarding remaining land from greedy developers and new migrants to defend their own investments. Despite the common emphasis on single-family homeownership as an ideal, only one version had positive connotations. One conjured notions of large-scale monotonous housing developments while the other an upstanding and independent homeowner. New developments had no chance of assimilating with existing social and spatial patterns. Defining the expansion of housing and population as a threat represented a core tenet and motivator of political action in the name of maintaining their quality of life.

With the state on display as an omen for the nation, California provided a hospitable testing ground for fears regarding the nation's environmental conditions to propagate. Alongside real estate developers, the state government itself behaved antagonistically toward critics. "Which do you want?" demanded a report from the state's Department of Fish and Game, "Growth and progress, or fish?"[41] Some placed hopes in urban planning to devise objective guidelines for growth since the "majority of people" wanted protection from the assaults of "special interest groups."[42] Residents viewed California as the place where "the signs and portents of approaching ecological disaster" were recognized as anything but unique to the state. What "man has done here stands out dramatically: black oil contrasts with bleached sand, dry summer, grass and trees don't cover much, litter on the freeway, and slurbs spreading across thousands of square miles." These conditions may have been similar in other places, but critics contended that they looked worse in California since "this state is central in the dreams and myths of the nation and the world." For those reasons, freeways, smog, DDT, and ugly, sprawling urban plans were more noticeable than elsewhere. Moreover, waves "of the future break first on the rocky California coast."[43] Despite the state's singular qualities, no American could risk being unaware of California's difficulties or ponder about their origins. The overarching problem was population. Every "facet of the land and its life, from the conservation of wilderness . . . to the restoration of meaning and pleasure to life in the cities" experienced the consequences of population pressures.

Establishing boundaries to maintain the integrity of a place was an oblique way of advocating for racial and social segregation—often under the cover of progressive or environmentally responsible language. Dasmann observed that a "properly planned city with adequate opportunity for all would not breed the strife and turmoil that emanates from a Harlem or a Fillmore district."[44] He looked admiringly upon Santa Barbara—"one of the most charming places"—and how residents preserved "its quiet beauty" by excluding industrial growth, limiting housing developments, and implementing minimum lot sizes. Unlike other cities that encouraged any and all growth, Santa Barbara focused on welcoming "brainy gentlemen in smokeless industries" in a locale where "great minds are at home."[45] Concurring with Dasmann, urban planners and critics Christopher Tunnard and Boris Pushkarev insisted that justifying modern American civilization to its population and the world beyond required "the creation of a more appropriate physical shape."[46] They reiterated a common complaint that designers, by failing to place human beings at the center of the American environment, had left it "either empty or cluttered with waste."[47] This lamentable situation was a recent development. Economic imperatives not only prompted a laissez-faire attitude on the forces shaping the environment but also caused "a confusion in men's minds between personal liberties and wider freedoms." Nature's "automatic limits" to human freedom implied a need for solitude, privacy, health, and rest. In Santa Barbara, Tunnard and Pushkarev looked favorably on the effort to "preserve a pastoral or handsomely landscaped residential haven" free from urban clutter despite the risk of higher taxes.[48] Santa Barbara's natural surroundings in and of themselves provided unassailable justification against development.

Retaining the state's environmental attractions and avoiding external pressures for continual urban development required a variety of legal and social curbs. Residents framed the ongoing development of previously open land as environmental destruction through well-known and repeated sentiments. A report released by the Allied Protection and Improvement Association, an umbrella organization that represented Santa Barbara homeowners, argued that once-beautiful areas of California "have become blanketed with ugly urban sprawl, smog ridden, water contaminated, traffic congested, air polluted, and burdened with excessive taxes" that overdevelopment required.[49] Poor planning and a narrow perspective that privileged crude forms of growth and progress resulted in a blighted landscape. Given how much these circumstances affected the daily lives of average citizens, it was predictable that they would be proactive in their desire to "regulate the destiny" of their immediate environments.

In addition to spatial transformations, suburbanization and the expansion of private homeownership engendered shifts in social and economic life. Young families with children and relatively high incomes found new habits and ways to spend their time and money. For commercial interests, suburbs offered not only "more new customers but better customers."[50] New building types, such as shopping centers surrounded by parking lots, and new roads facilitated the ability of populations to live farther from central cities.[51] Americans who equated civilization with electronics and bathroom fixtures foretold significant changes in the values attached to affluence. Taking pride in quantity and growth, Americans wanted the "biggest and the highest office buildings; he wants the most books in his libraries; he wants two cars, two telephones, and two television sets . . . in every American home."[52] Yet this growth generated its own set of problems. These problems, however, had an air of familiarity. As industry, stores, and offices moved outward, the suburbs, according to observers, changed into cities and gave "the erstwhile country dwellers a second taste of city life with all the familiar problems of heavy traffic, congestion, even slums." New suburban dwellers who moved out of cities often found less of an idyll than the same problems in a changed environment.

Actions taken in the name of neighborhood interests had large-scale equivalents. Calls to "regulate the destiny" of a place worked as a convenient euphemism for population control. Although the idea of natural limits had the veneer of reasonable common sense, some took the idea in a more radical direction. Garrett Hardin played an instrumental role in bringing such arguments to a wide audience through his provocative and widely debated essay, "The Tragedy of the Commons," published in 1968 in *Science*.[53] Looking squarely at population as a planetary-scale dilemma, Hardin believed too many well-meaning people minimized "the evils of overpopulation." These individuals simply did not understand how overpopulation meant relinquishing "the privileges they now enjoy." Comprehending the world's land and resources as finite with no possible escape through extraterrestrial colonization meant acknowledging an unavoidable expansion in human misery. Hardin concluded that finite resources meant that zero population growth was the only solution.[54]

Zero population growth policies, Hardin argued, allowed humans not just to survive but to flourish. "All forms of enjoyment, from swimming . . . to playing music and writing poetry" required limiting population. Contrariwise, if maximizing population was the goal, there would be "no gourmet meals, no vacations, no sports, no music, no literature, no art." Proclaiming himself a truth-teller, Hardin declared that he had parsed human opinions and came to an objective definition of the good. Squaring differences of opinion—one person's wilderness was another's ski lodge—demanded measuring those choices on a criterion of survival. Ultimately, limiting individual freedom to procreate offered the clearest and most likely solution. In the most famous example from "The Tragedy of the Commons," he asked readers to imagine a pasture open to all in which individual herdsmen attempted to keep as many of their own animals on the commons. This was satisfactory while society was unstable since tribal wars, poaching, and disease would manage the land's carrying capacity. Unfortunately, when that society reached a period of stability, the "inherent logic of the commons remorselessly generates tragedy." All people who sought to maximize their own gain added animals to their herds. However rational an individual choice, the increased stress on the land diminished conditions for the many. "Therein is the tragedy," Hardin concluded. If all pursued their own best interests without considering the whole, ruin would come to everyone.[55]

Pollution, waste, and the loss of natural beauty all resulted from the misuse of the commons. Hardin pondered how to confront a family, religion, race, or class that "adopts overbreeding as a policy to secure its own aggrandizement?" Coupling the freedom to breed with the belief that everyone had an equal right to the commons meant locking "the world into a tragic course of action." The freedom to procreate was codified not only in American values but universally in the United Nations' Declaration of Human Rights, which described the family as the natural and fundamental unit of society. For Hardin, the social arrangements that "produce responsibility are arrangements that create coercion, of some sort." Despite his argument that the increase in population caused the destruction of the commons, his own understandings of the commons, its uses and changes, were not always explicitly linked to population. He cited technological shifts to buttress his argument. Automobiles, factories, pesticides, fertilizers, and atomic energy were by-products of population growth. Ultimately, Hardin admitted that his own life and those of other Americans had not yet reached the point of tragedy. Nevertheless, he saw pathways that portended the restriction of several human pleasures, such as noise pollution from music or supersonic travel, even if they seemed far off. "We are a long way from outlawing the commons in matters of pleasure. Is this because our Puritan inheritance makes us view pleasure as something of a sin, and pain (that is, the pollution of advertising) as a sign of virtue?" he mused.[56] Acknowledging that every new enclosure of the commons involved circumscribing personal liberty, he argued that strictures would be accepted well enough in time for the sake of quality of life.

Several years after the publication of "The Tragedy of the Commons," Hardin provided further analysis of his general standpoint, under the phrase "lifeboat ethics." First published in *Psychology Today* in 1974 and then expanded on the same year for *Bioscience*, lifeboat ethics offered a framework for understanding the "problem of the survival of the human species" that no generation before had faced.[57] Meant as a partial correction of a then-popular idea attributed to economist and theorist Kenneth Boulding of the earth as a spaceship, lifeboat ethics offered a framework to avoid the "suicidal" inevitability of the tragedy of the commons. Hardin argued that two-thirds of the world's population was "desperately poor" and the remainder was wealthy. Imagining the earth as a lifeboat clarified its limited capacity. Strategies to resolve these restrictions, through foundation-sponsored activities associated with the Green Revolution, merely assured the exacerbation of the central problem. "The land of every nation has a limited carrying capacity," Hardin argued. The aftermath of the OPEC oil crisis convinced more and more people that "we have already exceeded the carrying capacity of the land." Addressing these actual limits meant choosing between unpleasant alternatives. One could swamp the boat with an ever-increasing number of passengers until everyone drowned or simply admit no more than a safe number. For those on the boat who felt guilty about the latter choice, Hardin offered a simple answer: "Get out and yield your place."[58] Not everyone on earth had an equal right to an equal share of the earth's resources.[59] Some needed to sacrifice for others.

Concerns about compulsory aid and resources on the part of some coincided with the rising power of global anti-imperialist movements for self-determination in the Global South.[60] In this context, the impulse toward altruism revealed an "enthusiastic but unrealistic generosity" on the part of wealthy nations since the bulk of need went to poor nations. Hardin reasoned, "What happens if some organizations or countries budget for accidents and others do not?" As it stood, poor nations that had trouble managing their population growth had a world food bank—essentially a commons in disguise—to save them. Hardin was not alone in this assessment. He quoted Alan Gregg, a vice president at the Rockefeller Foundation, who likened the growth and spread of humanity over the surface of the earth to the spread of cancer. This growth required food, but Gregg added that "they have never been cured by getting it." Despite the harshness of the statements, Hardin dismissed criticism of this point of view as misplaced bigotry. Extrapolating outward, he asked whether Americans of "non-Indian ancestry can look upon ourselves as the descendants of thieves who are guilty morally, if not legally, of stealing this land from its Indian owners" and should then give land back to living descendants. Hardin answered in the negative since "however morally or logically sound this proposal may be," the consequences would be "absurd." When "intoxicated with a sense of pure justice, we should decide to turn our land over to the Indians. Since all our other wealth has been derived from the land, wouldn't we be morally obliged to give that back to the Indians too?"

Prominent individuals including management professor at MIT Jay Forrester, president of the National Academy of Sciences Philip Handler, and Paul Ehrlich articulated similar ideas.[61] Ehrlich, a Stanford biologist and author of *Population Bomb*, also from 1968, was inspired to write on overpopulation while traveling with his family in India. Responses to lifeboat ethics included critics who noted that it was "nothing less than a deliberate decision to allow people who might otherwise survive, at least for a time, to die of starvation and disease" and characterized by a willful ignorance since most did not have to observe "their emaciated bodies, or help dig the mass graves necessary to cover those millions of corpses."[62] The idea that rich nations were self-sufficient was disproven by the oil crisis. Those in wealthy nations might "of course" become "self-sufficient by the expedient of radically lowering our own standard of living." Nevertheless, Americans seemed to lack any inclination for less abundance because it meant "ours would no longer be a rich lifeboat, and who wants that?" Ultimately, "every life saved this year in a poor country diminishes the quality of life for subsequent generations." Hardin's extremist views had a moderate version in neighborhoods close to his own where residents believed that their spaces had clear limits to the number of people they could accommodate with existing resources. Those who had received their share believed they had a right to protect it from others.

The belief that expanding sprawl and living beyond carrying capacity threatened to spoil a nation's social and environmental fabric contrasted with optimistic prospects ushered in by newfound economic and social prosperity after 1945—at least for certain parts of the population. In the face of these new comforts and technologies, individuals questioned their psychological and material consequences.[63] While critics lamented the loss of open space to meet housing demands, others saw positive directions. Increased affluence and the resources that accompanied it offered visions of the future that included more leisure and a higher quality of life. At a workshop held by the California Park and Recreation Society in the mid-1950s, participants heralded this coming destiny and projected their fantasies about the coming years.[64] Higher living standards meant a reduction in the number of "slum dwellers" and "sharecroppers." In the coming decade, new parks, playgrounds, churches, senior citizens' centers, and arts organizations would be joined by the possibility of driving from one coast to another without encountering a single traffic light.[65] A steady decline in the work week from 37.5 hours to 35 and then 30 meant that by the 1970s, millions of workers would go to the factory or office four days a week. The problem—if one could describe it as such—would be what to do with the extra time. Meeting the demands of increased leisure time among a wide swath of the population touched on issues regarding environmental access, energy, and land use. The rise in popularity of golf accelerated the construction of courses. Between the mid-1950s and 1970, the number of golf courses rose by at least fifty-five hundred courses.[66] Gardening developed into a popular, or possibly necessary, hobby as new homes included yards that required regular maintenance.[67] Horticulturists developed new shrubs and grasses, including those chemically treated for slow growth. Inside the home, updated appliances promised to make their predecessors look "like an old fogy."[68] Other visions of the future had a more fantastical tenor, with helicopters replacing buses to allow further expansion into rural areas alongside high-speed trains.

Fossil fuels—an integral part of fertilizers, cars, and helicopters—linked these changes and made them conceivable. The twentieth century's explosive increase in fossil fuel use is difficult to underestimate. Half of the coal consumed in the United States had been burned since 1920 and nearly half of all gas and oil since 1940.[69] Ellis A. Jarvis, a deputy superintendent with Los Angeles City Schools, acknowledged that the United States accounted for a substantial portion of global use, but much of the "free world" had been "living high" off the accumulated capital energy in coal, oil, and gas reserves. But those reserves had limits. In the face of coming scarcity, nuclear energy seemed an attractive—and unlimited—alternative. The ability of nuclear power to generate resources for centuries indicated yet unimagined transformations in daily life, with massive increases in automation and therefore even more time for leisure.

For many, the dream of automation proved especially compelling.[70] By 1965, ran a common assertion, people would only work four days a week with a guaranteed salary. The shift inspired visions of entertainment centered around the home with two color televisions and a "pay as you watch system" for about a dollar a night. Paraphrasing economist Stuart Chase, a businessman mused that Americans would thus be able to develop a culture that "does not depend upon work to give meaning to our lives." The coming wave of time outside of wage labor raised serious questions about the human constitution and how to live "with a degree of leisure unknown to any human culture." After all, man was "not a loafing organism. Without something to engage his mind and muscle, he rapidly degenerates . . . automation after its introductory period may well mean more leisure than the human organism by nature is able to tolerate." On a more modest and less philosophical scale, activities oriented toward filling increased free time often centered on the home and improving its immediate environment. Rather than existential questions about the nature and use of time, a more atomized vision of leisure developed around individual homeownership.

Detractors viewed new lifestyles as evidence of a "throw-away civilization" where craftsmanship had been forgotten and things fell apart in a deliberate attempt to force the population to buy something new. The realization that natural places had become, in the words of Barnard College English professor John Kouwehoven, a "technological landscape," divided by wire fences, "smoothed by tractors, tied to the urban-industrial world by wires, roads, and rails."[71] Rural areas displayed their ties to urban locales through the increasing height of antennae. Man's technology modified the texture of the earth itself, so in some corners, protecting the landscape emerged as the pressing issue.

"One of the marks of a civilized society is the extent to which it protects the public interest," declared a writer in the *New York Times* in 1969.[72] Whether in Ipswich, Massachusetts, Marin County in Northern California, or Santa Barbara, public interest in environmental quality signaled a proper civil society and path toward recognizing allied individuals.[73] Across the nation, assaults from yellow smog, overcrowding, and worsening living conditions kindled anxieties, but land use and housing raised some of the most acute concerns among middle-class and upper-middle-class Americans. Advocating for the conservation of open space and the reduction of pollution as well as questioning the benefits of growth provided residents with ethical and environmental justifications for protecting their material interests. Undeveloped green space and similar locations became a recognized service and infrastructure, alongside water and a police department, that many believed a well-run and high-quality community should provide.

With its distance from both Los Angeles and San Francisco, Santa Barbara contained characteristics of both and neither. While not technically a suburb, residents sensed a perilous possibility that Santa Barbara could soon have the characteristics of those lamentable settlements. Categorizing Santa Barbara and similar cities along the coast confounded easy definitions. The writer Remi Nadeau described these nonsuburban spots between San Francisco and Los Angeles as part of the California "rimland." The thread that connected these locales remained consistent up and down the coast. The mayor of Carmel, 240 miles north of Santa Barbara, expressed his main wishes for his city to have "no new building" and "no improvements of any kind."[74] According to Nadeau, the one thing inhabitants of the rimland had in common across the "social elite of Santa Barbara to the cattle ranchers of Modoc County" was that they were "off the beaten path of California growth, and, generally speaking, they like it."

Residents of this stretch of coastline separated from the state's population centers embraced a resistance to change. This battle meant standing in opposition to "what most other Californians affirmatively embrace as economic progress."[75] Nevertheless, in the early 1960s, Santa Barbara was the fastest-growing community among this cluster, though "it may be said to have grown in spite of itself" since its strongest assets were its rustic residential setting and "geared-down tempo of life." While not wishing to attract ever-greater growth, one local proclaimed that "no reasonable person who can make a good living in Santa Barbara would voluntarily live anywhere else."[76] Because of their "recaptured heritage," Nadeau observed that residents had been "less than enthusiastic at the appearance of the postwar tract subdivisions." Thus with "more foresight and courage" than other Southern California communities, Santa Barbara County placed restrictions on development to preserve the region's prewar charm. Heavy industry was generally considered a plague, and in some corners "even research centers with no industrial nuisance factors and with personnel of high income and educational levels have sometimes been resisted as a threat to community character."

The incursion of technology in particular incensed critics. Writer and editor Robert Cubbedge lamented that Santa Barbara "for all its Old Worldly charm" had been sorely afflicted by "electronic eyesores in particular." The city had a local television station, but many residents erected large aerials on their rooftops to receive signals from Los Angeles. As a result, when one stood in the hills adjacent the Santa Barbara Mission, the water and Channel Islands could only be seen "through a conglomeration of four-tiered television aerials.... It seemed a sacrilege."[77] Cubbedge spoke for many when he described suburbs as "vast aesthetic wastelands cluttered with millions of monotonous houses," a man-made America with a "near-criminal disgrace of vast proportions." He placed his hopes in an "enraged citizenry" ready to restore "physical America to the community of civilized nations."[78] The nation may not have the resources to legislate beauty, but enough minds could be changed to avoid "cultural barbarism."

Cubbedge placed culpability on individual behavior. "Have you ever been guilty of being a slob?" he demanded.[79] You have if you have ever "discarded litter in anything but a proper waste receptacle . . . if you've ever walked on the grass in a public garden, shaken a rug out a door or window, or built a fire on a public beach." His definition expanded further. One could not claim immunity from being a slob if one had ever condoned, even because of indifference, "an act of slobbism, public or private, which might have been prevented through vehement protest." Worse than being a monument to nothingness, American cities were monuments to individual greed.

Residents appreciated Santa Barbara's natural surroundings, but also found them to be politically useful, especially with rising environmentalist attitudes. The increased spread and legitimacy of environmentalism as a social movement provided opportunities for broad interpretations of its scope and outlook. Conceptions of environmentalism with a radical temper, such as those who embraced population control or anti-humanist ideas, contrasted with moderating voices that could include hunters, fishers, and others who participated in recreational activities "with a masculine edge" that encouraged popular acceptance for preserving natural areas.[80] For Santa Barbara's homeowners, especially in particular neighborhoods, environmentalism could be neutralized of any radical political or social content to justify protecting their piece of the city.

By recognizing environmental quality as a vital component of their lives, Santa Barbarans constructed a tacit framework for thinking about the relationship between nature and society, largely informed by their own immediate environs. In their rendering, maintaining the natural and urban environment required limiting the number of human inhabitants and the type of housing constructed. Trampling over remaining land for new subdivisions or multifamily housing not only desecrated the land; it would potentially bring undesirable new inhabitants. Instead of regarding increasing needs for affordable housing for a rising population as important enough to require complex reflection and action, a significant number of residents simply concluded that their city had reached its maximum size. Advocating for protections for existing homeowners gave rise to an environmental determinism that settled into a common sense and justified the belief that the most valued regions of California were already full.

As much as denizens of so-called rimland cities wished for a clear divide between their own environments and external developments, the outside world crept in. Santa Barbara experienced a particularly rapid increase in population. The influx of new arrivals stemmed from the 1958 reactivation of Camp Cooke, sixty-five miles west of the city, as Vandenberg Air Force Base; the expansion of the University of California, Santa Barbara; and associated growth of research and defense industries.[81] Impending and imagined transformations provoked anxieties among existing residents. Prospective plans for the city included development in the Mesa Hills, which residents believed should remain a "permanent green belt" without realizing the tracts were privately owned and remained undeveloped because of a lack of technologies to build on its steep slope while its surrounding level land had been developed.[82] Soon afterward new technologies made the hills a possible location for housing. Homes had been built on the sides of San Roque canyon and were "creeping up the foothills." The Foothill Preservation League warned that the San Roque foothills could endure a tripling of its population and the loss of scenic spaces to condos and housing tracts.[83] The league proposed a rezoning to one house per acre as a solution. In Goleta Valley to the east of the city, "conventional cookie cutter type subdivisions" came out of bulldozed lemon groves. In response to the rapidity of tract construction, the Santa Barbara County Planning Department hoped to implement a development plan that would work more in "harmony with the land" so "the landscape will not be completely destroyed."[84]

Linked by circumstances of proximity and by their status as homeowners, local citizens came together and formed neighborhood associations to assert their financial and social stakes, often against local and county governments. Motivated primarily by the desire to protect their existing conditions, these associations nevertheless staged their work as beneficial to the entire city. The neutrality embodied in statements about promoting "the welfare, betterment, and prosperity of our individual districts in particular and of the city and the community as a whole" belied the political power of these associations.[85] Pushing for land use limits to a small set of defined interventions in the name of securing "proper and most beneficial development" became the primary way the associations presented themselves as urban and environmental stewards. To gain further influence to fight inappropriate land uses, the individual neighborhood associations formed umbrella groups, such as the Allied Improvement Association (AIA), to collaborate and advocate for their interests. They hoped their efforts would inspire others in similar places to show how relatively small and informal organizations could manage urban growth.[86]

A wide range of environmental issues, including flood and mudslide prevention, maintenance of air quality, the development of an oil sanctuary, and freeway development, fell under their sphere of interest. But protecting neighborhood character—a euphemistic term for property values—took precedence. In the face of projections that showed Santa Barbara's population doubling by the 1980s, Standish Palmer, the research director for a local nonprofit called the Citizens Planning Association, argued that improvement associations be granted greater decision-making powers. If a residential area was "threatened" by a service station or a restaurant, neighborhood associations could take a proactive role in rejecting its construction rather than simply lodging a public relations campaign. Fighting "the encroachment of business into living areas, the granting of variances and conditional uses running contrary to existing zoning, the intrusion of apartments into residential areas" all helped prevent the deterioration of the city's attractions. Even existing private homes turned into potential Trojan horses, such as when a proposed ordinance suggested that up to two rooms of a family home could be rented for a family day care, foster family, or other home occupations.[87] The rhetoric of invasion and threats, as well as the necessity of constant vigilance, characterized their perspective. This was especially important for improvement associations since the city planning office would "almost always" decide in favor of the variance.[88]

The antagonism between a city government that would "almost always" decide against the wishes of current residents came into clearest relief regarding multifamily housing. Individuals representing the Mesa Improvement Association on the western coast of the city informed their neighbors of a developer who received conditional approval for a zoning variance to build multifamily housing. The association countered that one of the major justifications for granting an exception was for developments that improved a neighborhood. There was always the possibility that variances would go too far. When the developer proposed a design for thirty-two apartments, the association's newsletter demanded, "It is supposed to be compatible with adjacent properties!!" The association viewed conditional approval of this sort of project as a slippery slope. "We're told we should be happy with the 'lesser of two evil,' really now, why should we be faced with any evils!!!!????"[89]

A particular anti-growth attitude prevailed in these associations. An issue of the Mission Canyon Association newsletter declared that "what is good for industrial interests harm and deteriorate" the city's residential areas.[90] In contrast, single-family homes offered stable values over time in contrast to the fluctuations of businesses. On the Mesa, residents presented themselves as part of a "very trying and varied history" due to the presence of oil wells and an image of being on the wrong side of the tracks, but the Mesa Improvement Association organized to protect its interests.[91] The Mesa had often, the associated claimed, been considered the city's "stepchild" due to its location in the western part of the city.[92] Going unmentioned was the fact that Japanese and Mexican immigrant families lived along portions of the Mesa along Cliff Drive in the 1920s and 1930s. By the mid-1960s, white locals worried that their "old residential neighborhood" came under threat. The Mesa Improvement Association acknowledged that developers had very good reasons for finding their neighborhood attractive. There was "stable weather" and the city's "most inspiring" view of the ocean. Introducing apartments would only exacerbate the idea of the neighborhood as a less-than-desirable location. The newsletter asked forcefully, "Do we want to go toward a complex of Apartments, Boarding Houses and Rest Homes? Are our streets adequate for the additional traffic load? Will our tax base of single dwelling homeowners be broadened to compensate for the additional Fire, Police and School Services enjoyed by the Apartment dwellers? Will our antiquated sewer system carry the additional load of Multiple apartments?" The neighborhood's demographics would shift from "homeowners" to "Apartment dwellers." Only the former represented a desirable resident. Resources and services were scarce, and instead of asking for more public services, the settled conclusion was that there was not enough to go around. Someone's gain in housing would always result in another's loss in quality of life.

Zoning issues put into relief the fact that city government posed a major hazard to their domestic conditions by shoving "their density and problems" on the neighborhood. This realization catalyzed activism and political intervention. "Do you think that we can get by without participating in civic issues and problems in this day and age!!!" demanded the association newsletter. Civic matters reached a point "where more and more attention and participation is necessary by all of us." In one case, an LA-based developer purchased a ten-acre tract near Arroyo Burro beach with plans to build up to four hundred apartments adjacent to single-family homes and a beach that was "already handling capacity crowds."[93] Without careful attention, outside developers could, residents argued, ruin landscapes across Santa Barbara.

Similar concerns occupied other neighborhoods. The Peach Grove Improvement Association fought to prevent an automobile sales and service center adjacent to members' homes.[94] The Hope-La Cumbre Improvement Association located in the northwestern part of Santa Barbara, with over two hundred members, characterized its neighborhood as an ideal "combination of City and Country" and was once the location of racially restrictive covenants.[95] In response to a zoning variance proposed by the City Planning Commission to expand parking adjacent neighborhood beaches, the association countered that the city wanted to sacrifice green space near one of its most "valuable high priority strips of beach property." John Carroll, president of the Federated Council of Improvement Associations, another umbrella organization, placed an advertisement in the *Santa Barbara News-Press* against a proposed civic auditorium and amusement park.[96] The advertisement proclaimed that an amusement park especially would be detrimental to the city and its general welfare, spurring "great devaluation" of property and "especially cheapen[ing]" its immediate surroundings. Moreover, amusements parks "frequently attract the undesirable and disorderly element for many miles in the surrounding county." Alongside diminishing property and cultural values came increased costs to cover an inevitable rise of police protection due to juvenile delinquency and "dirt and filth" to the area's beaches. The City Planning Commission denied the permission to build.

While most of the action against development occurred in residential areas, the entire city was subject to citizen protests against construction that threatened the urban character. City regulations limited the height of buildings to 45 feet or three stories, but in 1968, a developer proposed building a 120-foot-high, eleven-story condo on a downtown block.[97] Drawings of the building showed that open spaces around high-rise developments could not be seen half a block away and that trees lost their importance. In voicing opposition to the proposed high-rise building two blocks from State Street,

Clark Howell, the president of the Upper Eastside Improvement Association, wrote on behalf of the organization to the City Planning Commission that the organization was "not opposed to growth and well-conceived change."[98] Instead, the association believed that changes "should come as part of the orderly development of the community." Howell stressed that neither he nor the organization had a categorical objection to high-rises. He simply wished to state that he believed their approval should come only after careful consideration of their effect on the entire city and then only in limited areas so as not to be "detrimental to the best interest of the people."

The Santa Barbara Women's Club concurred with Howell's statement and added that it believed a high-rise would have a most undesirable impact, "psychologically and aesthetically," on residents, visitors, and the unique character of the community.[99] Judith Dodge Orias, the vice president of the Hidden Valley Protective and Improvement Association, whose motto was "where comfort, culture, and excellence are a way of life," wrote that "no one" would want to lose their privacy or view to a tall tower. Orias added that her association concluded that a high-rise would have a detrimental effect on the value of adjacent properties, mostly "well-designed apartments and private residences," unless they all received the same ability to construct tall structures, which would inevitably result "in a maze of high rise structures."[100] This would be an unacceptable change in the city's environment.[101] High-rise buildings, a resolution from the AIA stated, were "totally out of character" with the Santa Barbara environment "as a whole, and with the surrounding neighborhood, single-family dwellings, apartments, and churches."[102] Although opponents recognized that high-rises might be appropriate in other parts of the city, it was "not appropriate in this part of the Santa Barbara community which prides itself on a distinctive architectural style and mood compatible with its beautiful natural surroundings and treasured historic background." Ultimately, a "very dangerous precedent" would be created if the building was approved.

The work of applying constraints on housing, building type, and commercial activities in particular neighborhoods (Figure 4.1) often, but not always, sidestepped the fact that their strategies curbed the entry of unwanted people as well. Associating multifamily housing with an infestation that introduced an undesirable population to a neighborhood advanced notions similar to Hardin's tragedy of the commons or lifeboat ethics. For those who believed in inherent limits to the qualities that first attracted residents to Santa Barbara, restricting access was a necessity. Any proposed expansion for a wider population was framed as a seizure of rights. This point of view even applied in cases that putatively increased resources for all.

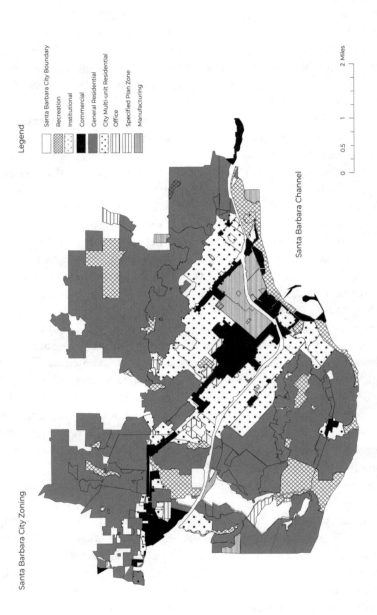

FIGURE 4.1. Current zoning map of Santa Barbara. Information from the City of Santa Barbara Planning and Zoning Counter. Map by Sierra Chmela, edited by Shelby Doyle.

In addition to multifamily housing developments, high-rises, and certain types of commercial structures, the associations mobilized against oil. In 1963, the AIA recommended an amendment to the City Charter to ban oil drilling within the city.[103] Noting the enemy was "unknown and powerful," the AIA only knew that the interests were economic, and if the organization's members could find additional sources of revenue, the city could forget the "easy money" from oil drilling.[104] The opening up of Santa Barbara's famed coastline and beaches to wider public access in the years before the establishment of the California Coastal Commission in 1972 puts into relief how ideals of a public good could be integrated and redeployed in the interests of property owners. A 1959 amendment to a subdivision ordinance put forward to the Santa Barbara County Board of Supervisors called for new developments abutting tidelands to include twenty feet of rights-of-way for beach access no more than six hundred feet apart.[105] Attorneys for owners of ocean-fronting land protested the amendment as "socialism" and "public thievery." They continued that such a rule would unfairly burden and annoy property owners since it transformed beaches into public spaces but without the supervision and services provided at official public beaches. Editors for the *Santa Barbara News-Press* countered that the public "as a whole has a right to enjoyment of the tidelands in every safe and reasonable way" and "it would be contrary to the long-range best interests of the county as a whole to permit long stretches of California coast line to be barred to public access in the future when coastal areas are thickly populated residential neighborhoods." For property owners, resisting wider public accessibility to beaches meant protecting the state's amenities for themselves but not others.

In 1970, the Allied Protection and Improvement Association released a resolution clarifying its commitments. Santa Barbara's residents, the resolution began, had an "obligation to those who have strived so faithfully in the past, to the citizens living here today, and to the future Santa Barbarans."[106] The city had, the resolution continued, "reached a critical point in its growth." Years of allowing building projects "unrelated to a coherent plan of development" was "certain to result in the degradation of the community." Freeways, traffic, and housing the less privileged presented problems that were an "affront to those Santa Barbarans whose political imagination gave this community the character and reputation it now enjoys." From their perspective, the city endangered its reputation and was fast becoming a "shoddy facsimile." Instead of focusing on the present, the city's goals needed to be oriented "to the future"—"it is today when we must begin serious, long range planning to ensure a successful tomorrow." Disorderly sprawl, earth-moving technology to create subdivisions on formerly open land, and the automobile represented connected aspects of a harmful emphasis on growth. Ordered and orderly development through restraints on growth were antidotes to the marred landscapes in evidence throughout the United States.

Rising affluence and suburbanization after 1945 often receive credit for the ascendance of modern environmentalism. In this narrative, increasing awareness about the destruction of open space and diminished access to nature resulted from individual experiences of chaotic suburban growth and consequent infrastructure and population pressures. This path to environmental awareness not only provided a framework for critiquing suburban growth but also justified socially exclusionary attitudes. Who belonged within the association's definition of "we" was not explicitly stated but could be easily inferred. The priorities of long-standing, white homeowners took precedence, and as a result, homeowners became an important political constituency and social identity.[107] Through organizing into homeowners and neighborhood associations, residents influenced the outlines of local concerns and methods of diagnosing problems, and they defined the scope of acceptable solutions. Associations of like-minded, property-owning neighbors constituted a political and social formation that emphasized an individualized set of interests. The environment became a way of bridging disagreements and creating an ideological consensus. Appealing to existing or recent environmental conditions and the hazards of change endorsed certain types of development, while others fell outside the sphere of acceptability.

Claims over property and ownership, both of specific homes and the character of the city's neighborhoods, sat at the heart of the contest over control in Santa Barbara. Residents who considered Santa Barbara as an exceptional rather than conventional locale in need of protection raised the stakes to a matter of civilizational survival. Despite locating Santa Barbara within California's unique and ostensibly isolated "rimland," the growth factors that marked other locations—from the defense industry to higher education—stood close at hand. Tensions between residents and local government bodies put into relief how both groups conceived of their obligations to their neighbors and themselves. Neighborhood associations simultaneously acknowledged and rejected their own ties to the region and their greater communities. Expansions in social and political equity, they argued, not only fell outside their purview but were ultimately undesirable intrusions into their neighborhoods. The problems facing Santa Barbara homeowners were framed as nuisances for other locations.

The belief in fundamental limits of environmental resources and the populations who could benefit from them undergirded responses to the landscape transformations wrought by social and environmental changes after 1945. Debates over possible responses to this predicament took place on a global scale and in localized contexts of neighborhoods and communities. Whether at the scale of a neighborhood or a nation, each place had a point where people believed conditions inexorably shifted from positive to negative. Global arguments about population, food, and natural resources had local parallels. The dominant solution remained the same: prohibitions on accommodating a larger population. Advocating for limits to population and settlement based on supposed resource constraints framed the response as inevitable and unavoidable. From small cities to hemispheric expanses, embracing population control provided a solution to maintain the status quo. Those who benefited from existing conditions could continue to benefit while justifying the exclusion of others as a necessity.

5

The Worst Place

> Surely, the future beauty of our environment is more important than a few hundred million dollars.[1]

The twelfth page of the *Los Angeles Times* on May 6, 1969, carried three short articles on military actions in Lebanon, Israel, and Cambodia (Figure 5.1).[2] Advertisements took up most of the page's column inches, including one trumpeting a book promising the "candid confessions of the girl who married the SPOILED PRIEST," assurances that a "top executive of a well-known book publisher" was interested in works by local authors, and a commitment from Berlitz that "You can speak Spanish by July 21st." But just one advertisement took up about half the page. It featured an array of photographs depicting couples and families on the beach, playing tennis, looking at art, and sitting in front of a historic mission, above the photos the advertisement's text read, "Santa Barbara like it is today." Below a single line contained a simple request: "Come play with us this summer." A longer text in smaller type made readers aware that Santa Barbara, just ninety minutes from Los Angeles, was as enjoyable as it was a year earlier and "all the years before." The city was a "sunny, cool, smiling vacationland" offering "85 happy things to do and see."

The advertisement's cheerful disposition sparked irritation and anger among some in Santa Barbara. But not because they disagreed. In fact, they acknowledged the accuracy of the depictions. The city indeed offered a pleasant, sunny locale filled with activities for young and old. Instead, the exasperation stemmed from a glaring omission. Less than four months earlier, oil from a blowout on an offshore platform that started on January 28, 1969, blackened the Santa Barbara Channel's beaches. This was not a small incident; rather, it was the largest oil spill in the nation's history to that point

FIGURE 5.1. Page twelve of the *Los Angeles Times* on May 6, 1969. © 1969 *Los Angeles Times*. Used with permission.

Lebanese Army Says It Will Fight Guerrillas

BEIRUT — The Lebanese army announced Monday it has decided to crack down severely on Palestinian guerrillas in southern Lebanon.

The army's communique followed weekend clashes between the guerrillas and Lebanese troops in which one soldier was killed and three army trucks were destroyed.

The announcement was the first official admission of mounting friction between the army and the guerrillas who want to use Lebanon as a base for commando raids into Israel.

Almost two weeks ago Premier Rashid Karameh resigned following fighting between government troops and guerrilla sympathizers that left 18 dead and more than 100 wounded.

The army blamed the latest fighting on members of the Syrian-backed Al Saika group which is affiliated with that country's ruling Baath Party.

The Lebanese government, fearing Israeli retaliation, has been reluctant to give the guerrillas a free hand to conduct raids into Israel.

Arabs Not War-Ready, Israeli Premier Says

JERUSALEM — The Arabs are not prepared for a full-scale war with Israel, Prime Minister Golda Meir declared Monday, but she added that Israel's armed forces are ready in case she is wrong.

"Occasionally our region is portrayed as being on the point of an explosion which may spread beyond this area," Mrs. Meir said in a State of the Union message to the Knesset, Israel's parliament.

"There is no justification for this contention. We live in this region and we are perfectly familiar with the actual state of affairs.

"Israel cannot permit herself to err in her evaluation of the situation or underestimate the gravity of the dangers, nor can it exaggerate them. We have learned not to create pipe dreams.

Is Best Judgment

"To the best of our judgment the Arab countries cannot at the present permit themselves to wage a total war."

She added, however, that while she believes her government's assessment to have a firm foundation, Israel's military forces "are ready for any eventuality, even for the eventuality of a mistake in this forecast."

Mrs. Meir's address followed some expressions of concern that fighting along the Suez Canal and Jordan River cease-fire lines could escalate into another wide-open conflict in the Middle East.

Mrs. Meir renewed Israel's terms for settlement of the Middle East problem through direct negotiations with the Arabs. These terms call for an end to the state of belligerence in force since Israel's foundation in 1948, agreements on boundaries and free navigation of waterways, such as the Suez Canal.

She dismissed claims by President Gamal Abdel Nasser in his May Day speech that Egypt has destroyed 60% of Israel's Suez Canal fortifications.

"All I can say is I hope that in the future his so-called victories are of the same type as claimed in this false report," she said.

Mrs. Meir also assailed Jordan's King Hussein, who put forth a six-point peace proposal in Washington April 10.

She said: "Anyone glancing at those six points will soon realize that they contain nothing but an Arab interpretation of the Security Council resolution, and, indeed, they were so described by King Hussein himself on his return to Amman..."

Meanwhile, sporadic firing between Israeli and Arab forces was reported Monday along the canal and near the Allenby Bridge just north of the Dead Sea.

An Israeli spokesman said artillery, light arms and mortar fire was exchanged across the waterway at the Kantara region.

N. Viet Troops Hit U.S. Base; 125 Reds Killed

SAIGON — North Vietnamese troops launched a heavy attack today against an American base near Cambodia and lost at least 125 soldiers dead and 25 captured, military spokesmen reported.

Some of the 400 North Vietnamese broke into the American base, defended by about 200 men. They seized six bunkers and held them for about an hour until they were driven back, U.S. spokesmen said. U.S. casualties were put at nine killed and 59 wounded.

The target of the assault was Fire Base Carolyn of the U.S. 1st Cavalry Division (Airmobile) 65 miles northwest of Saigon and about 12 miles from Cambodia.

Troops of the North Vietnamese 1st and 7th Divisions are concentrated nearby in War Zone C. American forces are trying to root them out with a massive B-52 bombing campaign and ground sweeps originating from a string of bases like Carolyn.

Storming out of bamboo jungles, the North Vietnamese hit the base from two sides about 2 a.m. after a heavy rocket barrage aimed at pinning down the defenders.

The fighting was hand-to-hand at times and artillerymen inside the base lowered their 105-mm. howitzers to fire point-blank at the charging enemy.

The battle lasted four hours until 6 a.m. Field reports said most of the 25 prisoners seized were wounded.

Supporting North Vietnamese troops fired antiaircraft guns at helicopter gunships that fired rockets at the assault troops. U.S. spokesmen said none of the helicopters was hit.

The attackers blazed away with machine guns, small arms and bazooka-type rockets.

Twenty miles to the southeast of Carolyn, other troops of the division came under a heavy rocket and mortar assault and a standoff attack from enemy troops firing small arms. Helicopter gunships attacked the enemy firing positions, but the results were not known. U.S. casualties were termed light.

The U.S. command put four more B-52 raids into the Cambodian border area overnight—making a total of 55 in the past two weeks, with about $20 million worth of bombs.

In Saigon's Chinese district, police raided an apparent terrorist headquarters and seized two women and a man identified as hard-core members of a spy and terror network.

A big cache of arms was found including explosives, documents, medicine and seven flags of the Viet Cong. Police also arrested three suspected terrorists besides the three identified as hard-core.

Elsewhere, reported ground action was minimal. The allied commands reported only six overnight attacks by rocket or mortar, an indication that enemy forces unable to cross South Vietnam's borders to resupply may be running short of material.

The raiding police also turned up Monday 52 miles north of Saigon, U.S. spokesmen said. It was another setback for the Communist command, which American officials say has lost 38,000 men and 20,000 weapons since its offensive was launched Feb. 23.

---

to all WRITERS in the area...

A top executive of a well-known book publisher will soon be coming to Los Angeles from New York to interview writers. His purpose is to uncover manuscripts worthy of publication. Fiction, non-fiction, poetry, juveniles, collections of short stories or articles, religious, specialized and even controversial subjects will be considered.

If you have a manuscript ready (or almost ready) for publication and would like to discuss it with the executive, please telephone the number below, free of charge. Call between 9:00 a.m. and 10:00 p.m., and leave your name and address. You will be contacted later.

Telephone: 800/553-9550. This is a free call.

If you prefer, write to the Editorial Director,
Dept. CA-15, P.O. Box 2119, G.P.O., New York, N.Y. 10001

6% HAMILTON THRIFT & LOAN

per annum paid or compounded quarterly

FREE 500 BLUE CHIP STAMPS FOR NEW OR ADDED FUNDS OF $100 OR MORE

At Hamilton Thrift your money earns 6% per annum paid or compounded quarterly on Passbook Installment Thrift Certificates. $10 to $15,000 acceptable. Funds received by the 12th earn from the 1st of the month.

7111 PACIFIC BLVD. • HUNTINGTON PARK, CALIF.
Thrift by Mail—Free Postage Both Ways
LUdlow 2-5451

The candid confessions of the girl who married the SPOILED PRIEST

I MARRIED A PRIEST

A Bantam Book/95¢

VIVA PÉPE LOPEZ

...and the Tequila Revolution!

The Spirit of Mexico
$5.69 FIFTH

80 PROOF. PEPE LOPEZ IMPORT CO., LTD., LOUISVILLE, KENTUCKY, ©1969

You can speak Spanish by July 21st

The trick is how we teach you. On May 12th, when the course starts, you start right in with simple words. El almuerzo. Lunch. Más vino. More wine.

After the first lesson, you're speaking easy sentences. Useful stuff, like ¿Quién es esa señorita? Who is that young lady?

And by the time the course ends, on July 21st, you'll know enough Spanish to get around. Camarero, esta cuenta es increíble. Waiter, this check is outrageous.

At this point, we feel it's only fair to warn you that not more than 10 people can take each Spanish group course at Berlitz". (The cost is $140). The same goes for our French, Italian, German and English courses, which start the same day. So maybe you should call us en seguida. Or in other words, right now.

Berlitz
Practical language lessons

1908 Wilshire Blvd., Los Angeles, Calif. 90057, Phone: (213) 483-7722
321 North Beverly Dr., Beverly Hills, Calif. 90210, Phone: (213) 276-1101
81 Town & Country, Orange, Calif. 92668, Phone: (714) 547-9351
4526 Sherman Oaks Ave., Sherman Oaks, Calif. 91403, Phone: (213) 783-8194
170 South Lake Avenue, Pasadena, Calif. 91101, Phone: (213) 795-5888

Santa Barbara like it is today.

Come play with us this summer.

Santa Barbara is as enjoyable today as it was last year and all the years before. A sunny, cool, smiling vacationland offering you and your family 85 happy things to do and see. Mountain grandeur. Botanic gardens. Boating and fishing. Historic landmarks. Golf and tennis. Shopping adventures. An undersea aquarium. Wonderful accommodations at moderate rates. Come play with us this summer.

Visit Santa Barbara

90 minutes near via U.S. 101 north

and remained so until the 1989 Exxon Valdez spill in Prince William Sound, Alaska. The advertisement, detractors argued, invited visitors to a deception. The leisure-filled portrayal belied the fact that for weeks the city's residents had been in open conflict with the oil industry and the federal government.

Alongside the scenic environment and pleasant climate, Santa Barbara had another distinctive feature: an affluent and well-connected population. With its most prominent attractions tainted and malodorous by an unwelcome industry, residents who previously had little reason for direct political action mobilized as fervent environmental activists. This conflict led historian Hal Rothman to describe the event as a political awakening for those who had previously "luxuriated in their Eden" inadvertently minimizing the decades of work that went into creating such a haven.[3] Coinciding with direct action, local, state, and federal government officials held hearings and proposed legislation not just on oil pollution but on a wide range of environmental issues. At federal legislative hearings, some of which took place in Santa Barbara, residents conveyed not only their rage and vulnerability but also, occasionally, their support for the industry's role in the region's conditions. Santa Barbara's mayor at that time, Gerald Firestone, testified in federal hearings in February 1969 and repeated a common refrain that residents felt helpless and upset because "of this tragic action that has been brought to their shores." The community had not wanted drilling in such proximity to home and so became oil's "innocent victims."[4] Living in Santa Barbara was meant to provide a high quality of life and protection from the ill effects of modern life. Realizing that buffer might be illusory roused inhabitants to action.

The event has remained a flashpoint for American environmentalism, inspiring the first Earth Day and a host of federal environmental legislation.[5] Surveying legislative and legal accomplishments on environmental issues after the oil spill, Paul Sabin notes that it had "an important, but diffuse impact on environmental law" and "did not drive the key energy proposals of the early 1970s."[6] New environmental policies and a galvanized political awareness did little to alter the nation's dependence on oil. At times, Santa Barbara residents seemed unwilling to confront their own dependence on fossil fuels and simply wished that extraction would move to less ostensibly exceptional places.

The blowout's public impact stood less for questioning dependence, consumption, and ubiquity of fossil fuels than the realization that even a privileged community was not immune from devastating environmental disasters. If it happened in Santa Barbara, then presumably very few places could assume protection. The environmental historian and Santa Barbara resident Roderick Nash declared that the city "was probably the worst place in the United States for an oil spill to happen from the standpoint of the oil companies. The worst place. This is a town famous for its beauty."[7] Depicting the oil industry and the government agencies that abetted them as the enemy enabled residents to step around questions about their own entanglements with oil. Constructing a clear division between residents and industry evaded scrutiny of their ties. Paradoxically, residents' inward focus on environmental quality close to home made environmentalism palatable to a wider public.[8] Media portrayals depicted Santa Barbara residents in a relatable light to an audience that included those inclined to regard environmental issues with skepticism. Unlike pollution at industrial sites, which could be considered an unfortunate but unavoidable occurrence, the sullying of beaches in an affluent tourist and residential haven had an air of a place desecrated against its will. Citizen activism elevated Santa Barbara as a setting that deserved freedom from the polluting nuisances of oil.

The language of victimization not just from oil but from a government meant to protect residents minimized questions about the priorities that stood behind the words decrying oil. Understanding environmentalism as centrally concerned with maintenance of a way of life, aesthetic conditions, and the privileges of property had broad consequences for public acceptance and political priorities of the movement. Sincere anxieties about the environment as a general matter ran up against the oil spill painted as a highly local issue for people who lived in exceptional circumstances. Nevertheless, this event resonated to attract a wide audience. This was a popular environmentalism offered in marked contrast to social conflicts in American society during the 1960s such as struggles over civil rights, urban renewal, and environmental justice. Despite direct actions on the part of Santa Barbara residents, ownership environmentalism made no demands for radical changes in society.

Yet the limits marked off by this strain of the movement hampered the argument for environmental quality as a public good. With the social and economic interests of affluent, white Americans at the forefront, environmentalism could achieve mainstream acceptance while contracting its social and political ambitions. Reinforcing natural beauty, community distinctiveness, exclusivity, and property ownership as substantive justifications for environmental projects reflected the preferences not just of Santa Barbara's residents but of similar communities across the nation. Environmental quality was undoubtedly a public good, but for whom? The anger over the advertisement's omissions illustrates the tensions regarding not just the city's image and quality of life but also who controlled the narrative and who ultimately deserved to live in environmentally healthy places.

For most of its length, the western United States' coastline trends on a north–south axis. But from Washington through Northern California, curvatures along the coast called bights form short indentations that temporarily shift the axis to create south-facing portions of shore.[9] The Southern California Bight stretches for 270 miles from Point Conception in Santa Barbara County to San Diego. At its more pronounced northern terminus, the bight gives Santa Barbara County its predominantly south-facing orientation. The Transverse Ranges, mountains named for their east–west orientation, intersect with this portion of the bight and extend into the waters of the Santa Barbara Channel, a body seventy-five miles long and twenty-four miles wide with an area of about eighteen hundred square miles. The channel separates the mainland from the Channel Islands, once inhabited by the Chumash in the northern islands near Santa Barbara and Tongva in the south closer to Los Angeles. The city of Santa Barbara sits about fifty miles from the start of the bight's western end near the midpoint of the channel's length. Like much of the Pacific coast, the California current's warm and cold water masses generally flow north or south. The Santa Barbara Channel is a brief departure from that reigning direction. The channel marks a transition zone between the warm waters of the Southern California countercurrent and the cool Northern California current. The convergence results in a wide diversity of marine life around the Channel Islands. Species common in Northern California, Oregon, and even Washington are found in the western islands of San Miguel and Santa Rosa, but twenty nautical miles away the eastern islands of Santa Cruz, Anacapa, and Santa Barbara shelter life associated with Southern California and into Baja California. Blue, gray, and humpback whales congregate in high concentrations in the transition zone, as do sea otters, seals, pelicans, dolphins, and sea lions.

At the very end of the nineteenth century, a new development began altering the channel's marine environment. Humans started drilling for oil underneath the channel. This oil field developed from the Repetto Formation, an oil-rich area of sediment that took shape during the Pliocene Age, five to ten million years ago. After sitting unnoticed for millions of years, twentieth-century geologists estimated that up to 1.4 billion barrels of oil sat beneath the channel.[10] In the eighteenth century, Spanish explorers entering the Santa Barbara Channel noted a tar-like substance in the water and beaches that Indigenous inhabitants used to waterproof boats.[11] Summerland, a small settlement seven miles east of Santa Barbara, became an early site for offshore oil drilling from piers via slant drilling in 1897. That modest effort grew into a series of lucrative offshore oil strikes. By the end of the 1930s, California, Louisiana, and Texas enacted legislation to control mineral extraction and resulting revenues on their coasts. In California, the 1938 State Lands Act permitted oil leases in state tidelands up to the three-mile limit that marked the border between state and federal waters. The act's passage sparked federal challenges to clarify jurisdiction. Offshore platforms replaced piers by the 1950s. State involvement escalated a decade later when the California state government began awarding oil leases on land beneath the sea up to three miles from shore. With an estimated 710 billion barrels of recoverable oil and 1,630 trillion cubic feet of natural gas contained in the undersea land off the United States' coasts at stake, state and federal governments quarreled over their respective legal and financial claims.[12]

Federal responses came first through congressional action and then from the Supreme Court in 1945 when the federal government sued California to determine control over submerged lands and mineral rights under the three-mile boundary. In 1947, the Supreme Court sided with the federal government, which then began a process of defining state and federal boundaries in greater detail.[13] Subsequently, the Submerged Lands Act of 1953 gave states title to lands and natural resources beneath waters within their boundaries. But three months later, the Outer Continental Shelf Lands Act established federal jurisdiction over the seabed and subsoil beyond the limits of state control, defined as three miles from the line of mean high tide.[14] From the perspectives of state and federal governments, territorial control translated to a straightforward desire for mineral rights and revenue. But the region's inhabitants had different concerns.

After World War II, during which Santa Barbarans experienced a nearby land attack by Japanese forces targeting the Ellwood Oil Field about twelve miles east of the city that directly contributed to the forced internment of the nation's Japanese population, unease rose about the adverse effects of oil development on tourism. In response, residents and conservationists lobbied for a marine refuge to protect the city's ocean views from seismic exploration and offshore oil platforms.[15] The state created a sixteen-mile-long sanctuary along the coast near Santa Barbara up to the three-mile state boundary in the Pacific and prohibited oil development within its borders unless deemed in the state's best interests by the State Lands Commission. The 1955 Cunningham-Shell Tidelands Act restricted leases and created sanctuaries in scenic areas along the coasts of Los Angeles, Santa Barbara, and San Luis Obispo Counties.[16] Despite these sanctuaries, much of the adjacent area remained available for oil drilling. Between 1953 and 1965, the state of California supervised the drilling of about five hundred core holes in the channel on state and federal lands, as well as areas of disputed jurisdiction.[17] Standard Oil of California constructed the Santa Barbara Channel's first offshore platform, named Hazel, in 1958 in Summerland. By 1969, the federal government received about $3 billion from thirteen hundred oil and gas leases and about four thousand wells on Outer Continental Shelf Lands.[18] Overall, California received about $5 million a year in royalties.[19] Santa Barbara County earned $98 million from oil and gas business with about 2 percent of that total from offshore developments. Some of the oil money went to environmental conservation programs. After 1964, the National Park Service administered a Land and Water Conservation Fund financed by royalties on state and local projects to preserve natural landscapes and resources. The success of lease sales off the Gulf Coast led federal officials, with Lyndon Johnson's blessing, to pressure the secretary of the interior, Stewart Udall, to open more federal lands off California for leases.

Whose claims to the land had greater precedence set competing economic interests against one another. After the blowout, one legal scholar wrote that "nature does not merely permit, but rather commands that the sea shall be held in common."[20] In the eyes of government agencies, what the sea held in common was reducible to mineral resources. Linking financial profit to conservation via fossil fuel extraction created a dilemma for environmental activists, whereas oil companies secured recognition for supporting conservation activities. In Santa Barbara, disputes between federal and state jurisdictions and who would profit from the economic benefits of oil beneath the nation's shores encountered another interest: tourism and recreation. Into the 1960s, the region's oil development revenues continued to outpace proceeds from tourism and related sectors including retirement services and education. Although residents' commitment to environmental quality and aesthetic conditions conflicted with government financial priorities, they faced an obstacle of imagination. The inability to quantify environmental quality compared to potential profits highlighted the limits of economic metrics. Opposition to oil development in the Santa Barbara Channel came primarily from local rather than national groups who argued on aesthetic grounds against offshore oil drilling in their region. For the local population, the quality of the beaches alongside the climate and other features of the natural environment had paramount importance. Envisioning opposing sides—federal, state, and local—as simply contrasts between equally legitimate interests played down disparities in available leverage and resources. Those with greater influence conveyed that environmental quality had a subordinate position compared to mineral resource development and the accompanying revenues. The money made that clear. Nevertheless, underlying the commitment to clean beaches was the belief that some public goods could and should stand outside economic forces.

Having faith in the competence and priorities of government institutions depended in part on ease of access to political influence and living in a community that occupied a comfortable place in American society. In Santa Barbara and adjacent communities including Carpenteria, Summerland, and Montecito, many residents felt they had achieved that status. Never a hotbed for radicals or urban strife, Santa Barbara distinguished itself, according to resident and sociologist Harvey Molotch, within California from "sprawling Los Angeles" and the "avant-garde Bay Area" as a "calm, clean, and orderly" place inhabited by residents who had a "wide choice of places in the world to live" but chose that city for "its ideal climate, beauty, and sophistication."[21] Self-regard as "one of the nation's last outposts of graciousness and tranquility" and an alternative against the excesses and shortcomings of modern life and its "homogenizing trends" provided feelings of serenity on the surface.[22] Nevertheless, the oil industry continued to exist as an ever-present though uncomfortable feature of the landscape. Oil extraction's long presence in the region prompted complaints about its detrimental impacts on the view, as well as a general incongruity between natural beauty and heavy industry. Unlike people in many other parts of the country, Santa Barbarans had the ear of those with enough power to influence the region's offshore oil drilling. Alvin Weingand, a former California state senator and local hotel owner, recalled flying over the Santa Barbara Channel in 1964 with Stewart Udall, widely known as an ardent conservationist. Weingand, who also served as manager of the Montecito Protective and Improvement Association to "preserve and maintain Montecito as an area of beauty and charm, of a residential character," pointed to the "beautiful coastline" below and remarked that Californians were "terribly concerned all this may be ruined by the oil leases that are coming up."[23] Udall assured him that no leases would be granted "except under conditions that will protect your environment."[24] Such reassurances provided a sense of hope and authority, which later proved illusory.

The desire to profit from oil also came from within the city. In the early 1960s, then-mayor Edward Abbott hoped to offer an oil lease on a two-acre, triangle-shaped piece of land on the city's east side. Opponents countered that such a lease violated the Shell-Cunningham Act and disregarded both the city's dependence on aesthetic values rather than industrialization for its economy and an anti-drilling ordinance that labeled any property used for oil drilling a public nuisance.[25] Residents argued in letters to the editor in the *Santa Barbara News-Press* about oil's value to the city and the qualities that attracted people to make Santa Barbara home. Mrs. D.R. Miller Jr. remarked that she gazed out her window and marveled at the "clean sparkling city, the lovely palm-lined beaches, and the blue ocean." She moved to Santa Barbara from "smog-choked" Los Angeles and shuddered to think "what could happen if we lose our sense of values and sacrifice our beautiful city to industries of any type."[26] But Miss Maria Margelli believed that since "we are sitting on a gold mine of black oil," the revenues could obviate fees and other "prosaic" methods of raising money.[27] The prospect of gaining as much as $15 million for the city faced opposition through the view that "some things are beyond price" in "one of the few remaining islands of natural beauty in California."[28]

Residents regularly disputed with government bodies in a conflict that centered on the division between financial and aesthetic interests. Public outcry over the prospect of offshore oil platforms led to discussions in February 1967 with the Interior Department's assistant secretary for mineral resources, J. Cordell Moore, who agreed to examine the matter more closely.[29] Despite the lack of geologic and geophysical data and technical information about the safety of offshore drilling as well as the difficulty of finding experts without industry ties, federal officials found aesthetic arguments valid enough to institute a further two-mile-wide buffer, a reduced number of leases, and fewer platforms. Yet a push for further reductions prompted Moore to dismiss residents' claims. He could not "see how these people can expect us to absorb any additional revenue losses merely because of their further obsession to protect their view."[30] The crux of the juxtaposition between the ocean as a place of beauty, marine life, and recreation and as a source of oil settled on the capacity to assign a dollar value to one thing but not another.

Residents' commitment to Santa Barbara's environmental and aesthetic distinctiveness augmented the sense of harm and invasion. Sincere anxieties about oil's negative consequences for the environment substantiated beliefs that Santa Barbara deserved unique special protections. Writing in *Sports Illustrated*, Ross Macdonald, the pen name of mystery novelist Kenneth Millar, described how he and his wife, Margaret, often looked on the Santa Barbara Channel from their home. For Macdonald, who later published a novel, *Sleeping Beauty*, in 1973 that conspicuously featured an oil spill on the California coast, the oil platforms signaled something ominous. Although not visible from his home, Macdonald insisted that he had "been steadily aware of them." The platforms represented "a sense of impending change to our beaches and our sea and our eggshell-fragile way of life." Even on quiet and pristine evenings, he felt a change and "there was nothing we could do about it."[31] The inability to control the conditions of one's home and the realization its circumstances were subject to external forces was intolerable.

The elevation of natural beauty, a long-standing concern of late nineteenth- and early twentieth-century preservationists, as a primary justification for environmental protections clearly figured highly in residents' expectations of life in Santa Barbara in 1969. In this case, the territory under threat was not forests and mountains but places that were part of urban daily life. Shared interests in protecting property and natural resources close to home brought together residents of assorted political commitments who held differing experiences with environmental issues. Some activists drew on backgrounds in local and regional politics, especially in the Republican Party, such as Alan Weingand, but others came to political involvement in response to the oil spill. Commitments to protecting the beaches and quality of life were tied up with a sense of home and community exclusivity.

Despite blowouts having been described as "the most spectacular, costly, and highly feared hazard of drilling," oil spills occurred with regularity.[32] During first six months of 1969, the United States recorded almost one hundred oil spills ranging in size from a few barrels to the blowout on Platform A.[33] The morning of January 29, 1969, a journalist with the *Santa Barbara News-Press*, Robert Sollen, received an anonymous phone call. "The ocean is boiling around Platform A," the voice told him, referring to a recently constructed offshore oil platform in the Santa Barbara Channel.[34] Platform A stood about three miles from the coast in the Outer Continental Shelf on Federal Tract 402. The top of its vertical rig reached 210 feet above the sea's surface and stood in water 188 feet deep. Union Oil Company of California operated the platform and had, in partnership with Texaco, Gulf, and Mobile, paid $61.4 million plus promised royalties of one-sixth of the market price per barrel of oil to the federal government for an annual rental on a lease of fifty-four hundred ocean-floor acres agreed on in February 1968. Union was one of twenty-six companies that paid the federal government more than $602 million for drilling rights in the channel. The US government stood to gain as much as $2.5 billion from royalties while oil companies spent over $100 million in development in the Santa Barbara Channel.

In 1969, Union, founded in Southern California with additional operations in Alaska, Indonesia, Hong Kong, and Louisiana, was the eleventh-largest oil company in the United States. It held assets of $2.4 billion and aspired to be among the top ten. Developing offshore oil drilling in the Santa Barbara Channel was part of a strategy for joining those ranks. Twelve platforms operated by different oil companies stood on a fifty-mile length of the Santa Barbara Channel, with eight in state waters within three miles of shore. The other four, including Platform A, were situated in federal waters.

After approval for exploratory drilling by the US Geological Survey, Union began drilling wells in February 1968. The following month, Union workers discovered oil from an exploratory well and soon requested permits from the US Army Corps of Engineers to construct a platform. Santa Barbara's city government initially asked for public hearings regarding the platform's construction but later withdrew the request. Over the summer of that year, officials discussed Platform A's design, location, and number of wells. The platform cost about $5 million to construct, and each of its fifty-six planned wells would cost $250,000 more.[35] At the start of the new year, with permits in place, workers began drilling from the platform.[36]

On land, the year 1969 began with a different set of local challenges. Southern California experienced some of its worst flooding in decades.[37] Over a week of heavy rains caused massive floods, and subsequent mudslides resulted in the death of one hundred people, the displacement of several thousand, and $100 million in damages.[38] One newspaper feature posited that man and nature combined to cause the floods, man through construction and urban development and nature through nine days of rain.[39] The rains had just stopped when drilling began on the fifth well on Platform A.[40] In the late morning on January 28, after penetrating 3,479 feet into the earth, workers began removing 90-foot-long "stands" or lengths of the drill pipe from the well. One significant risk from offshore oil drilling arises from an excessive contrast in pressure between the drill from above and the oil-bearing strata below. In oil extraction, maintaining this balance meant that workers utilized a substance called "drilling mud," a chemical fluid of high specific gravity, to fill and maintain the hole as they drilled. A loss of mud circulation or change to proper density could disrupt the delicate balance of pressure. As workers removed a stand from the hole, a loud hissing signaled something was amiss. Dark gray mud shot out of the top and showered the men on the platform.[41] A change in pressure strained the well's casing and caused mud and gas to burst out at the surface.

The crew spent several minutes attempting to connect a blowout preventer on top of the drill pipe, but it could not withstand the volume of discharge. The workers then decided to plunge the drill pipe back down into the hole, which stopped the flow of mud and gas at the surface, but bubbles of gas indicated that the pressure simply transferred from one place to another. The blowout and the initial actions to stem its flow occurred a day before any public knowledge. The office of Daniel Grant, the Santa Barbara County supervisor, received a call that afternoon to inform him of the accident. But he was occupied visiting sites damaged from rain and mudslides with Governor Ronald Reagan, so he was left uninformed.[42] At the *News-Press* office on January 29, Sollen confirmed the event with a Coast Guard lieutenant, George Brown, and wrote a short news item about the blowout for the paper. Initially, Union spokesmen assured government officials that the well would be under control within a day. But over the next ten days, workers on the platform repeatedly tried and failed to control the flow of oil, with one hundred men eventually using eight hundred barrels of drilling mud and nine hundred sacks of cement to cap the hole.[43] The first day of the blowout created a fifty-square-mile oil slick, but favorable wind directions mostly kept the oil from reaching shore.[44] Around three thirty in the afternoon of February 4, winds shifted to the southeast and increased in speed.[45] Within two hours, crude oil covered Santa Barbara Harbor and adjacent beaches. Eventually twenty-eight miles of shoreline from Goleta to Ventura received a heavy coating of oil. On land, Sollen's short article swelled into a profusion of media coverage. This was an event some residents had feared would happen.

Given the vast sums of money that the oil companies invested in securing leases, developing oil explorations, and constructing platforms, industry representatives believed not only that the companies held certain rights over the land but also that they were major contributors to the nation's welfare. Disclosures about political machinations within the Department of the Interior augmented the sense that the federal government privileged immediate financial gain above any consideration for its citizens and their access to environmental quality. Fred Eissler, a Santa Barbara high school teacher as well as a national director for the Sierra Club, obtained copies of two memos written by Stanley Cain, a botanist and assistant secretary for Fish, Wildlife, and Parks under Stewart Udall. The first memo, issued on August 7, 1967, recommended making the Santa Barbara Channel a federal marine sanctuary. Three days later, after discussions with the president's Budget Bureau and J. Cordell Moore, Cain's position shifted.[46] In his second memo, Cain endorsed the installation of oil platforms in the Santa Barbara Channel with the justification that the platforms would be at least five miles from shore, thus reducing platform "visibility to land to negligibility." Cain professed that Moore objected to a proposed one-year moratorium on leasing to provide time for further study, adding that Moore would have agreed to the delay if Udall had been willing to accept criticism for the decision from oil companies and the Budget Bureau.[47] For residents, Santa Barbara's environmental destruction resulted from the government and oil industry's simple and misguided desire for a financial windfall.

Udall's involvement in approving the leases carried an additional air of betrayal. In retrospect, his promise merely emphasized for Weingand and others how little control the government had—or wanted—to assert over oil companies. In the decision to grant the leases, Udall contended that the Department of the Interior had registered no dissent in opening up the channel.[48] But Santa Barbara officials argued that they simply placed their trust in federal officials. George Clyde, a Santa Barbara County supervisor, testified in front of a US Senate subcommittee and was asked why local opponents did not stress spillage controls. He responded that the Department of the Interior repeatedly stated that there was nothing to fear.[49] Clyde maintained that Eugene W. Standley, a staff engineer for the Interior Department, admitted the department chose to handle its affairs through city, county, and state agencies rather than hold public hearings. Standley had warned the Los Angeles District Engineer of Corps, who faced similar challenges to offshore oil platforms, that he should not hold public hearings in order not to "stir up the natives" any more than necessary.[50]

These revelations shifted perceptions of residents' relationship to the government, which increasingly seemed to be an institution with desires antithetical to those it purported to represent. Local expectations that the federal government's primary obligation was as a custodian for its citizens' welfare ran against the desires of the oil industry, which, according to Allan Coates Jr., mayor of Carpenteria, "forcibly destroyed" and changed the entire character of the region.[51] Coates wondered why the entire Santa Barbara Channel could not become a reserve and why experts within the Interior needed to be "so partial to the oil industry?" The oil companies, Clyde believed, might have been within their legal rights to drill, but by doing so they perpetrated a crime against the public at large.[52] Government responsibility to provide for the general welfare of its citizens seemed far off the mark. A reporter from *Advertising Age* arrived in the city and spoke with twenty-four people from "8 to 80, in all walks of life." With one exception, the reporter found all disclosed feeling frustration, hopelessness, and despair with the repeated refrain that "the government just don't care—we can't beat the power of the oil company money."[53] An instantly recognizable "sadness" pervaded the city, much like "meeting up with a beautiful girl that you've long known and learning that she has contracted some dread disease." One Santa Barbara correspondent penned an open letter to Richard Nixon, inaugurated only eight days before the blowout, noting that as a Republican and major supporter of Nixon's previous campaigns, he deplored the events in Santa Barbara. But more upsetting were the actions of administration officials, which only gave credence "to what everyone suspects and that is that the oil industry has infiltrated the ranks" of the Interior Department.[54] Bereft of government allies, residents needed to protect themselves.

As Union employees repeatedly attempted and failed to stem the flow of oil, on shore the blowout conjured visions of a transformation from an oceanside haven to a mutilated version of itself. Gerald Firestone, the recently installed Santa Barbara mayor, learned about the blowout while working at his clothing store on State Street. The Santa Barbara–born mayor later recalled that his first thoughts went not toward economic consequences that a massive oil spill would engender but to "the threat to the entire personality of the city."[55] The environmental despoilation risked precipitating an existential crisis. War metaphors threw into relief residents' perceptions of the exceptional circumstances that faced their domiciles. Ross Macdonald and Robert Easton, a local journalist, declared that life in Santa Barbara was now "somewhat reminiscent of civilian life in a war zone."[56] Udall acknowledged his culpability for the blowout's occurrence, describing it as a "conservation Bay of Pigs."[57]

Depicting the oil spill as an act of senseless violence, with residents and the environment as helpless victims of oil companies, tacitly endorsed a view that some places and people held greater entitlement to environmental health than others. Santa Barbara represented goodness and resistance against dominant trends in American urbanization. Oil challenged the decades-long effort to present Santa Barbara as an environmental haven surrounded by natural beauty. What residents assumed that the government and oil companies could not fathom was that the environment could not have a cost attached to it—it was priceless. Mrs. Hallock Hoffman wrote to the *News-Press* that "this condition, this atmosphere, cannot be bought. If it is sold to oil wells, it can never be returned to us or our children."[58] On February 6, the *News-Press* published a photograph of eighteen-year-old Kathy Morales, with her hair in pigtails, looking down on the beach. The accompanying article noted that she was witnessing the final moments of the life of a convulsing, oil-soaked loon. With tears streaming down her face, she lamented that she could not imagine coming to the beach for a casual walk again. She added that she did not know "if it will ever be the same again, and no one can tell me."[59] Offshore oil drilling, another resident claimed was "absolutely incompatible with the environmental values" cherished in the city.[60] The *Sierra Club Bulletin* echoed the assertion that the city had a long tradition of concern for the environment.[61] Inhabitants shared a deep fear that Santa Barbara would lose its unique character and become just another "technological slum in a nation already overendowed with wasted urban regions."[62] For others, Santa Barbara's reputation as a place of leisure and beauty exacerbated the sense that if a disaster could happen there, then nowhere was safe. The destruction and violation that threaded these accounts together furnished traction for the belief that the oil spill represented American disregard for the environment and its reckoning.

The clash between residents on one side and the government and oil industry on the other generally avoided confronting questions about the role of economic growth in pushing oil consumption and how to account for the costs of environmental damage.[63] Garrett Hardin viewed the event differently. The blowout made clear his conviction that a substantive challenge to the oil industry needed to dismantle the "central core of business dogma"—namely, cost-benefit analysis.[64] By demonstrating that conservationist objectives better supported the bottom line than "commercial exploiters," Hardin believed he devised a sustainable alternative to those destroying the environment in the name of meeting the needs of a growing population. Focusing too closely on energy needs superseded other measurements for a good quality of life. "All too often," Hardin argued, humans believed that "every additional oil field" constituted a societal gain because "conventional economic analysis" did not take "'soft' concepts of natural beauty and peace of mind" into account. Despite difficulties in quantifying those concepts, it was "insanity" to assume those had no value, especially since the "gallon of gas that makes it possible for an individual to drive his automobile increases smog, increases traffic, wastes time, increases medical bills, decreases recreational areas, and increases nervous strain." Ecological justice dictated that "he who produces a cost should be responsible for paying it." In the case of the Santa Barbara Channel, Hardin maintained that since the sea belonged "neither to an agency of the Government, nor to the oil well drillers," the costs of drilling should include not only labor and raw materials but any resulting pollution as well. Santa Barbara's spill would be "neither the last accident nor the last battle," but sooner or later industries would be "forced to internalize so-called externalities." Rather than thinking about the oil spill as an unfortunate byproduct of oil, the spill was a product.

Along with musings and articulations of grief and violation, residents organized. The most prominent activist organization formed in the wake of the blowout originated in the minds of two men, one a graphic designer and one who worked in public relations, the day after the blowout.[65] James "Bud" Bottoms and Marvin Stuart met the day after public disclosure of the oil spill and began talking about their mutual opposition to oil development in the channel. Bottoms, once president of Santa Barbara Beautiful, an advocacy group formed to enhance the city's beauty, said to Stuart, "We've got to get oil out!" With that sentence, Stuart came upon the name for the group: Get Oil Out! Through Get Oil Out! (GOO!), some of Santa Barbara's prominent residents undertook actions that were at once seen as "militant opposition" and "guerrilla warfare on the most genteel level." By February 2, GOO! had taken out advertising space in newspapers, demanding, "Why do we see oil-soaked ducks struggling to survive on our beaches? How many oil slicks are needed to convince us that the wildlife of Santa Barbara and the natural beauty of its shore cannot survive with the present oil activity in the Santa Barbara Channel?" At times GOO! protests seemed, according to Robert Easton, "almost a futile gesture compared with the enormity of what was happening."[66] Mainstays of respectable political activity, such as writing letters, holding meetings, and issuing "Un-oil" stock certificates illustrated with polluting oil platforms, refineries, and wells to those who gave the group money, joined with protests that included public burnings of oil company credit cards. GOO! circulated a sheet of songs with titles such as "The Goo That Was Leaked for Two," "A Word from the Opposition," and "Dick, Please Check Our Slick," the latter of which asked, "Oh, why won't Dick inspect our slick?"[67] The blowout unified residents in unexpected ways that displayed environmentalism's political and cultural pliability. Martin Levine, Santa Barbara County's Deputy Counsel, saw that people "who couldn't otherwise agree on anything are getting together on this one." Another resident concurred that "ultra conservatives, the new left and the big gray middle agree against oil. John Birchers and leftist militants are writing letters . . . and you can't tell the difference."[68] The alignment of these groups stemmed from the fact that, in the words of one commentator, the "poisoning of the environment bothers more than weirdo naturalists in sneakers with butterfly nets."[69] The "irate local citizenry" were engaged in a battle that was "building into a revealing test of the national strength of the growing movement for environmental protection."

Local actions led some to conclude that the oil spill "radicalized" the community. Residents' actions supported such claims, at least outwardly. Historian Adam Rome points out that the oil spill "prompted many radicals to think harder about the environment."[70] The core of Santa Barbara's environmental activists contrasted with popular images of environmentalists and left wing or new left activists. In certain respects, the actions of the city's politically right-leaning inhabitants predated left or radical interest in environmental concerns.[71] These residents included a "strange mixture of hippies and solid establishment types, housewives, and scientists." College students attacked banks with ties to Union, but so did middle-aged Republicans, which created a "strange mixture" of activists.[72] Everyone from "button-down radicals" to the "grey flannel suit crowd" urged direct action in addition to conventional activities such as raising money and circulating petitions, including a lie-in at a city council meeting, a harbor blockade, and even conspiratorial murmurs of sabotaging Platform A. These discussions and their diverse audience added to the impression that anti-oil forces constituted a representative sampling of the citizenry.[73] Whether the intentions of this "strange mixture" posed a genuine challenge to the existing status of the environment remained unsettled.

The features that defined Santa Barbara as an undeserving place for a large-scale oil pollution event elicited fears regarding vulnerabilities for the entire United States. As a shorthand for clarifying the nation's concerns about the environment, the Santa Barbara oil spill represented the results of a troubling combination of weak government regulation or indifference and the oil industry's primitive technologies and greed. These factors aggravated worries since Santa Barbara was made up, in the words of Harvey Molotch, of "hard-rock Republicans" who were unused to "stark threats to their survival or arbitrary, contemptuous handling of their wishes. They are an unlikely group to be forced to confront brutal reality about how the 'normal channels' in America can be hopelessly clogged and unresponsive."[74] Those who lived in Santa Barbara had previously experienced outsized privileges including the benefit of ostensibly never having to choose between environmental harmony and economic prosperity.

If the luck they once had seemed to have run out, questions remained about the expectations of immunity from environmental devastation. Residents believed they made their homes in an exceptional place, a site of privileged exception, and much of their experience validated that notion. More broadly, the spill raised questions about the dominance of oil and other natural resources in modern life, the workings of political power, the role of citizen action, and the possibility of making claims on behalf of the environment. Ross Macdonald argued that the event "brought to a head our moral and economic doubts about American uses of energy and asked whether we really have to go on polluting the sea and land and air in order to support our freeway philosophy of one man, one car."[75] The idea that limits on human behavior and consumption might be necessary in order to guarantee a clean environment threatened one of the reigning assumptions about the ability of postwar Americans to have all they wanted without troubling over consequences.[76] If Santa Barbara before the oil spill represented the possibility that one could be insulated from the negative aspects of modern life while also enjoying its luxuries, including environmental ones, then its aftermath brought into relief the ways that forces seemingly external to the life and livelihood of the city were already embedded within it. The events of January 28, 1969, highlighted the tensions between a desire for a pristine and unpolluted environment alongside a high standard of living, and who ultimately believed they deserved both without cost.

The sense of violation and lack of control extended to the belief, as articulated in the *New York Times*, that even the simplest facts about the causes of the oil spill were "about as murky as the ugly, dark oil slick staining hundreds of square miles of the Pacific."[77] For Santa Barbarans, this statement applied most readily to the relationship between the oil industry and government. Casting the blowout simply as a technical failure meant that those failures had solutions, despite the paucity of even basic information about offshore drilling technologies. Nevertheless, officials could treat these oil spills as exceptional and unfortunate, but fundamentally manageable. "Oil spills are usually accidents" noted "The Oil Spill Problem," a report authored by a Nixon-appointed panel on oil spills chaired by John C. Calhoun Jr., a vice president at Texas A&M University.[78] Poor practices, improper designs, the state of technological advancement, and logistics could all stand for improvement. The panel argued that lack of available tools for effectively confronting oil spills shifted some responsibility away from government and industry. But they also acknowledged that government "generally ignored or underestimated" possible hazards, except when "the hazard to human life was high."[79]

Alongside dismissing hazards unless they met a threshold of damage, from the perspective of the oil industry and federal government the blowout constituted a technical malfunction of limited significance. The federal government mostly admitted to the "undesirable effects" of offshore oil drilling such as damage to environmental quality. But its inclination to address problems centered on improving existing methods and tools rather than inquiring into the broader effects of oil extraction and consumption.[80] Even this comparatively modest task of framing the oil spill as an aberration proved an obstacle. The more than one hundred spills that occurred in the United States during the first six months of 1969 belied the notion that they were "rather unique problems." If those who found oil spills near their homes focused on the immediate material event, those further away could treat them as an anomaly and dissolved them among "the larger set of environmental problems facing society today." Another disadvantage came when attempting to assign dollar values to the effects of pollution on citizens.[81] Public hearings gave citizens a chance to air their concerns to the government, but those were mostly no match for the fact that the Outer Continental Shelf provided an opportunity to "add needed fuels, energy, metals, and non-metals to our economy and monies to the Gross National Product." Those resources did not "lie on some vast and remote frontier" but were tantalizingly close to home. Almost half of the nation's population lived near the coast where suboceanic resources represented the single largest area of undeveloped mineral resources. The juxtaposition between towns and cities and natural resources put their competing interests into relief. These places were homes, to be sure, but also places of recreation, natural beauty, and energy. Locations that promised a bounty in natural resources simultaneously constituted a "unique ecological setting" and home to "kinds and types of wildlife that cannot exist elsewhere, and an environment difficult for man to work in."

Even the process of stopping oil spills suggested collusion between the federal government and the oil industry. On February 11, just under two weeks after the blowout began, Nixon appointed Lee DuBridge, his science adviser and former president of the California Institute of Technology, to head an eleven-member panel to devise the best course of action to stop the leak. On June 2, the DuBridge panel issued a two-page report on its findings with the recommendation to rapidly withdraw oil through further drilling in order to reduce pressure and "forever to prevent future spillage" in the Santa Barbara Channel.[82] William Pecora, head of the US Geological Survey, estimated that two years of pumping from up to fifty new wells might be needed to extract enough oil against further seepages, but he then acknowledged that if the oil pool was connected to another, the process might extend up to twenty years. Alternatives to pumping oil included shutting down all operations and paving up to twenty acres of the ocean bed to seal up fissures, but the panel concluded that pumping oil stood to be the least dangerous. With no means of independent verification, the decision to carry on with oil extraction appeared to allow Union to continue extracting profit from misfortune.

In response to the DuBridge report, one of California's US senators, Alan Cranston, announced that he attempted to obtain the information the panel consulted to base its conclusions. This mission failed because of the oil company's proprietary claims. Charges of conflicts of interest extended toward panel members, which included those with ties to the oil industry through commercial or academic relationships. John S. Steinhart, the panel's executive secretary, acknowledged that the data used to make their conclusions came from Union Oil, its partners, and the US Geological Survey, but only because they were the parties with data on the leased tracts. Despite oil industry ties, DuBridge insisted that the panel was of "unquestioned integrity."[83] A columnist for the *Los Angeles Times* responded to the panel by accusing the Department of the Interior of abdicating its responsibility of safeguarding the public interest by permitting oil companies to profit while denying citizens access to information. Although the Interior stood within its legal rights to shield information from the public, in this case "moral and Constitutional considerations [were] overriding." The department's unwillingness to speak on behalf of a community living "under constant threat of a disastrous oil blowout" was intolerable. This experience of marginalization in the face of decisions that affected the conditions of their homes altered residents' understandings of the federal government.

"One wonders," the *Los Angeles Times* reporter continued, "if the stamp 'proprietary' will come to be used in information dealing with civilian environmental problems the way 'secret' is used in the military domain." For the same reason that Californians could not find out how much DDT was being sprayed in the state, technologies for drilling and geological data about the Santa Barbara Channel remained under legal cover. Residents, an editorial in the *Santa Barbara News-Press* asserted, considered the arbitrariness or even maleficence of providing advantages to corporations over citizens as a violation of the "rightful interest of individuals or cities."[84] Like Senator Cranston, *Santa Barbara News-Press* journalists attempted to glean specifics about the DuBridge panel with no success. "Here, obviously, is government by men, rather than by laws," an editorial charged. A federal agency had "no right to deprive" Californians from "obtaining essential information to protect their natural resources from despoliation by the oil industry." Although Santa Barbara's civic life was at stake, criticism of the DuBridge panel called the legitimacy of government institutions into question with its inability to protect citizens from men who would hasten its destruction. In the absence of knowledge and information, people turned their attention to other types of arguments to appeal for support.

Confronting the consequences of taking oil extraction and development out of Santa Barbara included the extent to which local protests engaged with or ignored the centrality of energy consumption in everyday life. This was especially pertinent in a place like Southern California, which consumed about 20 percent of all gas produced in the nation. In 1950, Union Oil imagined a situation—the havoc—that would result if "by some catastrophic miracle" all American oil wells suddenly went dry.[85] Envisioning a world without oil was one with "highways without automobiles. Or modern industry without trucks. Agriculture without tractors . . . Life without a host of everyday products, plastics, solvents, paints, tires, detergents, cosmetics, inks." A single barrel of oil made all those ordinary luxuries possible. Conjuring memories from World War II, the company wondered if "free peoples defending themselves from the dictatorships" would even be possible without the "military striking power of the man-made global rivers of oil that turned the tide of victory?" That hyperbolic declaration contained a vital question for industry and environmentalists alike: To what extent would individuals acknowledge their ties to oil?

On February 4, when oil began lapping against the sand on the shores

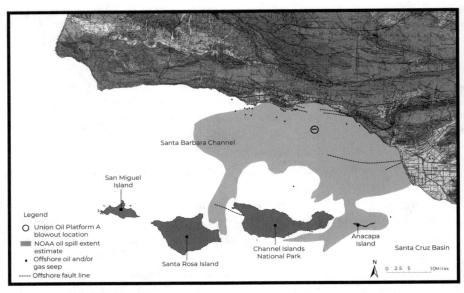

FIGURE 5.2. Estimated extent of oil spill from the blowout on Platform A that began on January 28, 1969, in the Santa Barbara Channel. Map by Sierra Chmela.

of Santa Barbara County, individuals indirectly addressed that question (Figure 5.2). National media outlets repeated a refrain echoed in moments of crisis, environmental or otherwise: How could one put a cost on this destruction? The nation was suddenly faced, according to the *New York Times*, "with the fact that one cannot measure in dollars the damage resulting from mass slaughter of birds, fish, whales and seals, to say nothing of the value of once sparkling beaches in danger of conversion to noisome, oil-soaked wastelands."[86] Suffering wildlife and, to all appearances, rather primitive modes of cleaning oil off birds and beaches with bales of hay exacerbated the initial shock. Gerald Firestone declared that the city's beaches looked like Dunkirk.[87] *Time* magazine described the spill as "a massive, inflamed abscess bursting with reddish-brown pus."[88] One resident echoed the sentiment as he went out on a workboat to examine the blowout and saw a "big yellow boil bursting with pus."[89] Just a few years earlier the government had been "too busy auctioning offshore drilling leases to the oil companies" to pay attention to local protests.[90] Six hundred million dollars seemed far too important than the abstract possibility that Southern California would experience its own *Torrey Canyon*, a reference to a supertanker accident off the coast of Cornwall in South West England that leaked 120,000 tons of crude oil into the English Channel in March 1967.[91] Now, it seemed the burden of justification would fall squarely on oil companies. If they could not guarantee drilling without inflicting environmental damage, then the government needed to cancel the leases and offer the oil companies a financial settlement. The nation could "afford no more risks in tampering with the ocean floor."[92]

The conservative and decorous features of some of Santa Barbara's most prominent activists gave the urgency about pollution a respectable cast. Lois Sidenberg of Carpenteria was one who found herself becoming an environmental activist. Described by the *New York Times* as a "feisty socialite grandmother," this daughter of a countess grew up in Greenwich, Connecticut, played field hockey at Northwestern University, and participated in foxhunts. She was a staunch Republican with personal connections that meant she "dined socially" with Stewart Udall, among others. Before the spill, her activism mainly consisted of volunteering for several civic and beautification organizations. Although "rational and eminently sensible," the oil spill inspired Sidenberg to take part in more aggressive activities. She was not the only woman pushed to such sentiments. At one of GOO!'s first mass meetings, a speaker asked the crowd if anyone from an oil company wanted to speak. Sidenberg recalled that she stood next to "literally a little old lady in tennis shoes" who said between gritted teeth that she would kill them if they were present. Stories also circulated about a "very staid, extremely fat lady" who proclaimed that she would put on a wetsuit, swim out to the platform, and install underwater demolition equipment, and at the "most prestigiously conservative club," a *"respectable* appearing elderly lady" came up to Sidenberg and whispered that the Mafia was headquartered in Southern California, so they should be hired to blow up the platforms.

Yet even at their most combative, these activists aimed at local corrections. A writer in the *Los Angeles Times* acknowledged that despite these words and actions, it would be an exaggeration to discuss this activism as evidence of the "radicalization of the rich."[93] Nevertheless, the spill provided a "crash course in practical politics" for the many residents who had "their comfortable faith in the basic rightness of the American political and economic system" rattled. GOO! members lamented their late discovery that "Oil is King." By demanding protections for their surroundings and homes, residents were forced to acknowledge some of the realities of the "intricate and shadowy relationships" between the oil industry and government. The writer even claimed that the "wealthy and usually conservative" residents with few experiences with "helpless rage" were now subject to the kind of "impotent anger that is familiar to poor people, black people, and university students."[94] Despite the wealth, public sympathy arrived from various parts of the world. A petition gained more than eighty thousand signatures by early May 1969 from fifteen states and other nations. A letter from an individual in Louisville, Kentucky, shared fears of oil pollution from the Ohio River. A writer from Stamford, Connecticut, stated that "there are many of us who appalled" by the industry's lack of concern for the "filth it pours into our atmosphere and waterways." Closer to home, a resident of Northridge in Los Angeles's San Fernando Valley pleaded with GOO! members to "keep up the fight" and "don't let anyone tell you that you are being 'hysterical' or 'unreasonable.'" The oil companies and those who approved drilling were "mad and should be treated as such."[95]

Coming to terms with this lack of access to political power motivated residents to pursue alternative paths to capture attention. On one of Nixon's visits to his "western White House" in San Clemente on the southern tip of Orange County, two GOO! members decided to deliver petitions against oil via a boat with a GOO! banner flying high. When the Coast Guard denied access, members "were content to bob in the ocean swells" just beyond the one-and-a-half-mile boundary ordered by the Secret Service. "We're meek militants," admitted Bud Bottoms, after the retreat.[96] This docile challenge to the situation had limits. Experiencing this adversity "familiar to poor people, black people, and university students" did not necessarily mean the creation of bonds of solidarity with the respectable, affluent Santa Barbarans. Protecting Santa Barbara's assets of natural beauty and quality of life often meant keeping a more tenacious grip on the community's exclusivity.

Despite being rebuffed in San Clemente, Santa Barbarans still had greater abilities to access influential individuals to voice political concerns than many Americans. Appeals to high-ranking officials in the federal government displayed the leverage and entitlement residents believed they wielded and deserved. Max Feldman, the president of the civic improvement organization Santa Barbara Beautiful, wrote to Nixon expressing that he had been appalled by Hickel, who ignored "every communication" from Santa Barbara residents.[97] Feldman implored the president to support an in-depth economic analysis to determine whether the nation actually needed oil from the Santa Barbara Channel since it would be "a sin to destroy the beauty and threaten the environment . . . for 'business as usual.'" In Feldman's rendering, "the environment" had limited geographic breadth and a distinct hierarchy. Recent oil discoveries in Alaska, he noted, would more than meet future needs. Returning to his own surroundings, Feldman noted that "on the surface and in selected locations, conditions appear to be back to normal along our beaches." But this was deceptive. With only a small amount of effort, one could find black rocks and dead sea creatures along the shore, or find oneself coated with crude oil just by taking a walk on the beach. Feldman found it difficult to believe that the federal government, with a "primary function" to protect the people and their environment, "should be the leader in threatening the destruction of ours."

The emphasis on citizen action as a rejoinder to government and industry partially obscured the fact that many activists found their lack of influence infuriating. A journalist for the *National Observer* noted that what "irks GOO! members the most is that they have been unable to gain President Nixon's ear."[98] John Wiester, a GOO! member and president of an engineering materials firm, insisted that American political leaders "must realize that priorities are shifting and that environment is the number one issue. If Nixon believes the environment is as important as he says, he couldn't start acting at any better place than here in his own backyard." One businessman lamented that the "whole democratic process seems to be falling apart. Nobody responds to us, and what we end up doing is progressively less reasonable." If the federal government failed to express some "reasonable attitude," Santa Barbara would "blow up" since nothing seemed to happen "except that we lose."[99]

Implicit and explicit reinforcements of Santa Barbara's distinctiveness and exclusivity revealed the limits of residents' environmental concerns based on the notion that some places—namely, their homes—deserved greater protections. Photographs of the location including the oil slick around Platform A, tarred beaches, dead birds, and attempts to sop up oil with hay published in newspapers and magazines elicited local and national fury.[100] "Most towns would welcome oil," wrote one journalist, but "most towns aren't in the business of being beautiful; being beautiful is Santa Barbara's reason for being."[101] In a bit of proto-NIMBYism, the *Los Angeles Times* observed that most GOO! leaders just wanted "protection for their back yard . . . their yachts, their harbor, their beaches, their ocean view." Maintaining the city as a "respite from the horrors of big cities—actually a respite from people who make big cities horrible" required vigilance to keep out features—or people—immediately detrimental to their way of life. Yet the *Berkeley Barb* noted that some years earlier, Gerald Firestone and other local officials had actually extolled the virtues of offshore oil.[102] Even now, the work of cleaning up the oil was "evidently . . . too dirty for our lily white politicians and businessmen" since mostly Black and Chicano prisoners did much of the menial labor such as spreading and collecting hay to clean the beaches. Environmental action mobilized to preserve a certain lifestyle divided people into those who belonged and those who did not. The divides connoted that environmental quality was for the white and well-off. Nevertheless, local concerns about individual yachts and yards with ocean views had the potential to move beyond their parochial origins to touch on national interests in maintaining natural beauty and lands.[103] The idea of being entitled to a clean and attractive natural environment did not necessarily have to remain the purview for the wealthy and well-connected.

The oil spill proved beyond any doubt that pollution was not a problem for somewhere else. The events elicited national sympathies and recognition from places markedly dissimilar to Santa Barbara. A Montana resident wrote to her local newspaper asserting that people where she lived "knew something of what pollution means" and the subsequent conflicts between business and the environment.[104] Finding solutions seemed intractable because "pollution is almost a way of life. It is expected. It is accepted. In the name of progress, or through carelessness and greed." The federal government created the conditions for privileging economic growth above all else, but its policies also "merely reflect what has been the value structure of American society." Only reevaluating and transforming national priorities and values would prevent more accidents like Santa Barbara. Would the spill "drive home the disastrous consequences of needless and careless tampering with the environment? Will it force an examination of the values of society? Or will man continue down the road of homicide and suicide in the name of progress? If he does, there will be other Santa Barbaras until there is nothing left." Rather than expressing bitterness for being subject to pollution with little attention, the letter writer hoped that Santa Barbara's experience opened an opportunity to address environmental hazards at a national scale.

Whether residents linked their own experience with oil pollution and environmental damage to those of others, questions regarding how to maintain those connections remained up for debate. To some, Santa Barbara "became a mecca for conservation, and every Santa Barbaran a naturalist, a conservationist, and an ecologist."[105] The oil spill opened space to discuss a host of other environmental ills. Norman Sanders, a geographer at University of California, Santa Barbara, insisted that California, with its "skyrocketing population," was "being assaulted" with a variety of problems, many of which could "happen elsewhere in the future."[106] In his guidebook to environmental activism published in 1972, Sanders indicted the nation's habits for exploiting natural resources in the name of the American way of life. But individuals did not work alone; the government and industry had major roles in shaping contemporary conditions. Based on his life in Santa Barbara, Sanders concluded that "neither big business nor big government" possessed the will to solve environmental problems. Grassroots action needed to play a greater part in protecting the environment and changing people's attitudes. Starting with problems close to home meant organizing against specific problems and demonstrating to "those in power that citizens mean business."

Nevertheless, other residents remained more charitable toward the government and oil companies and were forthcoming about their need for oil while additionally accusing the new crop of environmental activists of opportunism. Wayne A. Phelan of Avila Beach observed that "the same politically ambitious people have appointed themselves to represent" Santa Barbara, but "these extremists" only caused bad publicity. Surely, Phelan contended, Union Oil would have "preferred not to have the oil leak happen," and "in all fairness . . . have spent considerable time, money, and manpower, and have done a great job cleaning up the beaches."[107] The oil spill allowed the city to be "represented by a few greedy politicians and idle trouble makers rather than be fair about a very unfortunate incident." Phelan added that "most of us do not have the same feeling of desecration that our self-appointed saviors have expressed." Another resident agreed and stated that he was disturbed that the city was seeking an injunction against "those wicked, profit-seeking oil companies," thus inflicting "tremendous and irreparable damage to them." Would those who would want to destroy these companies "be very much amused if those same oil companies turned about and sued our fair city for the damage done to them?"[108] Others noted that oil companies provided revenues through taxes, and that those who wanted oil companies out of Santa Barbara forgot to consider the real consequences of losing oil and its by-products. One man sympathetic to the oil industry added that people "don't stop and think, but it would be a long ride to Los Angeles by horseback or wagon if there wasn't any oil, gas, or any of the other 54 byproducts made from crude."[109]

"No one intentionally pollutes the environment," wrote J. Jamison Moore of Beverly Hills to the *Santa Barbara News-Press*. Moore insisted that "we all contribute, in some manner or means, to depreciation of the states of nature either through inadvertence or thoughtlessness." Petroleum companies, he reasoned, "neither anticipated nor desired the incident." Since the blowout, their motivations concentrated on mitigating the problem and therefore they acted responsibly at "considerable expense" toward cleaning local beaches. Angry members of the public needed to recognize that oil companies had made a deep commitment to the Santa Barbara Channel through extensive economic investment. Rather than making a return on their investment, a moratorium on drilling constituted a "form of confiscation without due process of law which is a precedent that cannot be supported within our form of government." Steeping back from the actual events, Moore argued that the oil companies' "dilemma affects us all, whether or not we support their position."[110]

Despite charges of bias in favor of the oil industry, many government officials saw themselves as simply recognizing the utility between balancing oil consumption and care for the environment. The US Geological Survey's Pecora believed mediating between the risks of pollution and the need and desire for oil hinged on the question of "how great a level of pollution is tolerable."[111] He opined that Santa Barbara residents had "every right to want a city free of industry and oil"; nevertheless, the nation had "a limited supply of oil," and questions of priority usually were decided "politically in Congress." The idea of equity in protecting lands troubled others. Senator Frank Moss of Utah acknowledged this dilemma for Southern California, which had the highest per capita gasoline consumption of any comparable area in the world. Did Californians with their vast oil deposits have a legitimate reason for being "excluded from pollution risks involved in producing oil its citizens consume." Moss wondered why "should people in some areas be exposed to production pollution so that others can enjoy clean beaches and clean shores? What if the people in every area insisted on being free from the pollution risks created by their consumption."[112]

Commercial interests accepted the premise that aspects of the city that could arguably be thought of as externalities, such as its beaches, sunny weather, and scenic vistas, had financial value. Announcing a return to a normal made economic sense. To entice tourists back to Santa Barbara, the city's chamber of commerce purchased advertising space in the *Los Angeles Times* and other outlets. This led to the advertisement referred to at the beginning of this chapter, which announced that the city remained "every bit as delightful" as in previous years. Its "cheery optimism" brought the city "to the brink of a citizens' revolt." Compounding the offense was the fact that the advertisements were financed with a $50,000 donation from the Western Oil and Gas Association with the bulk of the funds supposedly from the four oil companies that jointly owned Platform A. The Western Oil and Gas Association responded that it provided the funds at the request of the chamber of commerce. Considering this disclosure, a group of residents picketed the chamber's office. Protesters alleged that this public relations campaign coincided with hearings in the US Senate to phase out federal oil leases in the Santa Barbara Channel, so the advertisement was meant to keep oil in the region by arguing that its presence ultimately did not affect life in the city. The uproar resulted in the city council announcing that the chamber of commerce could no longer include references or images of the ocean, beachfront, or water sports in promotional material.[113] Nevertheless, the chamber invited twenty reporters to go fishing with them to prove that the recreational conditions remained as good as ever.[114]

Oil's opponents did not dispute the content of the images—they affirmed them. They created a duality about how the images were used. In a letter in the *Los Angeles Times*, Alvin Weingand and Bud Bottoms acknowledged the truth of the advertisement's sunny depiction of Santa Barbara, agreeing that the beaches were pristine on most days, but on bad days "not even the slickest of advertising can make them good."[115] On those days, one could easily understand why the spill became a national disaster of a scale that was "enough to make you cry." The two men hoped visitors would continue to arrive, but with the awareness that on some days the beaches were "a mess" because of "tragic abuse," and conclude that they had come upon a "place to stand and fight against spoliation of the environment." Oil, despite its long-standing existence in Santa Barbara's modern history, needed to be written out of the narrative about the city's relationship with its environment. Other places could have oil, and Santa Barbarans, like the rest of Southern California, and the nation, obviously needed such places. This environmentalism that came to flourish in the wake of the oil spill marked out a boundary between a place that some believed deserved maintenance of its pristine nature and other, less seemingly exceptional places.

Eight months after the blowout, the *Los Angeles Times* described Santa Barbara still as "a city under siege."[116] Oil continued to leak into the channel, and discussions about further oil extraction carried on under the shadows of drilling platforms that stood like "a fleet of warships" commemorating "the greatest environmental disaster of the past decade." Residents regarded their environmental awakening as vital for themselves and the nation. Lois Sidenberg argued that the "tragedy . . . and the persistent efforts of its citizens to establish the right of the people to determine the sort of environment in which they wished to live" aroused citizens throughout the nation. That enthusiasm for the right to a healthy environment, Sidenberg argued, could very well be GOO!'s most valuable and enduring contribution. Fred Eissler agreed that Santa Barbara's experience "reinforced the nation's understanding about environmental protections," but "our message to the nation" should not be lost "upon ourselves as we continue to assert our right to maintain the quality of our local environment." Roderick Nash even went so far as to proclaim that "every locality" needed its equivalent of the Santa Barbara spill in order to open the eyes of the "vast majority." Despite human intelligence, Nash found that most were "unable to discern a problem until on the brink of catastrophe." Not everywhere could be Santa Barbara, but it would not be a complete tragedy if everywhere had its own environmental reckoning.

Such an assertion elided the fact that other locations experienced environmental catastrophes that predated the blowout. But many of those other places lacked the popular clout, reputation, and media coverage that Santa Barbara possessed. This pull was on display on the one-year anniversary of the blowout when numerous environmental groups and individuals ranging from local activist organizations to former cabinet members came together in the city for a day of speeches, seminars, and a banquet. Stewart Udall, Alan Cranston, Paul Ehrlich, and other elected officials in addition to the heads of the Sierra Club and Americans for Democratic Action made appearances. At the end of the day, Nash read aloud the Santa Barbara Declaration of Environmental Rights, cataloging the "misuses of environment and a call to correct the situation" so that all had access to an environment "capable of sustaining life and promoting happiness."[117] The declaration began with the possibility of a break from the immediate past of careless environmental neglect. The indictment leveled against human beings for offenses against the environment varied in scale and included littering; the loss of open space, wilderness, and wildlife; air and water pollution; overpopulation; and making "much of the physical world ugly and loud, depriving man of the beauty and quiet that feeds his spirit."[118] The litany of charges addressed specific events in Santa Barbara obliquely. If regulating the oil industry had once been a clear objective for activists, the Declaration of Environmental Rights and its expansive claims reflected at once the far-reaching resonance of these problems as well as the frustrations with a political process that demonstrated a lack of will to champion substantive changes in oil policy. The emphasis on "we" in framing the charges and principles in the declaration implied a universalism in responsibility and obligation.[119] The generalized culpability for littering, destroying wilderness, polluting water and air, overpopulation, and making "much of the physical world ugly and loud, depriving man of the beauty and quiet that feeds his spirit" failed to distinguish between the privileged and poor and developed and undeveloped parts of the world, as well as the dynamics between them. Nash himself, in a chapter included in the 1982 third edition of *Wilderness and the American Mind*, first published in 1967, included a graph charting the relationship between valuing nature and civilization over time framed by the concept of marginal utility.[120] Over time "civilization becomes plentiful and nature scarce," thus changing its value. As a result, civilization, not nature, constituted the "threat to people's mental and physical well-being."[121] Divisions between civilization and nature in Nash's analysis aligned with similar divisions between places that should not have oil extraction and those that could.

Nash, along with Ross Macdonald and Robert Easton, maintained in a piece for the *New York Times Magazine* that declaring the "11th Commandment" or "Thou shalt not abuse the earth" provided the community not only with national attention but with "an ideology and a creed."[122] Placing a catholic array of environmental concerns at the crux of the declaration furnished space to make more ambitious demands as alternatives to the prototypical tools of modern environmentalism—namely, policy and litigation. Paul Sabin notes that for many environmentalists, situating oil within a larger environmental crisis "seemed a bold political move that would address the fundamental imbalance in the relationship between humans and nature."[123] But that shift lessened the political focus on oil consumption and dependency. The environmental principles outlined in the declaration underscored popular acceptance for reformist ideas about man's relationship to nature, the meaning of progress, and how human beings inhabited land. Nevertheless, radical perspectives marked the commandment. Articulating man's place as "a member, not master" of the community of living things; arguing that when it came to the natural world, "private interests and corporate ownership should be so limited as to preserve the interest of society and the integrity of the environment"; and redefining progress toward "long-term quality rather than immediate quantity" indicated a "revolution in conduct" meant to pacify an "environment which is rising in revolt against us." This was a revolution proposed by those who had considered themselves anything but revolutionaries.

Tangible victories against oil's presence remained elusive. A year after the blowout and despite citizen action, lawsuits, and congressional hearings, residents lamented the likelihood that the city's scenic beauty would now include dozens of drilling platforms on the coast. "If our psyches are messed up from worrying about pollution and ugliness now, just wait," Bud Bottoms conceded to a reporter.[124] Although the federal government delayed approval of new platforms, several companies expected the resumption of offshore oil drilling in the Santa Barbara Channel in the near future. At the same time, "antipollution concern" developed from a "minor political issue to the hottest issue of our time, excluding war and peace."[125] The sweeping extent of the claims represented in the Declaration of Environmental Rights also worked as a shorthand for the environmental movement's detractors. If environmentalism's mainstream popularity, especially after the first Earth Day on April 22, 1970, with its twenty million participants, lent itself to a diversity of alliances, then its critics came from equally diverse sources. The criticism had common links. *Time* magazine quoted a "black militant in Chicago," who proclaimed that he did not "give a good goddam about ecology."[126] Those on the left and right believed the environmental movement resembled a "children's crusade of opportunistic politicians, zealous Ivy Leaguers, longhaired eco-activists, and scientists." Casting environmental issues as centrally focused on beaches in an affluent town revealed environmental quality as a diversion from more pressing concerns. Detractors argued that environmentalists failed to make a case that their "confused mix of unrelated alarms and issues" brought together under "the rhetoric of ecology" had anything to do with contemporary social and economic worries. At the very least, environmentalists needed to recognize that "curbing carbon monoxide in cities" must take precedence over "saving caribou in Alaska." In Santa Barbara, the resident-cum-activists who embraced the tensions between exceptional and typical gave voice to worth of environmental quality. In doing so, they animated local and national conversations about the environment. But these discourses also stabilized a particular vision of environmental concern focused on protecting the way of life and land of affluent Americans seemingly unconnected to the anxieties of others.

Although the federal government delayed granting approval to construct new platforms, several companies expected to be able to commence offshore drilling in the Santa Barbara Channel in the 1970s. George Clyde welcomed national attention on Santa Barbara but worried about the risk that the city would "remain the symbol that saves the rest of the country while we ourselves go down the drain with further polluting oil development."[127] At times the national significance of the residents' environmental actions stood uneasily with local concerns about maintaining the city's remarkable qualities. Distinguishing places as either exceptional or average gave credence to assumptions not only of place but also of inhabitants. Those used to pristine beaches and a high quality of life could hardly be expected to experience environmental hardships. Bud Bottoms evoked the repeated refrain that Santa Barbara prevailed as "the city symbolic of environmental hope" and a "model city" that placed "human values before economic gains, giving total priority to saving and restoring our natural resources, retarding our growth and isolating ourselves from further desecration."[128] Yet the promise of a reorientation in the nation's economic and social structures encompassed in the oil spill was premature. In July 1974, four oil companies settled out of court with the cities of Santa Barbara and Carpenteria, the state of California, and Santa Barbara County for $9 million.[129] While not admitting any responsibility for the blowout, a Union Oil spokesman stressed that the dollar figure was for "actual damages, not punitive damages. We have always been willing to pay actual damages." The settlement paved the way to lifted moratoriums and the resumption of drilling in the Santa Barbara Channel while the country experienced an oil crisis.

In August 1970, the first annual report of the Council on Environmental Quality, an executive-level office established by Richard Nixon, posited that "historians may one day call 1970 the year of the environment" while at the same time they were "almost certain to see evidence of worsening environmental conditions in many parts of the country."[130] Today, historians' repeated evocations of the Santa Barbara oil spill as a central catalyst for the emergence of modern environmentalism often stress the diffuseness of national attention for the movement. The shift in attention from the centrality of oil in the weeks following January 28, 1969, to the broad and vague vision of the Santa Barbara Declaration of Environmental Rights buttressed disappointed observations of waning influence and specificity. This shift displaced the possibility of substantive political changes in energy policy and highlighted limitations in political will in the spill's aftermath. Assumptions about the appearance of a place, the status of its residents, and privileges of belonging transcended partisan politics to activate an environmental politics focused on protection rather than justice. The environmentalism that emerged was a result rather than a cause of activity, aroused by the fear that no place could be immune from environmental harm.

CONCLUSION

The Ends of Environmentalism

On Santa Barbara's eastern boundary sits Montecito, a wealthy enclave where slightly more than eight thousand people reside on 9.2 square miles. "Are there Americans who *don't* have fantasies about a better life in California?" asked a *New York Times* story on Montecito in 2023.[1] In 2014, the *Financial Times* reported that homes for sale in Montecito had an average listing price of slightly under $7 million and that a small group met weekly for "billionaires' breakfast club." Thomas Mann's former estate, El Fureidis—designed by Bertram Goodhue, completed in 1906, and reportedly owned by a Russian billionaire who sold another nearby property to Prince Harry and Meghan Markle—was for sale that year for $35 million.[2] But even the massive amount of wealth—mostly domestic despite notable exceptions—cannot stop climate change and its associated risks from breaching its rarefied environs. In and around this secluded and exclusive landscape, the Thomas fire destroyed more than a thousand structures and caused more than $2 billion in damages. Oprah Winfrey and retired tennis player Jimmy Connors posted videos on Instagram of damage at their homes. Connors posted on Twitter that he had been evacuated via helicopter.[3] Efforts to fully extinguish the fire continued until June 2018.[4] Since then the frequency of major fires has accelerated, but the market for desirable real estate remains stable. In 2021, a reporter for the *San Francisco Gate* quoted a real estate agent who admitted that the Thomas fire and subsequent mudslides had already receded into memory. Home prices in Montecito continued to hold to a median of above $6 million in 2023.[5]

Yet many of the homes that can exceed eight figures in sale price are uninsurable. The risk of climate change–induced wildfires even in this idyllic location outpaces the willingness of standard insurance companies to issue policies to homeowners. After a series of brushfires and riots in the summer of 1968, the state of California set up an alternative insurance plan for homeowners. The plan subsidizes homes in fire-prone areas up to $3 million, much less than most houses in Montecito actually cost. As a result, Montecito residents must find other, more complicated means of procuring insurance. The real estate agent quoted in the *San Francisco Gate* noted he had just sold a $12 million house with an insurance plan of $160,000 a year. Confronting climate change in this situation becomes an individual matter of managing expectations and calculating whether one can afford the risk. "As you start to look globally," the real estate agent observed, "we have tornados, hurricanes, fires, floods, there's a natural disaster in almost every place you look. Choose what threshold of risk you put yourself in personally. We tell people when you come into the market, insurance is going to be expensive." Emphasizing personal expenses associated with climate change as a primary concern for affluent individuals indicates that some will continue to protect what they have despite all environmental risks. This includes building and living on climatically vulnerable land.

Fire officials refer to Montecito and adjacent Santa Barbara as a "Goldilocks zone," designating a place that can create perfect opportunities for fire and flood and other climate change–caused disasters to commingle and "make life untenable." Increasing numbers of these wildland-urban interface regions with homes built near flammable vegetation raise the risk of wildfires.[6] Insurance provides the fiction of protection from what inhabitants imagine as the worst that climate change will bring. For many, California still offers enough to make living on the coast worthwhile, despite the immeasurable environmental risks. But for how much longer?

Ever-increasing costs or nonexistent insurance policies in Santa Barbara and its immediate surroundings are harbingers of risks to come. Looking deeper in time, scientists examined mud sediments in the city to identify layers in attempts to officially mark the beginning of the Anthropocene.[7] But rather than singling out Santa Barbara as exceptional, this book has argued that the city provides a window into how the propertied, not just the fantastically wealthy, have attempted to manage their environments to give precedence to their individual interests and ideas of protection using environmental quality as justification. Similar activities took place across the United States and fundamentally shaped American environmentalism, its ambitions, and its limitations.

Understanding the ascendancy of what this book has described as ownership environmentalism requires placing ideas of home and domesticity at the center of the narrative. Throughout the twentieth century, Santa Barbara's residents focused their voluntary and civic efforts on local interventions in the landscape. As a result of this work, the city became a national template for an environmental movement centered on the political and social priorities of affluent, educated, homeowning, and mostly white Americans, one concerned chiefly with shaping and protecting environments close to home. Instead of considering environmentalism as a challenge to the status quo or a cry for a more expansive understanding of the public good, ownership environmentalism championed aspects of the movement compatible with the lives and culture of private homeowners. More broadly, this environmentalism protected the basis of American liberal order and its values of precedence, decency, and civility rather than questioning its underlying priorities. This point of view renders benign environmentalism's potential for critique and underscores the need to reinsert political obligations and demands into environmentalism if it is going to be anything more than a cover for the interests of the affluent.[8]

In reflecting on the history of conservation, historian Karl Jacoby notes that Americans have "often pursued environmental quality at the expense of social justice."[9] Likewise, the intersection of homeownership and environment separated environmental quality from social justice. This book began in the wake of the 1925 earthquake that destroyed much of Santa Barbara's downtown. Subsequent reconstruction privileged Spanish Colonial Revival architecture as the style most "naturally" compatible with the city's climate and environment. This revisionist undertaking emphasized aesthetic connections with the American northeast rather than with Indigenous, Spanish, or Mexican influences. Local organizations took responsibility for mobilizing residents and crystallizing priorities for the city's aesthetic qualities and community ideals. Concentrating on the domestic sphere rendered the racial and social assumptions of these activities as the natural result of interventions of urban improvement. The home lent a nonpolitical veneer or even insignificance to this project. Regardless, reinforcing the household as a primary locus for developing environmental awareness and community values masked political interventions and private initiatives.

The continual assertion of California's exceptional qualities and the drive to protect and enhance the landscape included more literal cultivation of the state's plants and gardens. In addition to activities focused on the home garden or local botanic gardens, prominent conservationists and theorists of human genetics viewed native plants and trees as models for engineering and improving human societies—most ominously through eugenics. Botanic life offered a seemingly natural and objective order for human society to emulate. As California's population increased rapidly after 1945, models from the natural world appeared to confirm pessimistic outlooks made by several commentators. Numerous architectural and cultural critics latched onto "environment" as a driving concern, especially when lamenting that urban sprawl and population growth were threatening the aesthetic features that made California so exceptional. Californians found themselves enmeshed in debates that exposed a central implication of environmentalism—the idea that humans should limit growth for the sake of the earth. Responses to where and how those limits should be implemented revealed and confirmed social preferences of long-standing residents to the detriment of newly arriving populations. The 1969 oil spill catalyzed national environmental activism and presented an existential threat to Santa Barbara's public image as an environmental haven. In its wake, the city's politically conservative residents concluded that the best way to protect the environment was by tackling local problems through local citizen action. Santa Barbara hoped to avoid the excesses of modern affluence while enjoying the results of prosperity. Yet protections from too much external migration could not prevent the worst type of environmental disaster to arrive so close to home. This belief lent credence to an anti-statist vision of environmental responsibility stemming from a personal sense of injury and loss.

When refracted through the lens of homeownership, environmental concerns took on a conservative or even reactionary orientation. Maintaining individual and community comforts gave many the impression of environmental quality as a zero-sum game. The resources and attributes that cities on the California coast and other affluent places throughout the country offered were limited and could not be distributed equitably. Expanding access to those resources represented a clear threat to the environment and its long-standing population. The expansion of homeownership throughout the twentieth century proved a decisive influence on the place of environmental issues in American life. Although modern environmentalism's priorities often stemmed from the political and social priorities of affluent Americans, its ascendance as a social and political force suggests an alternate path centered on transforming existing orders. Environmentalism can accommodate a range of political outlooks. This is one of its major constraints, but also a source of its broad acceptance and power.

"In this country, we don't sacrifice for anything."[10] The attitude that privileged individual affluence even in the face of major crises helped shift American politics to the right.[11] "Can anyone wonder that Western Man—particularly *Homo Americanus*—has marched to the brink of an energy crisis?" asked journalist Sterling G. Slappey in 1971. Given the extent of energy use of the recent past with, as Slappey wrote, energy use since 1940 exceeding all previous years put together. The United States had an oversized role in global energy use, having consumed more gas, coal, oil, and nuclear power than the USSR, United Kingdom, West Germany, and Japan combined. Despite the extent of use and looming threat of "the brink of an energy crisis," he minimized the possibility. "Certainly, we may have brownouts in some areas this summer . . . and next winter we may have some failures in heating supplies."[12] Instead of indicating large-scale vulnerabilities with profound political and economic consequences, brownouts and winter heating failures could be minimized as isolated and minor inconveniences for consumers.

Framing current and future national energy issues as matters of technical capacities, regulatory delays, and logistics that could be improved avoided treating these matters as political problems or even subject to policy interventions to reduce oil consumption. Moreover, by identifying energy consumption as a necessary component of quality of life absolved it of any problematic consequences. More bluntly, access to energy resources took precedence over environmental quality. This was, according Slappey, an American story from the first time a settler in Jamestown cut down a tree in 1607. In the face of criticism regarding oil as a pollutant and source of broader environmental damage, oil executives countered with data testifying to the necessity of their industry. One business journal reported that the oil industry faced "the predicament of settlers facing attackers coming over every wall" with the industry under "heavy siege" almost anywhere that had "a whiff of exhaust fume or an oil splotch on the water." In 1971, oil supplied 44 percent of the United States' total energy and provided one-quarter of industrial energy, almost half of commercial and household heating requirements, and almost all energy for transportation. And the nation's oil needs only continued to increase.[13] Consumers' need for cheap and convenient oil, executives argued, eclipsed the desires of "extreme environmentalists" to prevent exploration, drilling, and extraction.

To be sure, numerous Americans with environmentalist sympathies had little interest in challenging patterns of oil extraction and consumption. Ambivalent responses followed questions regarding who could enjoy the results of California's prosperity, including its environmental quality. One continuity over time is the belief that some resources must be protected by restricting access. A culmination of this attitude came in 1978 when Proposition 13 passed in California, cutting property taxes by more than half and limiting future tax increases. Described by one historian as the "Watts riot of the white middle class," its social and economic reverberations continue to the present.[14] Yet attempts to circumscribe access and opportunity by race eventually led to diminished access among members of the very population those restrictions were supposed to protect. Informal, indeed illegal, means to restrict access to spaces persist as well. In March 2024, at least six Montecito residents received orders to remove boulders and plants obstructing public parking near popular trailheads under the threat of civil or criminal prosecution.[15] Other Californians have received fines and penalties for blocking access to legally public beaches. Wealthy homeowners have battled for years with the California Coastal Commission to continue blocking public access to beaches near their homes in Malibu.[16]

These activities suggest the necessity of alternative ways of thinking about the economic and social structures governing American society and who can access environmental quality. An environmental critique grounded in maintaining comforts for the relatively privileged benefits from a diminished understanding of political action's effectiveness. Weaponizing nature to protect the quality of life for the few shows how environmentalism can be complicit with maintaining or even exacerbating social and spatial inequalities. But marking out how ownership environmentalism came about demonstrates that the movement does not carry any intrinsic ideological content or inevitable conclusions. Shrouding political work under the guise of nature belies the power it has for ordering social expectations and even encouraging quietism. It is time we see it for what it is and what it has done in order to strive for alternative paths.

Acknowledgments

In the years since I began the research that became this book, I have accrued many debts, and I am profoundly grateful to have the opportunity to thank the people whose work and friendship supported this process. The project began at Columbia University, a time filled with an excess of happiness and camaraderie. I had the extra good fortune to work under the close guidance of Felicity Scott, Karl Jacoby, Reinhold Martin, Mabel Wilson, and Phoebe S. K. Young, all of whom are model scholars and human beings. My deepest thanks for Felicity's generosity and support over many years. Members of a writing group headed by Karl provided critical insights and commiseration. I also owe thanks to Gergo Baics, Gwen Wright, Kenneth Frampton, Mary McLeod, and the late Alan Brinkley.

Research would not have been possible without the dedicated labor of archivists and librarians, especially Daisy Muralles and Raul Pizano with the Special Research Collections at the University of California, Santa Barbara Library. Many thanks as well to archivists, librarians, and staff at Avery Architectural and Fine Art Library and the Rare Book and Manuscript Library at Columbia University, American Philosophical Society, Dumbarton Oaks, the Gledhill Library at the Santa Barbara Historical Museum, the Huntington Library, Sacramento State University, and UCLA Library Special Collections.

The people I met while at Columbia made the time wonderous. It is an absolute joy that in the years since, these individuals have become excellent travel companions, indispensable scholarly interlocutors, readers of drafts, and evermore valued friends: Alissa Anderson, Óscar Arnórsson, George Aumoithe, Daniel Barber, Elizabeth Biggs, Caitlin Blanchfield, Mara Caden, Marta Caldeira, Charlette Caldwell, Laura Carter, Erik Carver, Catherine Chou, Chris Cowell, Sam Daly, Mary Freeman, Addison Godel, James

Graham, Anna Danziger Halperin, Charles Halvorson, Robin Hartano, Nick Juravich, Hollyamber Kennedy, Mookie Kideckel, Miranda Kiek, Katy Lasdow, Craig Lee, Ayala Levin, Ruen-Chuan Ma, Alicia Maggard, Ariel Marcus, David Marcus, Laura Marsh, Jacob Moore, Ginger Nolan, Vyta Pivo, Mars Plater, Jason Resnikoff, Lindsey Resnikoff, Jonah Rowen, Heather Russo, Chelsea Szendi Schieder, Kara Schlichting, Ben Serby, Asheesh Siddique, Danny Steinmetz-Jenkins, Elliott Sturtevant, Norihiko Tsuneishi, Allison Powers Useche, Aaron White, and Becca Wright. Thank you all for the reading and writing groups, the travel adventures, hanging out, and so much more.

A group of people supported me through their friendship, offering places to stay during research trips and opportunities to pursue other types of writing over the years: Magda Biernat-Webster and Ian Webster, Stephenie Doyle and Mike Doyle, Jason Escalante, Carrie Bobo Gibbs and Jason Gibbs, Debra Hayreh and Sant Hayreh, Daniel Hendrickson, Amy Howell, Karen Kubey, Amy Mielke and Steve Mielke, Paul Schneider and Helen Wilson, and Mimi Zeiger.

The book took its current shape at the University of Illinois at Urbana-Champaign, where I had the unbelievable luck to spend two years at the Humanities Research Institute as a Mellon Postdoctoral Fellow in Environmental Humanities, basking in the brilliance of Leah Aronowsky and Bob Morrissey, two of the very best people. HRI was a wonderful intellectual home due to the inspirational leadership of Antoinette Burton and Nancy Castro. I gained an enormous amount from conversations with faculty and graduate students at Illinois, who were also subjected to various drafts of this book and are some of the most excellent friends a person could ask for, especially Susan Ask, John Levi Barnard, Christina Bollo, Clara Bosak-Schroeder, Katherine Burge, Eric Calderwood, Colleen Chiu-Shee, Jennifer Chuong, Eleanore Courtmanche, Carolyn Fornoff, Andrew Greenlee, Kristin Hoganson, Kate Holliday, Doug Jones, Jamie Jones, Craig Koslofsky, Lilah Leopold, Rebecca Oh, Alex Paterson, James Pilgrim, Amy Powell, Dana Rabin, Kristin Romberg, Charles Sing, Carol Symes, Sophia Warner, Shelley Weinberg, and Rod Wilson. Maria Gillombardo is the secret weapon of every scholar at the University of Illinois. Her tenacious support and willingness to read endless drafts of anything that crosses her path is awe-inspiring.

The ability to stay at Illinois to join the faculty of the Department of Landscape Architecture has meant the world to me. I am so grateful to have amazing colleagues in Brian Deal, John Clark, Lori Davis, Brian Deal, Aneesha Dharwadker, Marti Gortner, David Hays, Jie Hu, Kelley Lemon, Karen May,

ACKNOWLEDGMENTS   169

Mary Pat McGuire, Conor O'Shea, Dede Ruggles, Beth Scott, Stephen Sears, and Bill Sullivan. Thanks as well to Kevin Hamilton, dean of the College of Fine and Applied Arts at Illinois.

A wider circle of scholars offered advice, feedback, and friendship, including Daniel Abramson, David Bennett, Alek Bierig, Netta Cohen, Hazel Cowie, Macarena de la Vega, Michael Faciejew, Anna Kornbluh, Sarah Kunjummen, Charlotte Leib, Jasper Ludewig, Katharine Mershon, Mariya Rusak, Andrew Seaton, Phoebe Springstubb, Cass Turner, Matt Wells, and Sam Wetherell.

Critical financial support over the years came from the American Philosophical Society, the Buell Center for the Study of American Architecture at Columbia University, the Campus Research Board at the University of Illinois, the Mellon Foundation, the Huntington Library, Dumbarton Oaks, and the Wadsworth Endowment Funds of the Department of Landscape Architecture at Illinois. I especially appreciate getting to know Adrianna Link at the American Philosophical Society and Thaïsa Way, Anatole Tchikine, Elgin Cleckley, and Anna Livia Brand at Dumbarton Oaks. The first draft of this manuscript was sent off while I was in Brisbane as a visiting fellow at the Architecture Theory Criticism History Centre at the University of Queensland. I am so very grateful to Ashley Paine for facilitating that visit and the faculty affiliates of ATCH for making my time there so pleasant.

Dede Ruggles and the Unit for Criticism and Interpretive Theory at Illinois provided generous funding for a manuscript workshop. My unending gratitude goes to Amanda Ciafone, Marc Doussard, Paige Glotzer, and Keith Woodhouse, who read the entire manuscript and reoriented my thinking around it. Their insights renewed my resources and marked paths forward that helped me see the manuscript anew. Thanks, additionally, to Keith for being a trusted and wise source of advice since my first year on the job market. Reviewers for the University of Chicago Press, including Finis Dunaway, who waived anonymity, provided the best kind of collegiality through their amazingly generous and constructive feedback.

The brilliant Becky Nicolaides has been a source of constant support since the day we met while I was in graduate school. Among other things, I am especially grateful to her for introducing me to Timothy Mennel at the University of Chicago Press, who has been an enthusiastic supporter of this project since it was a few half-drafted chapters. Andrea Blatz and Anne Strother shepherded this manuscript with great expertise. Many thanks to Allison Gudenau and Beth Ina for copyediting. Varsha Venkatasubramanian provided the index. Working with Sierra Chmela on the maps was delightful.

Finally, thank you to Antony Crossfield for reading the manuscript when he didn't have to, for his artistic talent on images, and for the excellent chat, among many other things. Shelby Doyle, Shelley Hayreh, Justin Jennings, and Eleanor Pepper sustained me through years of friendship before this project began.

There is no adequate way to express my gratitude to my family, especially to my brother Tae Young and my 고모 in Tokyo, as well as aunts, uncles, and cousins from Seoul to Toronto. This book is dedicated with all my love to my parents, who gave me everything and are the best teachers I will ever have.

Notes

Introduction

1. Adam Rome, *The Genius of Earth Day: How a 1970 Teach-In Unexpectedly Made the First Green Generation* (New York: Hill and Wang, 2013).

2. Office of Response and Restoration, National Oceanic and Atmospheric Administration, "Largest Oil Spills Affecting U.S. Waters since 1969," https://response.restoration.noaa.gov/oil-and-chemical-spills/oil-spills/largest-oil-spills-affecting-us-waters-1969.html, accessed April 29, 2024.

3. Radio talk, September 9, 1931, Community Development and Conservation Collection, Subseries A, Community Arts Association Records, Plans and Planting Branch Collection, SBHC Mss 1, Box 25, Folder Radio Talks 1931, UCSB Department of Special Research Collections (hereafter cited as CDCC).

4. Robert O. Self, *American Babylon: Race and the Struggle for Postwar Oakland* (Princeton, NJ: Princeton University Press, 2003), esp. 16–17.

5. Jeffrey L. Rabin and Daryl Kelley, "'Slow Growth' Has Come at a Cost in Santa Barbara," *Los Angeles Times*, March 6, 2006, https://www.latimes.com/archives/la-xpm-2006-mar-06-me-slowgrow6-story.html, accessed February 19, 2024.

6. Discussions of property often start with John Locke, *Two Treatises of Government*, ed. Peter Laslett (Cambridge: Cambridge University Press, 1988 [1698]). General histories include Stuart Banner, *How the Indians Lost Their Land: Law and Power on the Frontier* (Cambridge, MA: Harvard University Press, 2005); Stuart Banner, *American Property: A History of How, Why, and What We Own* (Cambridge, MA: Harvard University Press, 2011); Stuart Banner, *Possessing the Pacific: Land, Settlers, and Indigenous People from Australia to Alaska* (Cambridge, MA: Harvard University Press, 2007); Andro Linklater, *Owning the Earth: The Transforming History and Land* (New York: Bloomsbury, 2015); Robert M. Fogelson, *Bourgeois Nightmares: Suburbia, 1870–1930* (New Haven, CT: Yale University Press, 2005); Hendrik Hartog, *Public Property and Private Power: The Corporation of the City of New York in American Law, 1730–1870* (Chapel Hill: University of North Carolina Press, 1983); Allan Greer, *Property and Dispossession: Natives, Empires, and Land in Early Modern North America* (Cambridge: Cambridge University Press, 2017); C. B. Macpherson, ed., *Property: Mainstream and Critical Positions* (Toronto: University of To-

ronto Press, 1978). For property in legal and philosophical scholarship, see Lawrence C. Becker, "The Moral Basis of Property Rights," *Nomos* 22 (1980): 187–220; Morris R. Cohen, "Property and Sovereignty," *Cornell Law Quarterly* 13, no. 1 (1927): 8–20; Cheryl I. Harris, "Whiteness as Property," *Harvard Law Review* 106, no. 8 (June 1993): 1707–91; Carol M. Rose, "Possession as the Origin of Property," *University of Chicago Law Review* 52, no. 1 (Winter 1985): 73–88; Carol M. Rose, *Property and Persuasion: Essays on the History, Theory, and Rhetoric of Ownership* (Boulder, CO: Westfield, 1994); Jeremy Waldron, *The Right to Private Property* (Oxford: Clarendon Press, 1988); Jeremy Waldron, *The Rule of Law and the Measure of Property* (Cambridge: Cambridge University Press, 2012), 1–41.

7. On the formation of bourgeois identity, see Christof Dejung, David Motadel and Jürgen Osterhammel, eds., *The Global Bourgeoisie: The Rise of the Middle Classes in the Age of Empire* (Princeton, NJ: Princeton University Press, 2019), esp. 1–40.

8. Self, *American Babylon*, esp. 16–17.

9. Etienne Benson, *Surroundings: A History of Environments and Environmentalisms* (Chicago: University of Chicago Press, 2020), 1–2.

10. Quoted in Benson, *Surroundings*, 3; Jenny Price, "Remaking American Environmentalism: On the Banks of the LA River," *Environmental History* 13, no. 3 (July 2008): 540; Keith Mako Woodhouse, "After Earth Day: The Modern Environmental Movement," *Reviews in American History* 42 (2014): 558.

11. On radical environmentalism, see Keith Makoto Woodhouse, *The Ecocentrists: A History of Radical Environmentalism* (New York: Columbia University Press, 2018).

12. Robert Darnton, *The Great Cat Massacre and Other Episodes in French Cultural History* (New York: Basic, 2009 [1984]), xvi.

13. Richard White, *The Republic for Which It Stands: The United States during Reconstruction and the Gilded Age, 1865–1896* (New York: Oxford University Press, 2017), 5.

14. Amy Kaplan, "Manifest Domesticity," *American Literature* 70, no. 3 (September 1998): 581–606; Susan Matt, *Homesickness: An American History* (Oxford: Oxford University Press, 2011). For context, see also Kristin L. Hoganson, *Consumer's Imperium: The Global Production of American Domesticity, 1865–1920* (Chapel Hill: University of North Carolina Press, 2007).

15. Kaplan, "Manifest Domesticity," 582; see also Antoinette Burton, "Toward Unsettling Histories of Domesticity," *American Historical Review* 124, no. 4 (October 2019): 1332–33; and Kristin Hoganson, "Inposts of Empires," *Diplomatic History* 45, no. 1 (January 2021): 6.

16. On the relationship between cities and nature, see Matthew Klingle, *Emerald City: An Environmental History of Seattle* (New Haven, CT: Yale University Press, 2007); Michael Rawson, *Eden on the Charles: The Making of Boston* (Cambridge, MA: Harvard University Press, 2010); Catherine McNeur, *Taming Manhattan: Environmental Battles in the Antebellum City* (Cambridge, MA: Harvard University Press, 2014).

17. On the concept of home in relation to modern American attitudes about wilderness, see William Cronon, "The Trouble with Wilderness: Or, Getting Back to the Wrong Nature," *Environmental History* 1, no. 1 (January 1996): esp. 21–25.

18. Better Homes in America, Statements by Members of the Advisory Council, 1925. Better Homes in America Collection, SBHC Mss 1, Subseries A, Box 1, Folder 14, CDCC.

19. Better Homes in America, Statements by Members of the Advisory Council, 1925. Better Homes in America Collection, SBHC Mss 1, Subseries A, Box 1, Folder 14, CDCC.

20. This analysis draws from Marc Edelman, "Social Movements: Changing Paradigms and Forms of Politics," *Annual Review of Anthropology* 30 (2001): 285–317; and Gemma Edwards, *Social Movements and Protest* (Cambridge: Cambridge University Press, 2014).

NOTES TO PAGES 7–9

21. Samuel Hays, *Beauty, Health, and Permanence: Environmental Politics in the United States, 1955–1985* (Cambridge: Cambridge University Press, 1987); Woodhouse, "After Earth Day," 562-63.

22. Raymond Williams, *Keywords: A Vocabulary of Culture and Society*, rev. ed. (New York: Oxford University Press, 1983 [1976]), 11.

23. Ted Nordhaus and Michael Shellenberger, *Break Through: Why We Can't Leave Saving the Planet to Environmentalists* (Boston: Mariner, 2009), 6.

24. Hays, *Beauty, Health, and Permanence*, 2–3. Adam Rome, *Bulldozer in the Countryside: Suburban Sprawl and the Rise of American Environmentalism* (Cambridge: Cambridge University Press, 2001), 5-12; Christopher C. Sellers, *Crabgrass Crucible: Suburban Nature and the Rise of Environmentalism in Twentieth-Century America* (Chapel Hill: University of North Carolina Press, 2012), 3–5.

25. Adam Rome, "Give Earth a Chance," *Journal of American History*, 2003, 526. Pollyanna Rhee, "Calculating Nature's Bill: Environmental Quality and the Critique of Economic Growth in the 1970s," *Global Perspectives* 5, no. 1 (April 2024): 1–11.

26. Sellers, *Crabgrass Crucible*, 7; Lawrence Culver, "Confluences of Nature and Culture," in *Oxford Handbook of Environmental History*, ed. Andrew C. Isenberg (Oxford: Oxford University Press, 2014), 564.

27. Elizabeth Grennan Browning, *Nature's Laboratory: Environmental Thought and Labor Radicalism in Chicago, 1886–1937* (Baltimore, MD: Johns Hopkins University Press, 2022).

28. Ellen Griffith Spears, *Rethinking the American Environmental Movement Post-1945* (New York: Routledge, 2020); Paul Sutter, "Putting the Intellectual Back in Environmental History," *Modern Intellectual History* 18 (2021): 604. See also Chad Montrie, *The Myth of Silent Spring: Rethinking the Origins of American Environmentalism* (Berkeley: University of California Press, 2018); Deagan Miller, *This Radical Land: A Natural History of American Dissent* (Chicago: University of Chicago Press, 2018); Michael Rawson, *Eden on the Charles: The Making of Boston* (Cambridge, MA: Harvard University Press, 2010); Rome, *Genius of Earth Day*; James Morton Turner, *The Promise of Wilderness: A History of American Environmental Politics* (Seattle: University of Washington Press, 2012); James Morton Turner, "'The Specter of Environmentalism': Wilderness, Environmental Politics, and the Evolution of the New Right," *Journal of American History* 96, no. 1 (June 2009): 123–48; Stephen Fox, *John Muir and His Legacy: The American Conservation Movement* (Madison: University of Wisconsin Press, 1985); Thomas Jundt, *Greening the Red, White and Blue: The Bomb, Big Business, and Consumer Resistance in Postwar America* (Oxford: Oxford University Press, 2014).

29. Sutter, "Putting the Intellectual Back in Environmental History," 604–5.

30. Michael Jones-Correa, "The Origins and Diffusion of Racial Restrictive Covenants," *Political Science Quarterly* (Winter 2000–2001): 541–68. Carol M. Rose, "Possession as the Origin of Property," *University of Chicago Law Review* 52, no. 1 (Winter 1985): 73–88; Carol M. Rose, *Property and Persuasion: Essays on the History, Theory, and Rhetoric of Ownership* (Boulder, CO: Westfield, 1994).

31. Carey McWilliams, *Southern California: An Island on the Land* (Santa Barbara, CA: Peregrine Smith, 1973 [1946]), 82–83; Genevieve Carpio, "Zorro Down Under: Settler Colonial Architecture and Racial Scripts En Route from California to Australia," *Aztlán: A Journal of Chicago Studies* 46, no. 1 (Spring 2021): 111–42.

32. For the role of women in the environmental movement, see Carolyn Merchant, *Earthcare: Women and the Environment* (New York: Routledge, 1996); Adam Rome, "'Political Hermaphrodites': Gender and Environmental Reform in Progressive America," *Environmental His-*

tory 11, no. 3 (2006): 440–63; Nancy C. Unger, *Beyond Nature's Housekeepers: American Women in Environmental History* (New York: Oxford University Press, 2012).

33. Richard White, "'Are You an Environmentalist or Do You Work for a Living?'" in *Uncommon Ground: Toward Reinventing Nature*, ed. William Cronon (New York: W. W. Norton, 1995), 171–85.

34. Quoted in Keith M. Woodhouse, "The Politics of Ecology: Environmentalism and Liberalism in the 1960s," *Journal for the Study of Radicalism* 2, no. 2 (2008): 53. For a further elaboration, see Woodhouse, *Ecocentrists*, 3–5.

35. On the relationship between conservatism and environmentalism, see Brian Allen Drake, *Loving Nature, Fearing the State: Environmentalism and Antigovernment Politics before Reagan* (Seattle: University of Washington Press, 2013); Adam Duane Orford, "The Creation of Enemies: Investigating Conservative Enviromental Polarization, 1945-1981," PhD dissertation (University of California, Berkeley, 2021); James Morton Turner and Andrew C. Isenberg, *The Republican Reversal: Conservatives and the Environment from Nixon to Trump* (Cambridge, MA: Harvard University Press, 2018). On environmental justice, see Robert D. Bullard, *Dumping in Dixie: Race, Class, and Environmental Quality* (Boulder, CO: Westview, 1990); Stephen Lerner, *Sacrifice Zones: The Front Lines of Toxic Chemical Exposure in the United States* (Cambridge, MA: MIT Press, 2010); David Naguib Pellow, *Garbage Wars: The Struggle for Environmental Justice in Chicago* (Cambridge, MA: MIT Press, 2004); Julie Sze, *Noxious New York: The Racial Politics of Urban Health and Environmental Justice* (Cambridge, MA: MIT Press, 2006); Dorceta Taylor, *Toxic Communities: Environmental Racism, Industrial Pollution, and Residential Mobility* (New York: NYU Press, 2014); Carl A. Zimring, *Clean and White: A History of Environmental Racism in the United States* (New York: NYU Press, 2016).

36. Woodhouse, "After Earth Day," 562.

37. This formulation is influenced by Lily Geismer, *Don't Blame Us: Suburban Liberals and the Transformation of the Democratic Party* (Princeton, NJ: Princeton University Press, 2014), esp. 3–4.

38. Ramachandra Guha, "Radical American Environmentalism and Wilderness Preservation: A Third World Critique," *Environmental Ethics* 11, no. 1 (Spring 1989): 71–83.

39. Rob Nixon, *Slow Violence and the Environmentalism of the Poor* (Cambridge, MA: Harvard University Press, 2011), 4–5.

40. For example, see Etienne Benson, *Surroundings: A History of Environments and Environmentalisms* (Chicago: University of Chicago Press, 2020); Jedidiah Purdy, *After Nature: A Politics for the Anthropocene* (Cambridge, MA: Harvard University Press, 2015); Paul Warde, Libby Robin, and Sverker Sörlin, *The Environment: A History of the Idea* (Baltimore, MD: Johns Hopkins University Press, 2018).

41. Cronon, "Trouble with Wilderness," 7–28.

42. Joseph Serna, "Southern California Edison Power Lines Sparked Deadly Thomas Fire, Investigators Find," *Los Angeles Times*, March 13, 2019, https://www.latimes.com/local/lanow/la-me-ln-thomas-fire-edison-cause-20190313-story.html, accessed August 30, 2021.

43. Brittny Mejia et al., "The Inferno That Won't Die: How the Thomas Fire Became a Monster," *Los Angeles Times* (Online); December 11, 2017, https://search.proquest.com/docview/1975603752/abstract/9412B974FE4941FBPQ/5.

44. Eric Sondheimer, "For Disaster-Stricken Santa Barbara, a Feel-Good Story on the Soccer Field," *Los Angeles Times*, March 4, 2018.

45. Hugo Martin, "Santa Barbara Tourism Officials Wrestle with Promoting the Region after Disaster," *Los Angeles Times*, January 31, 2018.

NOTES TO PAGES 13-15

46. Joseph Serna, "For Some, Thomas Fire Triggers 'Controlled Fright,'" *Los Angeles Times*, December 11, 2017.

47. Helen Delpar, *The Enormous Vogue for Things Mexican: Cultural Relations between the United States and Mexico, 1920–1935* (Tuscaloosa: University of Alabama Press, 1995); Todd Cronan, *Nothing Permanent: Modern Architecture in California* (Minneapolis: University of Minnesota Press, 2023); William Deverell, *Whitewashed Adobe: The Rise of Los Angeles and the Remaking of Its Mexican Past* (Berkeley: University of California Press, 2004); Richard L. Kagan, *The Spanish Craze: America's Fascination with the Hispanic World, 1779–1939* (Lincoln: University of Nebraska Press, 2019); Harold Kirker, *Old Forms on a New Land: California Architecture in Perspective* (Niwot, CO: Roberts Rinehart, 1991); Henry Knight, *Tropic of Hopes: California, Florida, and the Selling of American Paradise, 1869–1929* (Gainesville: University Press of Florida, 2013); Elizabeth Kryder-Reid, *California Mission Landscapes: Race, Memory, and the Politics of Heritage* (Minneapolis: University of Minnesota Press, 2016); Phoebe S. K. Young, *California Vieja: Culture and Memory in a Modern American Place* (Berkeley: University of California Press, 2006); Merry Ovnick, *Los Angeles: The End of the Rainbow* (New York: Chronicle, 1994); Kevin Starr, *Material Dreams: Southern California through the 1920s* (New York: Oxford University Press, 1990); David Wrobel, *Promised Lands: Promotion, Memory, and the Creation of the American West* (Lawrence: University Press of Kansas); Phoebe S. K. Young, "The Spanish Colonial Solution: The Politics of Style in Southern California, 1890s–1930s," in *Design in California and Mexico, 1915–1985*, ed. Wendy Kaplan (Los Angeles: Los Angeles County Museum of Art, 2017), 46–83.

48. Darnton, *Great Cat Massacre*, 116.

49. Arif Dirlik, "The Global in the Local," in *Global/Local: Cultural Production and the Transnational Imaginary*, ed. Rob Wilson and Wimal Dissanayake (Durham, NC: Duke University Press, 1996), 22; Doreen Massey, "A Global Sense of Place," in *Exploring Human Geography: A Reader*, ed. Stephen Daniels and Roger Lee (London: Routledge, 1995), 241.

50. Doreen Massey, "Questions of Locality," *Geography* 78, no. 2 (April 1992): 144–45.

51. On California's environmental history, see Douglas Cazaux Sackman, *Orange Empire: California and the Fruits of Eden* (Berkeley: University of California Press, 2001); Elsa Devienne, *Sand Rush: The Revival of the Beach in Twentieth-Century Los Angeles* (Oxford: Oxford University Press, 2024); Andrew C. Isenberg, *Mining California: An Ecological History* (New York: Hill and Wang, 2005); Carolyn Merchant, *Green versus Gold: Sources in California's Environmental History* (Washington, DC: Island, 1998); Char Miller, *Not So Golden State: Sustainability vs. the California Dream* (San Antonio, TX: Trinity University Press, 2016); Connie Y. Chiang, *Shaping the Shoreline: Fisheries and Tourism on the Monterey Coast* (Seattle: University of Washington Press, 2008); Linda Nash, *Inescapable Ecologies: A History of Environment, Disease, and Knowledge* (Berkeley: University of California Press, 2006); Sara C. Fingal, "Designing Conservation at the Sea Ranch," *Environmental History* 18, no. 1 (January 2013): 185–90; Char Miller, ed., *Cities and Nature in the American West* (Reno: University of Nevada Press, 2010); Marguerite S. Shaffer and Phoebe S. K. Young, eds., *Rendering Nature: Animals, Bodies, Places, Politics* (Philadelphia: University of Pennsylvania Press, 2015); Lawrence Culver, *The Frontier of Leisure: Southern California and the Shaping of Modern America* (Oxford: Oxford University Press, 2012).

52. For context, see Lisa McGirr, *Suburban Warriors: The Origins of the New American Right* (Princeton, NJ: Princeton University Press, 2001); Bethany Moreton, *To Serve God and Wal-Mart: The Making of Christian Free Enterprise* (Cambridge, MA: Harvard University Press, 2010); Andrew Needham, *Power Lines: Phoenix and the Making of the Modern Southwest* (Princeton, NJ: Princeton University Press, 2014); Lisa Sun-Hee Park and David Naguib Pellow, *The Slums*

of Aspen: Immigrants vs. the Environment in America's Eden (New York: New York University Press, 2011); James S. Duncan and Nancy G. Duncan, *Landscapes of Privilege: The Politics of the Aesthetic in an American Suburb* (London: Routledge, 2003).

Chapter One

1. Herbert Nunn, "Municipal Problems of Santa Barbara," *Bulletin of the Seismological Society of America*, December 1925, 308.
2. Nunn, "Municipal Problems of Santa Barbara," 309.
3. Nunn, "Municipal Problems of Santa Barbara," 310.
4. Nunn, "Municipal Problems of Santa Barbara," 310–11.
5. Edward G. Lowry, "Santa Barbara's Charm and Appeal Equaled Nowhere Else in Country," *Morning Press*, March 8, 1925.
6. "Santa Barbara as the Nomad Saw It," *Transcript*, c. 1925, clipping, Community Arts Association Records, Administrative Records, SBHC Mss 1, Subseries A, Box 4, Folder 9, CDCC.
7. Pearl Chase, "Santa Barbara Resurgent," *Survey Graphic* 54, no. 9 (August 1, 1925): 472.
8. Chase, "Santa Barbara Resurgent," 472.
9. "Santa Barbara's Opportunity," typewritten speech, Architectural Advisory Committee Records, SBHC Mss 1, Subseries A, Box 1, CDCC.
10. Linda Gordon, *The Second Coming of the KKK: The Ku Klux Klan of the 1920s and the American Political Tradition* (New York: Liveright, 2017); Carol Medlicott, "Constructing Territory, Constructing Citizenship: The Daughters of the American Revolution and 'Americanisation' in the 1920s," *Geopolitics* 10, no. 1 (2005): 99–120; Mae M. Ngai, *Impossible Subjects: Illegal Aliens and the Making of Modern America* (Princeton, NJ: Princeton University Press, 2004).
11. Philip J. Deloria, "American Master Narratives and the Problem of Indian Citizenship in the Gilded Age and Progressive Era," *Journal of the Gilded Age and Progressive Era* 14, no. 1 (January 2015): 3–12; Jeanette Wolfley, "Jim Crow, Indian Style: The Disenfranchisement of Native Americans," *American Indian Law Review* 16, no. 1 (1991): 167–202; Kevin Bruyneel, *The Third Space of Sovereignty: The Postcolonial Politics of US–Indigenous Relations* (Minneapolis: University of Minnesota Press, 2007); Mae M. Ngai, "Nationalism, Immigration Control, and the Ethnoracial Remapping of America in the 1920s," *OAH Magazine of History* 21, no. 3 (July 2007): 11–15; Margaret D. Jacobs, "Seeing Like a Settler Colonial State," *Modern American History* 1 (2018): 257–70.
12. Cathleen Cahill, *Federal Fathers and Mothers: A Social History of the United States Indian Service, 1869–1932* (Chapel Hill: University of North Carolina Press, 2011); K. T. Lomawaima, "The Mutuality of Citizenship and Sovereignty: The Society of American Indians and the Battle to Inherit America," *American Indian Quarterly* 37, no. 3 (2013): 333–51.
13. Kyle Powys Whyte, "Indigenous Experience, Environmental Justice, and Settler Colonialism," in *Nature and Experience: Phenomenology and the Environment*, ed. B. Bannon (Lanham, MD: Rowman & Littlefield, 2016), 3.
14. For context on this period, see Benjamin Madley, *An American Genocide: The United States and the California Indian Catastrophe, 1846–1873* (New Haven, CT: Yale University Press, 2017); Lisbeth Haas, *Saints and Citizens: Indigenous Histories of Colonial Missions and Mexican California* (Berkeley: University of California Press, 2013); Leonard Pitt, *Decline of the Californios: A Social History of the Spanish-Speaking Californians, 1846–1890* (Berkeley: University of California Press, 1999).
15. Madley, *American Genocide*, esp. 35–68.

16. Madley, *American Genocide*, 27.

17. Madley, *American Genocide*, 3; James A. Sandos, *Converting California: Indians and Franciscans in the Missions* (New Haven, CT: Yale University Press, 2008), 14.

18. Madley, *American Genocide*, 34–35; Sandos, *Converting California*, 157.

19. Phoebe S. Kropp, *California Vieja: Culture and Memory in a Modern American Place* (Berkeley: University of California Press, 2006).

20. Owen H. O'Neill, *History of Santa Barbara County* (Santa Barbara: H.M. Meier, 1939), 203–35; Charles Nordhoff, *California: For Health, Pleasure, and Residence: A Book for Travellers and Settlers* (New York: Harper and Brothers, 1873).

21. Pitt, *Decline of the Californios*; Kevin Starr, *Americans and the California Dream, 1850–1915* (New York: Oxford University Press, 1986 [1973]).

22. O'Neill, *History of Santa Barbara County*, 231.

23. O'Neill, *History of Santa Barbara County*, 287.

24. Elmer Grey, "Architecture in Southern California," *Architectural Record* 17, no. 1 (January 1, 1905): 1.

25. Grey, "Architecture in Southern California," 2.

26. Grey, "Architecture in Southern California," 14–15.

27. A canonical text here is Henry Nash Smith, *Virgin Land: The American West as Symbol and Myth* (Cambridge, MA: Harvard University Press, 1971). See also Annette Kolodny, *The Lay of the Land: Metaphor as Experience and History in American Life and Letters* (Chapel Hill: University of North Carolina Press, 1984); William Cronon, "The Trouble with Wilderness: Or, Getting Back to the Wrong Nature," *Environmental History* 1, n. 1 (January 1996): 7–28; Roderick Nash, *Wilderness and the American Mind* (New Haven, CT: Yale University Press, 2014 [1967]), esp. 24–43.

28. Grey, "Architecture in Southern California," 15.

29. "Santa Barbara's Opportunity," typewritten speech, SBHC, SBHC Mss 1, Architectural Advisory Committee, Box 1, Folder Speeches.

30. Grey, "Architecture in Southern California," 15–17; William Bell Langsdorf Jr., "The Real Estate Boom of 1887 in Southern California" (master's thesis, Occidental College, 1932).

31. Kenneth L. Roberts, "California's War on Ugliness," *Saturday Evening Post*, July 10, 1926.

32. Henry H. Saylor, "Home Building on the Pacific Coast," or "The Emergence of a Definite and Distinctive Styles which Meets Climatic and Present Day Needs," *Gardeners and Home Builder*, December 1925.

33. See Patrick Wolfe, "Settler Colonialism and the Elimination of the Native," *Journal of Genocide Research* 8, no. 4 (2006): 387–409.

34. Henry S. Pritchett, "Earthquake Days in Santa Barbara," *Scribner's* 79 (1926): 593.

35. On the San Francisco earthquake, see Johanna L. Dyl, *Seismic City: An Environmental History of San Francisco's 1906 Earthquake* (Seattle: University of Washington Press, 2017); Kevin Rozario, *The Culture of Calamity: Disaster and the Making of Modern America* (Chicago: University of Chicago Press, 2007), esp. 67–74.

36. Arthur C. Alvarez, "The Santa Barbara Earthquake of June 29, 1925: Effects of Buildings of Various Types, Conclusions," *University of California Publications in Engineering* 2, no. 6 (November 17, 1925): 206.

37. "The Earthquake Havoc at Santa Barbara," *North China Herald and Supreme Court and Consular Gazette*, August 1, 1925, 101.

38. "Pictures by Wire," *Chicago Daily Tribune*, June 30, 1925, 1.

39. "Tremors Continue All Day," *New York Times*, June 30, 1925, 1.

40. Pritchett, "Earthquake Days in Santa Barbara," 594.

41. "Earthquake Disaster in America," *Daily Express*, June 30, 1925.

42. "Miss Julia Morgan's Account of the Earthquake," June 29, 1925, Earthquake Files, SBHC Mss 1, Series III, Box 1, CDCC.

43. "$30,000,000 Loss; 12 Known Dead as Quake Razes Santa Barbara," *Hartford Courant*, June 20, 1925, 1.

44. "$30,000,000 Loss," 1.

45. "Series of Earthquakes Wreck Business Center and Take Lives of Dozen in California City," *Atlantic Constitution*, June 30, 1925, 1.

46. "Earth Stretched, Yawned, Shook Buildings Down, Say Witnesses," *New York Herald Tribune*, June 30, 1925, 1.

47. Gertrude Wesselhoeft Hoffmann, "The Santa Barbara Earthquake," SBHC Mss 1, Subseries A, Community Arts Association Administrative Records, Box 11, Folder 5, CDCC.

48. "Building Ordinance of the City of Santa Barbara, California, Ordinance No. 1234," effective May 23, 1925; Vern Hedden, "Building Department Problems after the Santa Barbara Earthquake," *Bulletin of the Seismological Society of America* 15 (December 1925): 32.

49. S. Hurst Seager, "Santa Barbara Earthquake," *The Builder* (October 23, 1925), 601.

50. Kenneth L. Roberts, "California's War on Ugliness," *Saturday Evening Post*, July 10, 1926.

51. Earnest Elmo Calkins, "Beauty the New Business Tool," *Atlantic Monthly*, (August 1927), 145-156. For context on advertising in this period see Roland Marchand, *Advertising the American Dream: Making Way for Modernity, 1920-1940* (Berkeley: University of California Press, 1985).

52. Charles H. Cheney, "Architectural Control in Relation to Zoning," *Annals of the American Academy of Political and Social Science* 155 (May 1931): 162.

53. George W. Marson to Bernhard Hoffmann, July 10, 1925. City of Santa Barbara Records, Series 1, Subseries A, Architectural Advisory Committee Correspondence, Box 1, CDCC.

54. Joseph M. Siry, "The Architecture of Earthquake Resistance: Julius Kahn's Truscon Company and Frank Lloyd Wright's Imperial Hotel," *Journal of the Society of Architectural Historians* 67, no. 1 (March 2008): 96.

55. Louis H. Sullivan, "Reflections on the Tokyo Disaster," *Architectural Record* 55, no. 2 (February 1924): 114. For context, see Gregory K. Clancey, *Earthquake Nation: The Cultural Politics of Japanese Seismicity, 1868-1930* (Berkeley: University of California Press, 2006); Carola Hein, "Resilient Tokyo: Disaster and Transformation in the Japanese City," in *The Resilient City: How Modern Cities Recover from Disaster*, ed. Lawrence J. Vale and Thomas J. Campanella (Oxford: Oxford University Press, 2005), 213-34.

56. H. J., "The Earthquake in Japan," *Architects' Journal* 57, no. 1497 (September 12, 1923): 377.

57. "The Rebuilding of Japan," *American Architect and the Architectural Review*, October 10, 1923, 349.

58. W. A. Starrett, "Steel and Reinforced Concrete Structures Will Replace the Old Native Methods of Building in Japan," *Architecture* 48 (October 1923): 353.

59. W. G. Blake Murdoch, "Architecture in Japan," *Architects' Journal* 57, no. 1497 (September 12, 1923): 377.

60. Siry, "Architecture of Earthquake Resistance," 78.

61. For history of the commission and design, see Kathryn Smith, "Frank Lloyd Wright and the Imperial Hotel: A Postscript," *Art Bulletin* 67, no. 2 (June 1985): 296-310.

62. Smith, "Frank Lloyd Wright and the Imperial Hotel," 168.

63. Sullivan, "Reflections on the Tokyo Disaster," 115-17.

NOTES TO PAGES 31–39

64. Typewritten speech, c. 1925, City of Santa Barbara Records, Series 1, Subseries A, Architectural Advisory Committee, Box 2, CDCC.

65. Cheney, "Architectural Control in Relation to Zoning," 164–65.

66. Cheney, "Architectural Control in Relation to Zoning," 162.

67. Bernhard Hoffmann to T. W. Dibblee, August 24, 1925, City of Santa Barbara Records, Series 1, Subseries A, Architectural Advisory Committee Box 1, CDCC.

68. Except for the Union Oil service station, all structures listed are currently standing.

69. Pearl Chase to R. J. Timmons, April 2, 1936, Plans and Planting Committee Records SBHC Mss 1, Series 1, Subseries A, Outgoing Correspondence Box 8, Folder January–June 1936, CDCC.

70. Pearl Chase to P. J. Sullivan, June 29, 1936, Plans and Planting Committee Records SBHC Mss 1, Series 1, Subseries A, Outgoing Correspondence Box 8, Folder January–June 1936, CDCC.

71. "Worth of Beauty," letter to the editor, c. 1926, SBHC Mss 1, Series III, Subject Files, Earthquakes, Box 1, Clippings, CDCC.

72. Samuel P. Hays, *Conservation and the Gospel of Efficiency: The Progressive Conservation Movement, 1890–1920* (Pittsburgh, PA: University of Pittsburgh Press, 1999 [1959]).

73. "Good Architecture," *California Southland*, November 1926, 26.

74. M. Urmy Seares, "A Community Approaches Its Ideals," *California Arts and Architecture*, June 1930, 20.

75. C. M. Glover to Bernhard Hoffmann, July 13, 1925, SBHC Mss 1, Series 1, Subseries A, Architectural Advisory Committee, Box 2, Folder 1925.

76. Carey McWilliams, *Southern California: An Island on the Land* (Santa Barbara, CA: Peregrine Smith, 1973 [1946]), 86.

77. For surveys of Asian Americans in the United States, particularly in the American West, see Connie Y. Chiang, *Nature behind Barbed Wire: An Environmental History of the Japanese American Incarceration* (Oxford: Oxford University Press, 2018); Stuart C. Miller, *The Unwelcome Immigrant: The American Image of the Chinese* (Berkeley: University of California Press, 1969); Sucheng Chan, *This Bittersweet Soil: The Chinese in California Agriculture, 1860–1910* (Berkeley: University of California Press, 1986); Erika Lee, *At America's Gates: Chinese Immigration during the Exclusion Era, 1882–1943* (Chapel Hill: University of North Carolina Press, 2004); Jan Lin, *Reconstructing Chinatown: Ethnic Enclave, Global Change* (Minneapolis: University of Minnesota Press, 1998); Nayan Shah, *Contagious Divides: Epidemics and Race in San Francisco's Chinatown* (Berkeley: University of California Press, 2001).

78. Bailey Willis, "A Study of the Santa Barbara Earthquake," *Bulletin of the Seismological Society of America* 15 (December 1925), 258.

79. Oliver Towne, "Bigger and Better Than Ever," *Los Angeles Times*, August 30, 1925, 11.

80. "New Santa Barbara Earthquake Proof," *China Press*, February 6, 1926, 13.

81. "Santa Barbara Is Now One of the Safest Places," *Boston Daily Globe*, July 2, 1925, A24.

82. "Santa Barbara's Loss Was Due to Jerry Building," *New York Herald Tribune*, September 5, 1926, C22.

83. "Santa Barbara to Celebrate," *Los Angeles Times*, June 29, 1926, A10.

84. Thomas Tallmadge, *The Story of Architecture in America* (New York: W. W. Norton, 1936), 118. See also Keith Eggener, "Nationalism, Internationalism, and the 'Naturalisation' of Modern Architecture in the United States, 1925–1940," *National Identities* 8 (September 2006): 243–58; David Gebhard, "The Spanish Colonial Revival in Southern California (1895–1930)," *Journal of the Society of Architectural Historians* 26, no. 2 (May 1967): 131. Matthew Bokovoy, *The San Diego World's Fairs and Southwestern Memory, 1880–1940* (Albuquerque: University of New Mexico

Press, 2005); William Deverell, *Whitewashed Adobe: The Rise of Los Angeles and the Remaking of Its Mexican Past* (Berkeley: University of California Press, 2004); Kropp, *California Vieja*; Carpio, "Zorro Down Under." On ideas of Anglo-Saxon, see Duncan Bell, *Dreamworlds of Race: Empire and the Utopian Destiny of Anglo-America* (Princeton, NJ: Princeton University Press, 2020), 29.

85. On settler colonialism in the West Coast in this period, see Henry Knight Lozano, *California & Hawai'i Bound: U.S. Settler Colonialism and the Pacific West, 1848–1959*.

86. Tallmadge, *Story of Architecture in America*, 119.

87. Sheldon Cheney, *New World Architecture* (London: Green, 1930), 268–70.

88. Reginald D. Johnson, "The Development of Architectural Styles in California," *California Southland*, August 1926, 7–8.

89. Typewritten speech titled "Santa Barbara's Opportunity," n.d., SBHC Mss 1, Series 1, Subseries A, Architectural Advisory Committee Records, Box 1, CDCC.

90. Cited in Charles H. Cheney, "Preface," in *California Architecture in Santa Barbara*, ed. H. Philip Staats (New York: Architectural, 1929), iv.

91. "Quake Shaken City Rebuilds in One Year," *Los Angeles Examiner*, June 27, 1926, 7.

92. Charles Lummis, "Two Years Later and So You Did Queenly My Santa Barbara," Community Arts Association Records, Series 1, Subseries A, Administrative Files, Box 5, Folder 1, CDCC.

93. Roy W. Cheesman, "An Open Letter to the Merchants of Santa Barbara," April 30, 1941, SBHC Mss 1, Series 1, Subseries A, Santa Barbara Chamber of Commerce Records, Box 10, CDCC; *Survey Graphic*, March 1940.

94. Typewritten text, "A Five Year Promotion Program for Santa Barbara County," 1940, SBHC Mss 1, Series 1, Subseries A, Santa Barbara Chamber of Commerce, Box 10, CDCC.

Chapter Two

1. Alexis de Tocqueville, *Democracy in America*, ed. J. P. Mayer, trans. George Lawrence (Garden City, NY: Doubleday Anchor, 1969 [1835–40]), 513.

2. Charles Lummis, *Stand Fast, Santa Barbara* (Santa Barbara, CA: Community Arts Association, 1923), n.p.

3. Megan Black, *The Global Interior: Mineral Frontiers and American Power* (Cambridge, MA: Harvard University Press, 2018), 32–39. On US conservation history, see Stephen Fox, *The American Conservation Movement: John Muir and His Legacy* (Madison: University of Wisconsin Press, 1986); Samuel P. Hays, *Conservation and the Gospel of Efficiency: The Progressive Conservation Movement, 1890–1920* (Cambridge, MA: Harvard University Press, 1959); Roderick Nash, *Wilderness and the American Mind* (New Haven, CT: Yale University Press, 1967); Sarah T. Phillips, *This Land, This Nation: Conservation, Rural America, and the New Deal* (New York: Cambridge University Press, 2007); Susan R. Schrepfer, *The Right to Save the Redwoods: A History of Environmental Reform, 1917–1978* (Madison: University of Wisconsin Press, 2001); Benjamin H. Johnson, *Escaping the Dark, Gray City: Fear and Hope in Progressive-Era Conservation* (New Haven, CT: Yale University Press, 2017); Elizabeth Grennan Browning, *Nature's Laboratory: Environmental Thought and Labor Radicalism in Chicago, 1886-1937* (Baltimore: Johns Hopkins University Press, 2022); Miles A. Powell, *Vanishing America: Species Extinction, Racial Peril, and the Origins of Conservation* (Cambridge, MA: Harvard University Press, 2016).

4. On Theodore Roosevelt and national expansion, see Gary Gerstle, "Theodore Roosevelt and the Divided Character of American Nationalism," *Journal of American History* 86, no. 3

NOTES TO PAGES 44–50

(1999): 1280–1307; Gary Gerstle, *American Crucible: Race and Nation in the Twentieth Century* (Princeton, NJ: Princeton University Press, 2017).

5. On masculinity and Roosevelt's place in conservation, see William Cronon, "The Trouble with Wilderness," in *Uncommon Ground: Rethinking the Human Place in Nature*, ed. William Cronon (New York: W. W. Norton, 1996). For Roosevelt's relationship to race and nationalism, see Gary Gerstle, *American Crucible*.

6. Lummis, *Stand Fast, Santa Barbara*.

7. Amy Kaplan, "Manifest Domesticity," *American Literature* 70, no. 3 (September 1998): 581–606.

8. Kyle Whyte, "Indigenous Experience, Environmental Justice, and Settler Colonialism," in *Nature and Experience: Phenomenology and the Environment*, ed. B. Bannon (Lanham, MD: Rowman & Littlefield, 2016), 157–74.

9. Karen E. Altman, "Consuming Ideology: The Better Homes in America Campaign," *Critical Studies in Mass Communication* 7, no. 3 (1990): 287.

10. Kaplan, "Manifest Domesticity," 585.

11. Powell, *Vanishing America*, 24–28.

12. Evan McKenzie, *Privatopia: Homeowner Associations and the Rise of Residential Private Government* (New Haven, CT: Yale University Press, 1996); Marc A. Weiss, *The Rise of the Community Builders: The American Real Estate Industry and Urban Planning* (New York: Columbia University Press, 1987).

13. Louis Hyman, *Debtor Nation: The History of America in Red Ink* (Princeton, NJ: Princeton University Press, 2011).

14. W. Carey McWilliams, *The Idea of Fraternity in America* (Berkeley: University of California Press, 1973), 509.

15. McWilliams, *Idea of Fraternity in America*, 512.

16. Stuart A. Queen, "What Is a Community?" *Social Forces* 1, no. 4 (1923): 375.

17. E. T. Hiller, "The Community as a Social Group," *American Sociological Review* 6, no. 2 (April 1941): 189.

18. Quoted in Miranda Joseph, *Against the Romance of Community* (Minneapolis: University of Minnesota Press, 2002), vii–ix.

19. This analysis is based on Iris Marion Young, "The Ideal of Community and the Politics of Difference," *Social Theory and Practice* 12, no. 1 (Spring 1986): 1–26 and Audre Lorde "The Master's Tools will Never Dismantle the Master's House" in *Sister Outsider: Essays and Speeches* (Berkeley: Crossing Press, 1984), 110-114.

20. Young, "Ideal of Community," 1–2.

21. Etienne Balibar, "Racism as Universalism," *New Political Science* 8, nos. 1–2 (1989): 9–22.

22. Stuart Schrader, "Against the Romance of Community Policing," *Stuart Schrader* (blog), https://stuartschrader.com/blog/against-romance-community-policing, accessed May 20, 2020.

23. Thomas Bender, *Community and Social Change in America* (New Brunswick, NJ: Rutgers University Press, 1978), 67.

24. "Population of California by Minor Civil Divisions," *Census Bulletin* 134 (November 2, 1891).

25. Lee M. A. Simpson, *Selling the City: Gender, Class, and the California Growth Machine* (Stanford, CA: Stanford University Press, 2004), 51.

26. Charles Loring Brace, *The New West: Or, California in 1867–1868* (New York: G. P. Putnam & Son, 1869), 355.

27. George Wharton James, *Through Ramona's Country* (Boston: Little, Brown, 1908), 375.

28. Charles Mulford Robinson, "A Report on the Civic Improvement and Beautification of Santa Barbara, California" (Santa Barbara, CA: Printed for the Civic League by the Independent, 1909), n.p.

29. Charles Lummis, *Stand Fast, Santa Barbara* (Santa Barbara, CA: Community Arts Association, 1923), n.p.

30. Jon A. Peterson, *The Birth of City Planning in the United States, 1840-1917* (Baltimore: Johns Hopkins University Press, 2003), 108–9.

31. Ellen K. Knowles, "A Unifying Vision: Improvement, Imagination, and Bernhard Hoffmann of Stockbridge (New England) and Santa Barbara (New Spain)" (master's thesis, University of Southern California, 2011), 37–43.

32. On Craig, see Pamela Skewes-Cox and Robert L. Sweeney, *Spanish Colonial Style: Santa Barbara and the Architecture of James Osborne Craig and Mary McLaughlin Craig* (New York: Rizzoli, 2015).

33. For literature on the history of historic preservation in the United States, see Miles Glendinning, *The Conservation Movement: A History of Architectural Preservation* (London: Routledge, 2013); Daniel Bluestone, *Buildings, Landscapes, and Memory: Case Studies in Historic Preservation* (New York: W. W. Norton, 2011); Max Page and Randall Mason, *Giving Preservation a History: Histories of Historic Preservation in the United States* (London: Routledge, 2004); Robert E. Stripe, ed., *A Richer Heritage: Historic Preservation in the Twenty-First Century* (Chapel Hill: University of North Carolina Press, 2003); David Lowenthal, *The Past Is a Foreign Country* (Cambridge: Cambridge University Press, 1999).

34. Roxanne M. Barker, "Small Town Progressivism: Pearl Chase and Female Activism in Santa Barbara, California, 1911–1918," *Southern California Quarterly* 79, no. 1 (Spring 1997): 49.

35. Curtis J. Sitomer, "Octogenarian 'Pearl' Still Serving Community," *Christian Science Monitor*, November 15, 1971, 17.

36. Quoted in Simpson, *Selling the City*, 1.

37. Simpson, *Selling the City*, 111.

38. Henry H. Saylor, "Home Building on the Pacific Coast: The Emergence of a Definite and Distinctive Style Which Meets Climatic and Present-Day Needs," *Gardener and Home Builder*, December 1925.

39. Anthony King, *The Bungalow: The Production of a Global Culture* (Oxford: Oxford University Press, 1994).

40. Gustav Stickley, "Nature and Art in California," *Craftsman* 6, no. 4 (July 1904): 370.

41. Stickley, "Nature and Art in California," 371.

42. Helen Lukens Gaut, "Two Typical California Houses Showing Vigor and Originality in Plan and Construction," *Craftsman* 17, no. 4 (January 1910): 436.

43. William H. Whyte, *The Last Landscape* (Philadelphia: University of Pennsylvania Press, 2002), esp. 15–53; McKenzie, *Privatopia*, esp. 106–121.

44. Bernhard Hoffmann to Robert B. Canfield, April 18, 1922, SBHC Mss 1, Series 1, Subseries A, Community Arts Association Records, Plans and Planting Branch Files, Correspondence, Box 1, Folder January–April 1922, CDCC.

45. "The Morning Press Platform," *Santa Barbara News-Press*, July 2, 1926, 4. For context, see J. C. Nichols, "Housing the Real Estate Problem," *Annals of the American Academy of Political and Social Science* 51 (January 1914): 132–39; McKenzie, *Privatopia*; Marc A. Weiss, *The Rise of the Community Builders: The American Real Estate Industry and Urban Planning* (New York: Columbia University Press, 1987); Michael Jones-Correa, "The Origins and Diffusion of Racial Restrictive Covenants," *Political Science Quarterly* (Winter 2000–2001): 541–68; Luisa Godinez

NOTES TO PAGES 53-58

Puig, "White Fortressing: How Racial Threat and Conservatism Lead to the Formation of Local Governments," *Urban Affairs Review* 60, n. 1 (January 2024): 16-48.

46. "Planning a City for the Future," *Santa Barbara News-Press*, July 2, 1926, 4.

47. "Housing Conditions in Section of This City Are Not as Ideal as Citizens Generally Believe," *Santa Barbara Morning Press*, June 6, 1920, 11.

48. See Christopher Capozzola, *Uncle Sam Wants You: World War I and the Making of the Modern American Citizen* (Oxford: Oxford University Press, 2008), esp. 6–11.

49. See, for example, Sarah E. Igo, *The Averaged American* (Cambridge, MA: Harvard University Press, 2007).

50. Community Arts Association brochure, c. 1925, SBHC Mss 1, Series 1, Subseries A, Community Arts Association, Administrative Records, Box 11, CDCC. "Well Done, Santa Barbara," *American Magazine of Art* 22, no. 2 (February 1931): 143.

51. "First Report to Carnegie before Receiving Grant," c. 1922, SBHC Mss 1, Series 1, Subseries A, Community Arts Association, Administrative Records, Box 11, CDCC. "Community Arts Association of Santa Barbara: The First Decade, 1920–1930," SBHC Mss 1, Series 1, Subseries A, Community Arts Association, Administrative Records, Box 19, CDCC. Bernhard Hoffmann to Mrs. Linn, March 2, 1922, SBHC Mss 1, Series 1, Subseries A, Community Arts Association, Plans and Planting Branch Files, Correspondence, Box 1, January–April 1922.

52. "The Community Arts of Santa Barbara," *American Magazine of Art* 18, no. 2 (February 1927): 92.

53. Mary Parker Follett, *The New State: Group Organization and the Solution of Popular Government* (New York: Longmans, Green, and Co., 1918), 223–24. For a contrasting perspective on the formation of political groups, see Doug McAdam, *Political Process and the Development of Black Insurgency, 1930–1970* (Chicago: University of Chicago Press, 1982); and Erin Pineda, *Seeing Like an Activist: Civil Disobedience and the Civil Rights Movement* (New York: Oxford University Press, 2021).

54. For women involved in municipal actions before suffrage, see Adam Rome, "'Political Hermaphrodites': Gender and Environmental Reform in Progressive America," *Environmental History* 11, no. 3 (July 2006): 440–63; also Karen J. Blair, *The Clubwoman as Feminist: True Womanhood Redefined, 1868–1914* (New York: Holmes & Meier, 1980); Anne M. Boylan, *The Origins of Women's Activism: New York and Boston, 1797–1840* (Chapel Hill: University of North Carolina Press, 2002); Alison Isenberg, *Downtown America: A History of the Place and the People Who Made It* (Chicago: University of Chicago Press, 2004); Carolyn Merchant, "Women of the Progressive Conservation Movement, 1900–1916," *Environmental Review: ER* 8, no. 1 (Spring 1984): 57–85; Daphne Spain, *How Women Saved the City* (Minneapolis: University of Minnesota Press, 2001); Camilla Stivers, *Bureau Men, Settlement Women: Constructing Public Administration in the Progressive Era* (Lawrence: University Press of Kansas, 2002); Nancy Unger, *Beyond Nature's Housekeepers: American Women in Environmental History* (New York: Oxford University Press, 2012).

55. Mary Ritter Beard, *Women's Work in Municipalities* (New York: D. Appleton, 1915).

56. Follett, *New State*, 223–24.

57. Follett, *New State*, 202.

58. Follett, *New State*, 195–96.

59. "The Community Arts Association of Santa Barbara: The First Decade, 1920–1930," SBHC Mss 1, Series 1, Subseries A, Community Arts Association, Administrative Records, Box 11, CDCC.

60. "The Community Arts Association of Santa Barbara: The First Decade, 1920–1930," SBHC Mss 1, Series 1, Subseries A, Community Arts Association, Administrative Records, Box 11, CDCC.

61. Isenberg, *Downtown America*, 6.

62. John Merriam (president, Carnegie Institution of Washington) to James R. Angell, May 24, 1921; Elizabeth A. Alexander to Frederick Keppel, March 24, 1926. Carnegie Corporation of New York, Grant Files III.A, Box 208, Rare Book and Manuscript Library, Columbia University (hereafter cited as CCNY). *Carnegie Corporation of New York: Report of the Acting President, Year Ended September 30, 1923* (New York: 522 Fifth Avenue, 1923), 53. For background on Andrew Carnegie and Carnegie Corporation activities, see Stephen Wertheim, *Tomorrow the World: The Birth of U.S. Global Supremacy* (Cambridge, MA: Harvard University Press, 38–39); Duncan Bell, *Dreamworlds of Race: Empire and the Utopian Destiny of Ango-America* (Princeton: Princeton University Press, 2020); Oliver Zunz, *Philanthropy in America: A History* (Princeton, NJ: Princeton University Press, 2012), esp. 22–26.

63. "Community Arts Association of Santa Barbara, 5/9/44," Grant Files, Series III.A, Box 120, CCNY; "Community Building in Santa Barbara, California," *Christian Science Monitor*, October 1, 1925; *Carnegie Corporation of New York* (1923), 53, 55.

64. H. I. Brock, "A Modern Haven of the 'Humanities,'" *New York Times Magazine*, May 17, 1925, 8.

65. On Carnegie activities in supporting libraries, see Abigail Van Slyck, *Free to All: Carnegie Libraries and American Culture, 1890–1920* (Chicago: University of Chicago Press, 1995).

66. *Carnegie Corporation of New York* (1923), 53–54.

67. *Carnegie Corporation of New York*, 55.

68. Statement of the History of the MacDowell Association, sent with Howard Mansfield to Henry S. Pritchett, April 20, 1920, 2. Carnegie Corporation of New York Records, Grant Files III.A, Box 208, CCNY.

69. Edwin Carty Ranck, "The MacDowell Colony at Peterborough," *Musical Quarterly* 6, no. 1 (January 1920): 25.

70. "Peterborough: The Edward MacDowell Memorial Colony," *American Magazine of Art* 8, no. 10 (August 1917): 396.

71. Edwin Arlington Robinson, "The Peterborough Idea," *North American Review* 204, no. 730 (September 1916): 451.

72. Brock, "Modern Haven of the 'Humanities,'" 8.

73. For more on the revival of medievalism in this period, see T. J. Jackson Lears, *No Place of Grace: Antimodernism and the Transformation of American Culture, 1880–1920* (New York: Pantheon, 1981). Brock, "Modern Haven of the 'Humanities,'" 8.

74. Henry S. Pritchett, "The Meaning of a Community Arts Association," *California Southland*, July–August 1925.

75. Pritchett, "Meaning of a Community Arts Association."

76. Henry Pritchett to Rosenwald Foundation, March 1932, SBHC Mss 1, Series 1, Subseries A, Community Arts Association, Administrative Records, Box 11, Folder 1, CDCC.

77. Community Arts Association Bulletin, April 1925, SBHC Mss 1, Series 1, Subseries A, Community Arts Association Administrative Records, Box 3, Folder 2, CDCC.

78. Edward Sajous, "How a Community Arts Association Is Raising Architectural Standards," *American City*, July 1923, 39; Hamilton McFadden, "Community Arts Association, Santa Barbara, Calif.," *American Magazine of Art* 15, no. 6 (July 1924): 301.

79. Sajous, "How a Community Arts Association Is Raising Architectural Standards," 39.

80. Edward F. Brown, "Does Beauty Pay?" *American City*, February 1924, 165.

81. Bernhard Hoffmann to F. F. Peabody, April 14, 1922, SBHC Mss 1, Series 1, Subseries A,

Community Arts Association Records, Plans and Planting Branch Files, Correspondence, Box 1, January–April 1922, CDCC.

82. Bernhard Hoffmann to Charles H. Cheney, April 4, 1929, Carnegie Corporation of New York Records, Grant Files III.A, Box 120, CCNY.

83. Carleton Monroe Winslow and Edward Fisher Brown, *Small House Designs: Collected by the Community Arts Association of Santa Barbara, California* (Santa Barbara, CA: Community Arts Association of Santa Barbara, 1924), 7.

84. Winslow and Brown, *Small House Designs*, 36–37.

85. Pearl Chase, "From Adobe to Glass, a Review of Housing in Santa Barbara," n.d., SBHC Mss 1, Series 1, Subseries A, Community Arts Association Records, Plants and Planting Branch Files, Correspondence, Outgoing Chronological Box 1, 1924, CDCC.

86. Winslow and Brown, *Small House Designs*, 7; McFadden, "Community Arts Association, Santa Barbara, Calif.," 301.

87. Winslow and Brown, *Small House Designs*, 8.

88. Brown, "Does Beauty Pay?," 166.

89. "Report of the Community Arts Association of Santa Barbara to the Carnegie Corporation of New York for the Year October 1, 1925, through September 30, 1926," SBHC Mss 1, Series 1, Subseries A, Community Arts Association, Administrative Records, Box 11, Folder 6, CDCC.

90. C. Henry Hathaway to Plans and Planting Branch, November 24, 1926, SBHC Mss 1, Series 1, Subseries A, Community Arts Association, Plans and Planting Branch Records, Correspondence, Incoming, Box 3, Folder 1926, CDCC.

91. R. E. Harsey to Community Arts Association, January 16, 1927, SBHC Mss 1, Series 1, Subseries A, Community Arts Association, Plans and Planting Branch Records, Correspondence, Incoming, Box 3, Folder 1927, CDCC.

92. Letter from American Building Association to Community Arts Association, October 24, 1924; Letter from The White Company, Havana, Cuba, to Community Arts Association, June 9, 1924; Department of Agriculture, Canada, to Community Arts Association, July 14, 1924, SBHC Mss 1, Series 1, Subseries A, Community Arts Association, Plans and Planting Branch Records, Chronological Box 1, 1924, CDCC.

93. Helen Spotts to the Home Planning Service Bureau, September 27, 1924, SBHC Mss 1, Series 1, Subseries A, Community Arts Association, Plans and Planting Branch Records, Correspondence, Outgoing, Chronological Box 1, 1924, CDCC.

94. Pearl Chase to James Ford, August 13, 1931, SBHC Mss 1, Series 1, Subseries A, Better Homes in America Records, Box 10, Folder 1, CDCC.

95. Bernhard Hoffmann to Frederick P. Keppel, December 24, 1927, SBHC Mss 1, Series 1, Subseries A, Community Arts Association, Administrative Files, Box 11, CDCC.

96. Bernhard Hoffmann to Allison Owen, November 1, 1926, SBHC Mss 1, Series 1, Subseries A, Community Arts Association Records, Plans and Planting Branch Files, Correspondence, Outgoing Box 2, CDCC.

97. Irving Morrow, "A Step in California's Architecture," *Architect and Engineer* 70, no. 2 (August 1922): 48–49.

98. Christine Turner Curtis, "Community Arts Association, Santa Barbara," *Overland Monthly and Out West Magazine* 83, no. 5 (May 1925): 220.

99. Janet Hutchinson, "The Cure for Domestic Neglect: Better Homes in America, 1922–1935," *Perspectives in Vernacular Architecture* 2 (1986): 168; "Better Homes in America," *Delineator* 101, no. 2 (September 1922): 1. Other sources on Better Homes in America include Karen

Altman, "Consuming Ideology: The Better Homes in America Campaign," *Critical Studies in Mass Communication* 7 (1990): 286–307; Jeffrey M. Hornstein, *A Nation of Realtors: A Cultural History of the Twentieth-Century American Middle Class* (Durham, NC: Duke University Press, 2005), 118–55; Jonathan Massey, "Risk and Regulation in the Financial Architecture of American Houses," in *Governing by Design: Architecture, Economy and Politics in the Twentieth Century*, ed. (Pittsburgh: University of Pittsburgh Press, 2013), 21–46.

100. Dolores Hayden, "Revisiting the Sitcom Suburbs," *Race, Poverty, and the Environment* 9, no. 1 (Summer 2002): 39. Hutchinson, "Cure for Domestic Neglect," 173.

101. Massey, "Risk and Regulation in the Financial Architecture of American Houses," 25.

102. Hutchison, "Cure for Domestic Neglect," 178.

103. Janet Hutchison, "Building for *Babbitt*: The State and Suburban Home Ideal," *Journal of Policy History*, 185–91.

104. "A Force for a Better America," *Delineator* 104, no. 6 (June 1924): 2. On the politics behind BHA, see Manisha Claire, "The Latent Racism of the Better Homes in America Program," *JSTOR Daily*, February 26, 2020, https://daily.jstor.org/the-latent-racism-of-the-better-homes-in-america-program/, accessed February 15, 2024.

105. Better Homes in America, *Guidebook of Better Homes in America: How to Organize the 1926 Campaign* (Washington: Better Homes in America, 1926), 7.

106. "Report of the Better Homes Committee, 1925," SBHC Mss 1, Series 1, Subseries A, Better Homes in America Records, Box 1, CDCC.

107. Better Homes in America, *Guidebook of Better Homes in America*, 4.

108. James Ford, "Introduction," in *The Better Homes Manual*, ed. Blanche Halbert (Chicago: University of Chicago Press, 1931).

109. From Better Homes in America, "Statements by Members of the Advisory Council of Better Homes in America," SBHC Mss 1, Series 1, Subseries A, Better Homes in America, Box 1, CDCC.

110. "Report of Better Homes Week, Santa Barbara, Calif."; "Houses for Inspection, Better Homes Week, May 10–17," SBHC Mss 1, Series 1, Subseries A, Better Homes in America, Box 1, CDCC.

111. C. M. Andera, "Dedication of Demonstration House, May 10, 1925," SBHC Mss 1, Series 1, Subseries A, Better Homes in America Records, Box 1, CDCC.

112. "Memorandum No. 1 to 1928 Chairmen, The Demonstration Home," SBHC Mss 1, Series 1, Subseries A, Better Homes in America Records, Box 10, CDCC.

113. "Comments on House B, 821 West Valerio," SBHC Mss 1, Series 1, Subseries A, Better Homes in America Records, Box 1, CDCC. For more context on the homes, see Valerie Smith, "The Small House Movement of the 1920s: Preserving 'Better' Houses" (master's thesis, Columbia University, 2022).

114. Report on 1926 Better Homes Week, SBHC Mss 1, Series 1, Subseries A, Better Homes in America Records, Box 1, CDCC.

115. Better Homes in America, *Guidebook of Better Homes in America*, 11–12.

116. Report of the Health Department, 1919, SBHC Mss 1, Series 1, Subseries A, Community Arts Association Records, Administrative Records, Box 1, CDCC.

117. Grace Ruth Southwich to Pearl Chase, May 19, 1925, SBHC Mss 1, Series 1, Subseries A, Better Homes in America Records, Box 8, CDCC.

118. "The Story of Demonstration House No. 3," SBHC Mss 1, Series 1, Subseries A, Better Homes in America Records, Box 1, CDCC.

119. Janet Hutchison, "Better Homes and Gullah," *Agricultural History* 67, no. 2 (Spring 1993): 107.

NOTES TO PAGES 73–77   187

120. African American and Black Historic Context Statement, Prepared for the City of Santa Barbara, August 2022, 38, https://santabarbaraca.gov/sites/default/files/filesync/Advisory_Groups/Historic_Landmarks_Commission/Archive/2022_Archives/03_Staff_Reports/2022-08-31_August_31_2022_Item_1_Final_Draft_African_American_and_Black_Historic_Context_Statement.pdf, accessed February 1, 2023.

121. "Revised Declaration of Conditions, Covenants, and Charges Affecting the Real Property Known as Hope Ranch Park," 1924, SBHC Mss 1, Series 1, Subseries B, Box 14, Folder Santa Barbara Estates, CDCC.

122. Better Homes in America, *Guidebook for Better Homes Campaign*, 41–43.

123. Better Homes in America, *Guidebook for Better Homes Campaigns*, 19.

124. Hutchison, "Building for *Babbitt*," 203.

125. "First Report to Carnegie before Receiving Grant," SBHC Mss 1, Series 1, Subseries A, Community Arts Association Records, Administrative Records, Box 11, CDCC.

126. "Report of the Activities of the Plans and Planting Committee of the Community Arts Association, February 1, 1922–February 1, 1923," SBHC Mss 1, Series 1, Subseries A, Community Arts Association Records, Plans and Planting Branch Files, Administrative Records, Box 2 CDCC.

Chapter Three

1. Richard Hofstadter, *The Age of Reform* (New York: Knopf, 1955), 36.

2. "Santa Barbara's Most Important Tree," *Santa Cruz Sentinel*, June 28, 1955; "Santa Barbara Boasts Biggest Tree of Its Kind," *Los Angeles Times*, February 24, 1946, A2; "Santa Barbara's Famous Landmark Escapes Ax," *Los Angeles Times*, October 16, 1935, 8.

3. Maunsell Van Rensselaer, *Trees of Santa Barbara* (Santa Barbara, CA: Santa Barbara Botanic Garden, 1940), v; Merritt B. Pratt, *Shade and Ornamental Trees of California* (Sacramento: California State Board of Forestry, 1921).

4. Francesco Franceschi, *Santa Barbara Exotic Flora* (Santa Barbara, CA: n.p., 1895), 41–42. On the transportation of plants from the nineteenth to the early twentieth centuries, see Luke Keogh, *The Wardian Case: How a Simple Box Moved Plants and Changed the World* (Chicago: University of Chicago Press, 2020) and Gary Y. Okihiro, *Pineapple Culture: A History of Tropical and Temperate Zones* (Berkeley: University of California Press, 2009). For botanical exchanges between Australia and the United States, see Ian Tyrrell, *True Gardens of the Gods: Californian-Australian Environmental Reform, 1860–1930* (Berkeley: University of California Press, 1999).

5. Van Rensselaer, *Trees of Santa Barbara*, 14.

6. M. C. Nordhoff, "The Value of a Community Arts Association," *California Southland*, September 1925, 12.

7. Steven Stoll, "Insects and Institutions: University Science and the Fruit Business in California," *Agricultural History* 69, no. 2 (Spring 1995): 228–29.

8. Charles E. Randall and D. Priscilla Edgerton, "Famous Trees," *United States Department of Agriculture, Miscellaneous Publication* 295 (June 1938): 1.

9. Leila Weekes-Wilson, *Santa Barbara, California* (Santa Barbara, CA: Pacific Coast, 1919), 97.

10. Weekes-Wilson, *Santa Barbara, California*, 98; for context on trees as national symbols, particularly in the nineteenth-century United States, see Jared Farmer, "Taking Liberties with Historic Trees," *Journal of American History* 104, no. 4 (March 2019): 815–42; Jared Farmer, "Witness to a Hanging: California's Haunted Trees," *BOOM: A Journal of California* 3, no. 1 (Spring

2013): 70–79; Max Page, *The Creative Destruction of Manhattan, 1900–1940* (Chicago: University of Chicago Press, 2001), esp. 177–213; Kevin Waite, "The 'Lost Cause' Goes West," *California History* 97, no. 1 (2020): 33–49.

11. Jared Farmer, *Trees in Paradise: A California History* (New York: W. W. Norton, 2013).

12. Randall and Edgerton, "Famous Trees," 1. See also Daegan Miller, *This Radical Land: A Natural History of American Dissent* (Chicago: University of Chicago Press, 2018), esp. 105–12 and 161–212.

13. For an early modern account of trees as a natural resource, see John Evelyn, *Sylva* (Menston: Scolar, 1972 [1664]).

14. Randall and Edgerton, "Famous Trees," 1.

15. For one aspect of the process of these transfers, see Keogh, *Wardian Case*.

16. Elizabeth A. Logan, "Sweet Peas of Civility: The Cultural Politics of Environment in California, 1848–1915," *California History* 92, no. 2 (August 2015): 4–21; Elizabeth A. Logan, "Urbane Bouquets: A Floricultural History of California, 1848 to 1915" (PhD diss., University of Southern California, 2013); Christine Macy and Sarah Bonnemason, *Architecture and Nature: Creating the American Landscape* (London: Routledge, 2003).

17. Robert Wiebe, *The Search for Order, 1877–1920* (New York: Hill and Wang, 1967); Alan Trachtenberg, *The Incorporation of America: Culture and Society in the Gilded Age* (New York: Hill and Wang, 1982); Olivier Zunz, *Making America Corporate, 1870–1920* (Chicago: University of Chicago Press, 1990).

18. Adam Rome, "'Political Hermaphrodites': Gender and Environmental Reform in Progressive America," *Environmental History* 11, no. 3 (July 2006): 440–63; Carolyn Merchant, "Women of the Progressive Conservation Movement, 1900–1916," *Environmental Review* (1984): 57–85; Nancy Unger, *Beyond Nature's Housekeepers: American Women in Environmental History*; Ted Moore, "Democratizing the Art: The Salt Lake Women's Chamber of Commerce and Air Pollution, 1936–1945," *Environmental History* 12, no. 1 (January 2007): 80–106; Ben A. Minteer, *The Landscape of Reform: Civic Pragmatism and Environmental Thought in America* (Cambridge, MA: MIT Press, 2006).

19. Alfred James McClatchie, "Eucalypts Cultivated in the United States," *USDA Bureau of Forestry Bulletin* 35, (Washington, DC: Government Printing Office, 1902), 14–15; Ellwood Cooper, *Forest Culture and Eucalyptus Trees* (San Francisco: Cubery, 1876), 17; Farmer, *Trees in Paradise*, 124; Robin W. Doughty, *The Eucalyptus: A Natural and Commercial History of the Gum Tree* (Baltimore, MD: Johns Hopkins University Press, 2000), 24; Abbot Kinney, *Eucalyptus* (Los Angeles: B. R. Baumgardt, 1895), 138; Viola Lockhart Warren, "The Eucalyptus Crusade," *Southern California Quarterly* 44, no. 1 (March 1962): 31–42; Ian R. Tyrrell, *True Gardens of the Gods: Californian-Australian Environmental Reform, 1860–1930* (Berkeley: University of California Press, 1999), 57–83.

20. Tyrrell, *True Gardens of the Gods*, 57.

21. Kinney, *Eucalyptus*, 131–54.

22. McClatchie, "Eucalypts Cultivated in the United States," 3.

23. Rebecca J. H. Woods, *The Herds Shot Round the World: Native Breeds and the British Empire, 1800–1900* (Chapel Hill: University of North Carolina Press, 2017), chap. 2. For transfers of plant and animal life before the formulation of acclimatization, see Alfred W. Crosby Jr., *The Columbian Exchange: Biological and Cultural Consequences of 1492* (Westport, CT: Praeger, 2003), 64–121.

24. See, for example, Benjamin Kidd, *The Control of the Tropics* (New York: Macmillan, 1898). On American "tropical triumphalism" in Panama, see Paul S. Sutter, "Triumphalism and

Unruliness during the Construction of the Panama Canal," *RCC Perspectives* 3 (2015): 19–24. On the relationship between nature and civilization in the British empire see Tiffany Tsao, "Environmentalism and Civilizational Development in the Colonial British Histories of the Indian Archipelago (1783-1820)," *Journal of the History of Ideas* 74, n. 3 (July 2013): 449-71.

25. Paul Sutter, "The Tropics: A Brief History of an Environmental Imaginary," in *Oxford Handbook of Environmental History*, ed. Andrew C. Isenberg (Oxford: Oxford University Press, 2014), 185–86; Michael A. Osborne, "Acclimatizing the World: A History of the Paradigmatic Colonial Science," *Osiris* 15 (2000): 135–51; Thomas R. Dunlap, "Remaking the Land: The Acclimatization Movement and Anglo Ideas of Nature," *Journal of World History* 8, no. 2 (Fall 1997): 303–19; Warwick Anderson, "Climates of Option: Acclimatization in Nineteenth-Century France and England," *Victorian Studies* 35, no. 2 (Winter 1992): 135–57.

26. Walter Johnson (*Soul by Soul: Life inside the Antebellum Slave Market* [Cambridge, MA: Harvard University Press, 1999], 139) notes that a similar term, *acclimation*, was used to describe the vitality of slaves who survived the trade to the harsh conditions of the lower South. See also Mart A. Stewart, "'Let Us Begin with the Weather': Climate, Race, and Cultural Distinctiveness in the American South," in *Nature and Society in Historical Context*, ed. Mikuláš Teich, Roy Porter, and Bo Gustafsson (New York: Cambridge University Press, 1997), 240–56; Osborne, "Acclimatizing the World," 135–51.

27. Tyrrell, *True Gardens of the Gods*, 22–45.

28. Dunlap, "Remaking the Land," 317.

29. David Arnold, *The Tropics and the Traveling Gaze: India, Landscape, and Science, 1800–1856* (Seattle: University of Washington Press, 2015), esp. 62–150; Paul Sutter, "Nature's Agents or Agents of Empire?: Entomological Workers and Environmental Change during the Construction of the Panama Canal," *Isis* 98, no. 4 (December 2007): 724–54; Katherine Manthorne, "The Quest for a Tropical Paradise: Palm Tree as Fact and Symbol in Latin American Landscape Imagery," *Art Journal* 44, no. 4 (Winter 1984): 374–82; Rebecca Preston, "'The Scenery of the Torrid Zone': Imagined Travels and the Culture of Exotics in Nineteenth-Century British Gardens," in *Imperial Cities: Landscape, Display, and Identity*, ed. Felix Driver and David Gilbert (Manchester: Manchester University Press, 1999), 194–211.

30. Catherine Cocks, "The Pleasures of Degenerations: Climate, Race, and the Origins of the Global Tourist South in the Americas," *Discourse* 29, nos. 2/3 (Spring and Fall 2007): 215; Catherine Cocks, *Tropical Whites: The Rise of the Tourist South in the Americas* (Philadelphia: University of Pennsylvania Press, 2013), 16–17. For an examination of the tropics as a "natural laboratory," see Ashanti Shih, "The Most Perfect Laboratory in the World: Making and Knowing Hawaii National Park," *History of Science* 57, no. 4 (2019): 493–517.

31. Kidd, *Control of the Tropics*, 48.

32. Kidd, *Control of the Tropics*, 54.

33. Cocks, *Tropical Whites*, 17–22.

34. See, for example, Kidd, *Control of the Tropics*. On American "tropical triumphalism" in Panama, see Sutter, "Triumphalism and Unruliness," 19–24.

35. Tyrrell, *True Gardens of the Gods*, 22–45.

36. This view was not uniformly adopted; others were in favor of native plants and for the eradication of foreign plants within national borders, see Gert Groenig and Joachim Woschke-Bulmahn, "Some Notes on the Mania for Native Plants in Germany," *Landscape Journal* 11, no. 2 (Fall 1992): 116–26; Joachim Wolschke-Bulmahn, "The Search for 'Ecological Goodness' among Garden Historians," in *Perspectives on Garden Histories*, ed. Michel Conan (Washington, DC: Dumbarton Oaks, 1999), 161–80.

37. Quoted in Carey McWilliams, *Southern California: An Island on the Land* (Salt Lake City: Peregrine Books, 1973 [1946]), 96.

38. For more on California's agricultural production, see Douglas Sackman, *Orange Empire: California and the Fruits of Eden* (Berkeley: University of California Press, 2005).

39. Ernest H. Wilson, "Opportunities That Await Gardeners of California," *House and Garden*, 1930, 84.

40. Farmer, *Trees in Paradise*, 157; Doughty, *Eucalyptus*, 1–23.

41. Franceschi, *Santa Barbara Exotic Flora*, 10–12. For biographical details, see John M. Tucker, "Francesco Franceschi," *Madroño* 7, no. 1 (January 1943): 18–27.

42. Lester Rowntree, "California Wildflowers for the East," *House and Garden*, October 1929, 104.

43. Franceschi, *Santa Barbara Exotic Flora*, 1–3.

44. "On the Formation of the Southern California Acclimatizing Association for the Introduction and Propagation of Plants," pamphlet, December 15, 1893. Southern California Ephemera Collection (Collection 200). UCLA Library Special Collections, Charles E. Young Research Library, University of California, Los Angeles.

45. Franceschi, *Santa Barbara Exotic Flora*; Marritt B. Pratt, *Shade and Ornamental Trees of California* (Sacramento: California State Board of Forestry, 1921). For historical context, see Sonja Dümpelmann, *Seeing Trees: A History of Street Trees in New York City and Berlin* (New Haven, CT: Yale University Press, 2019).

46. Richard White, "From Wilderness to Hybrid Landscapes: The Cultural Turn in Environmental History," *Historian* 66, no. 3 (2004): 557–64.

47. Adam Rome, "Nature Wars, Culture Wars: Immigration and Environmental Reform in the Progressive Era," *Environmental History* 13, no. 3 (July 2008): 432–53.

48. Pearl Chase, "Conservation by Education," June 1935, SBHC Mss 1, Series 1, Subseries A, Community Arts Association Records, Plans and Plantings Branch Files, Correspondence, Incoming, Box 3, Folder C, CDCC.

49. Sarah Rutherford, *Botanic Gardens* (London: Shire Library, 2015), 6.

50. For more on the history of botanic gardens, see Arthur W. Hill, "The History and Function of Botanic Gardens," *Annals of the Missouri Botanical Garden* 2, nos. 1/2 (February–April 1915): 185–240; Joy M. Giguere, "'Too Mean to Live and Certainly No Fit Condition to Die': Vandalism, Public Misbehavior, and the Rural Cemetery Movement," *Journal of the Early Republic* 38 (Summer 2018): 293–324; Therese O'Malley, "'Your Garden Must Be a Museum to You': Early American Botanic Gardens," *Huntington Library Quarterly* 59, nos. 2/3 (1996): 207–31.

51. O'Malley, "'Your Garden Must Be a Museum to You,'" 216.

52. Staffan Müller-Wille, "Nature as a Marketplace: The Political Economy of Linnaean Botany," *History of Political Economy* 35 (2003): 154–72.

53. Alicia DeMaio, "Planting the Seeds of Empire: Botanical Gardens in the United States, 1800–1860" (PhD diss., Harvard University, 2020), 91–92.

54. Logan, "Urbane Bouquets," 110.

55. Liberty Hyde Bailey, *Garden-Making: Suggestions for the Utilizing of Home Grounds* (New York: Macmillan, 1898), 2.

56. Bailey, *Garden-Making*, 1.

57. E. H. Wilson, "Trees and the Heart of Man," *House and Garden*, November 1929, 99.

58. On indigenous erasure, see Miles Powell, *Vanishing America: Species Extinction, Racial Peril, and the Origins of Conservation* (Cambridge: Harvard University Press, 2016); Miller, *This Radical Land*; Whyte, "Indigenous Experience, Environmental Justice, and Settler Colonialism,"

NOTES TO PAGES 86-88

in *Nature and Experience: Phenomenology and the Environment*, ed. B. Bannon (Lanham: Rowman & Littlefield, 2016), 157-74.

59. Donald Worster, *Nature's Economy: A History of Ecological Ideas* (Cambridge: Cambridge University Press, 1977), 191.

60. Worster, *Nature's Economy*, 192.

61. For context on Richards, see Danielle Dreilinger, *The Secret History of Home Economics: How Trailblazing Women Harnessed the Power of Home and Changed the Way We Live* (New York: W. W. Norton, 2021); Pamela Curtis Swallow, *The Remarkable Life and Career of Ellen Swallow Richards: Pioneer in Science and Technology* (Hoboken: Wiley, 2014); Robert Clarke, *Ellen Swallow: The Woman Who Founded Ecology* (Chicago: Follett, 1973).

62. Ellen Swallow Richards, *Euthenics: The Science of the Controllable Environment* (Boston: Whitcomb & Barrows, 1910), 26.

63. Michelle Corrodi, "On the Kitchen and Vulgar Odors: The Path to a New Domestic Architecture between the Mid-Nineteenth Century and the Second World War," in *The Kitchen*, ed. Klaus Spechtenbauser (Basel: Birkhäuser, 2006), 21-28; Ellen M. Plante, *The American Kitchen, 1700 to the Present: From Hearth to Highrise* (New York: Facts on File, 1995); Glenna Matthews, *"Just a Housewife": The Rise and Fall of Domesticity in America* (New York: Oxford University Press, 1987). On household technologies, see Elfie Miklautz, Herbert Lachmayer, Reinhard Eisendle, hg. *Die Küche: Zur Geschichte eines architektonischen, sozialen und imaginativen Raums* (Wien: Böhlau, 1999); Plante, *American Kitchen*; Ruth Schwartz Cowan, *More Work for Mother: The Ironies of Household Technology from the Open Hearth to the Microwave* (New York: Basic Books, 1983).

64. William G. Whitford, "Art Education as Euthenics," *School Review* 46, no. 10 (December 1938): 746.

65. Raymond Unwin, *Town Planning in Practice: An Introduction to the Art of Designing Cities and Suburbs* (London: T. Fisher, 1909); William H. Wilson, *The City Beautiful Movement* (Baltimore, MD: Johns Hopkins University Press, 1989); Robert Fishman, *Urban Utopias in the Twentieth Century* (Cambridge: MIT Press, 1982); Standish Meacham, *Regaining Paradise: Englishness and the Early Garden City Movement* (New Haven, CT: Yale University Press, 1999); John Archer, *Architecture and Suburbia: from English Villa to American Dream House* (Minneapolis: University of Minnesota Press, 2005); Teresa Harris, "The German Garden City Movement: Architecture, Politics and Urban Transformation, 1902-1931" (PhD diss., Columbia University, 2012); Peter J. Schmitt, *Back to Nature: The Arcadian Myth in Urban America* (New York: Oxford University Press, 1969), 177-89.

66. Unwin, *Town Planning in Practice*, 1; Garden City Company of California, *Ideal Homes in Garden Communities: A Book of Stock Plans* (New York: Robert M. McBride and Company, 1916).

67. For the history of home economics, see Schwartz Cowan, *More Work for Mother*; Dreilinger, *Secret History of Home Economics*; Megan J. Elias, *Stir It Up: Home Economics in American Culture* (Philadelphia: University of Pennsylvania Press, 2008); Sarah Stage and Virginia B. Vincenti, eds., *Rethinking Home Economics: Women and the History of a Profession* (Ithaca, NY: Cornell University Press, 1997); Susan Strasser, *Never Done: A History of American Housework* (New York: Henry Holt, 2000).

68. Whitford, "Art Education as Euthenics," 745-53.

69. "Begins Euthenics Building," *New York Times*, October 26, 1925, 21.

70. Carl E. Seashore, "The Term 'Euthenics,'" *Science* 94, no. 2450 (December 12, 1941): 561-62.

71. H. G. Baker, "The Role of Euthenics in Eugenics," *Social Science* 1, no. 3 (May-July 1926): 249.

72. Gabriel N. Rosenberg, "No Scrubs: Livestock Breeding, Eugenics, and the States in the Early Twentieth-Century United States," *Journal of American History* 107, no. 2 (2020): 369.

73. W. D. Cornwall, "Eugenics vs. Euthenics as a Method of Race Betterment," *Canadian Medical Association Journal* 29, no. 4 (October 1933): 443–45.

74. For context, see Alexandra Minna Stern, *Eugenic Nation: Faults and Frontiers of Better Breeding in Modern America*, 2nd ed. (Berkeley: University of California Press, 2015 [2005]).

75. Stern, *Eugenic Nation*, 11; Francis Galton, *Essays in Eugenics* (London: The Eugenics Education Society, 1909), 35.

76. Gifford Pinchot, *A Primer of Forestry* (Washington, DC: General Printing Office, 1899).

77. Pinchot, *Primer of Forestry*, 44–45.

78. Pinchot, *Primer of Forestry*, 54–56.

79. Pinchot, *Primer of Forestry*, 62–63.

80. Interview with Freida Gervin by Andy S__, August 12, 1975. Charles M. Goethe Papers, Sacramento State University Library Special Collections.

81. "Sorrow at Dr. Goethe's Passing and Appreciation for Works Are Expressed," *Sacramento Bee*, July 11, 1966, A4.

82. C. M. Goethe to Anglo California National Bank, January 21, 1955, SBHC MSS 1966/01, box 13, folder 4, Charles M. Goethe Papers, California State University Sacramento Special Collections and University Archives, Sacramento (hereafter cited as CMG Papers); C. M. Goethe to American Museum of Natural History, September 10, 1942, box 13, folder 4, CMG Papers; C. J. O'Connor to C. M. Goethe, September 16, 1942, box 14, folder 7, CMG Papers; C. M. Goethe to Editor, *Nature* magazine, October 26, 1942, box 14, CMG Papers; Richard W. Westwood to C. M. Goethe, November 2, 1942, box 16, folder 6, CMG Papers; "Rotenone as an Insecticide," *Nature* 132, no. 3326 (July 1933): 167.

83. Baker, "Role of Euthenics in Eugenics," 248.

84. Gina Marie Greene, "Children in Glass Houses: Toward a Hygienic, Eugenic Architecture for Children during the Third Republic in France (1870–1940)" (PhD diss., Princeton University, 2011). Goethe never notes that *Ungemach* in German means "adversity" or "difficulty." Paul-André Rosental, *A Human Garden: French Policy and the Transatlantic Legacies of Eugenic Experimentation*, trans. Carolyn Avery (New York: Berghahn, 2019).

85. Rosental, *Human Garden*, 21.

86. William H. Schneider, *Quality and Quantity: The Quest for Biological Regeneration in Twentieth-Century France* (New York: Cambridge University Press, 1990), 125–28.

87. Charles M. Goethe, *War Profits . . . and Better Babies* (Sacramento: Keystone, 1946), 1–2.

88. Goethe, *War Profits . . . and Better Babies*, 42.

89. Charles M. Goethe to David Brower, January 12, 1956, SBHC Mss 1, Series 1, Subseries A, Community Arts Association Records, Plans and Planting Branch Files, Correspondence, Incoming, Box 3, Folder Goethe, CDCC.

90. Newsletter to friends, March 28, 1958, SBHC Mss 1, Series 1, Subseries A, Community Arts Association Records, Plans and Planting Branch Files, Correspondence, Incoming, Box 3, Folder Goethe.

91. Keith C. Barrons, "Streamlined Plants," *Scientific American*, March 1938, 133; "Streamlined Plants," *Atlanta Constitution*, May 15, 1938.

92. Frederic Clements, "The Modern Botanical Garden," typescript report, Santa Barbara Botanic Garden Papers.

93. Alfred Burbank, "World Botanical Garden Project," *Christian Science Monitor*, May 3, 1918, 7; "Two Thousand Mile Boulevard," *Christian Science Monitor*, May 4, 1918, 13.

94. "Big Botanical Garden Under Way in State," *San Francisco Chronicle*, January 27, 1918, 8.

95. Harold M. Finley, "California's Agricultural Melting Pot," *Los Angeles Times*, December 13, 1925, K3.

96. Clements, "Modern Botanical Garden."

97. For context on the Santa Barbara Botanic Garden's history, see Mary Carroll, "A History of the Santa Barbara Botanic Garden and Its Landscapes: A Report for the Santa Barbara Botanic Garden," 2003.

98. Clements, "Modern Botanical Garden."

99. Caroline Merchant, *The Death of Nature: Women, Ecology, and the Scientific Revolution* (San Francisco: Harper & Row, 1980).

100. "California Conservation Week, March 3–9, 1935," Mss 90, Box 10, Folder 9, M. Ashby Johnson Collection, Department of Special Research Collections, UC Santa Barbara Library, University of California, Santa Barbara (hereafter cited as MAJ).

101. "Conservation Work as Told by Pearl Chase," *Santa Barbara News-Press*, 1926, clipping in Mss 90, Box 10, Folder 9, MAJ; Anita Guerrini, "The Wild Garden: Landscaping Southern California in the Early Twentieth Century," *Notes and Records: The Royal Society Journal of the History of Science* 75 (2021): 259–76; Logan, "Urbane Bouquets," esp. 43–50.

102. "The Santa Barbara Committee to Clean Up and Beautify Our Community," April 1933, SBHC Mss 1, Box 8, Folder 1933.

103. "Santa Barbara County Report Sheet: Campaign to Clean Up and Beautify Our Community," April 1933, SBHC Mss 1, Series 1, Subseries A, Community Arts Association Records, Plants and Planting Branch Files, General Alphabetical, Box 8, Folder 1933.

104. "Clean Up Week," April 1933, SBHC Mss 1, Community Arts Association Records, Plants and Planting Branch Files, General Alphabetical, Box 8, Folder 1933.

105. Alfred J. Stewart, "Suggestions for La Primavera Lot Planting Contest," November 1940, SBHC Mss 1, Series 1, Subseries B Box 9, Folder La Primavera in Santa Barbara, 1940–7.

106. "La Primavera en Santa Barbara Lot Planting Contest," October 18, 1940, SBHC Mss 1, Series 1, Subseries B Box 9, Folder La Primavera in Santa Barbara, 1940–7, CDCC.

107. "To Property Owners in Santa Barbara," c. 1940, SBHC Mss 1, Series 1, Subseries B Box 9, Folder La Primavera in Santa Barbara, 1940–7, CDCC.

108. Margaret L. Dearing, "Methods of Presenting Nature Study," SBHC Mss 1, Series 1, Subseries A, Garden Club of SB and Montecito, Box 1, Folder 1937, CDCC.

109. John D. Wright radio talk, February 27, 1932, SBHC Mss 1, Series 1, Subseries A, Community Arts Association Records, Plans and Planting Branch Files, General Alphabetical, Box 25, Folder 1, CDCC.

110. "Garden Gossip Leaflet" X, Massachusetts Committee of Better Homes in America, n.d., SBHC Mss 1, Series 1, Subseries A, Better Homes in America Files, Box 10, Folder 14, CDCC.

111. "Garden Gossip Leaflet" VII, Massachusetts Committee of Better Homes in America, n.d., SBHC Mss 1, Series 1, Subseries A, Better Homes in America Files, Box 10, Folder 14, CDCC.

112. Margaret A. Hall, "The Fine Art of Landscape Architecture," *Southern California Gardens* 1, no. 2 (June 19, 1929): 9.

113. Hall, "Fine Art of Landscape Architecture," 16.

114. Charles M. Goethe to the Plans and Planting Committee, June 28, 1946, SBHC Mss 1, Plans and Planting, Correspondence, Incoming Box 3, Folder Goethe.

115. Frederick Law Olmsted, *Report of the State Park Survey of California* (Sacramento: California State Printing Office, 1929), 16.

116. Victoria Padilla, *Southern California Gardens: An Illustrated History* (Berkeley: University of California Press, 1961), 92.

117. Padilla, *Southern California Gardens*, 98.

118. Padilla, *Southern California Gardens*, 110–11.

119. Pearl Chase to P. J. Maher, February 9, 1942, SBHC Mss 1, Series 1, Subseries A, Community Arts Association Collection, Plans and Planting Files, Correspondence, Outgoing, Box 9, Folder Jan–July 1942.

120. Padilla, *Southern California Gardens*, 134.

121. Padilla, *Southern California Gardens*, 136.

122. Padilla, *Southern California Gardens*, 112.

123. Padilla, *Southern California Gardens*, 113.

124. Radio talk by Herbert W. Green, July 15, 1932, SBHC Mss1, Series 1, Subseries A, Community Arts Association Records, Plans and Planting Branch Files, General, Box 25, Folder 2, CDCC.

Chapter Four

1. Ada Louise Huxtable, "The Crisis of the Environment," *New York Times*, December 29, 1969, 28.

2. Frank K. Kelly, "Whither Santa Barbara?" clipping, c. 1973, SBHC Mss 1, Series 1, Subseries A, Citizens Planning Association, Box 4, Folder General Plan Revision, CDCC.

3. Kevin Starr, *Golden Dreams: California in an Age of Abundance, 1950–1963* (Oxford: Oxford University Press, 2009).

4. This argument is influenced by Lily Geismer, *Don't Blame Us: Suburban Liberals and the Transformation of the Democratic Party* (Princeton: Princeton University Press, 2014), esp. 97–121.

5. Evan McKenzie, *Privatopia: Homeowner Associations and the Rise of Residential Private Government* (New Haven, CT: Yale University Press, 1996).

6. Mike Davis, *City of Quartz: Excavating the Future in Los Angeles* (New York: Verso, 1990), 153. See also David M. P. Freund, *Colored Property: State Policy and White Racial Politics in Suburban America* (Chicago: University of Chicago Press, 2007).

7. On homeowners associations and their legal status, see James Duncan and Nancy Duncan, *Landscapes of Privilege: The Politics of the Aesthetic in an American Suburb* (New York: Routledge, 2003), esp. 59–148; McKenzie, *Privatopia*, esp. 122–49; Barbara Coyle McCabe, "Homeowners Associations as Private Governments: What We Know, What We Don't, and Why It Matters," *Public Administration Review* 71, no. 4 (July/August 2011): 535–42; Robert H. Nelson, "Homeowners Associations in Historical Perspective," *Public Administration Review* 71, no. 4 (July/August 2011): 546–49. On neighborhood associations, see Martin Ruef and Seok-Woo Kwon, "Neighborhood Associations and Social Capital," *Social Forces* 95, no. 1 (September 2016): 159–89.

8. Geismer, *Don't Blame Us*, 1–12; Duncan and Duncan, *Landscapes of Privilege*, 3–12.

9. Lisa McGirr, *Suburban Warriors: The Origins of the New American Right* (Princeton, NJ: Princeton University Press, 2001).

10. Robert O. Self, *American Babylon: Race and the Struggle for Postwar Oakland* (Princeton: Princeton University Press, 2005), 17.

11. For context on this, see Keith Makoto Woodhouse, *The Ecocentrists: A History of Radical Environmentalism* (New York: Columbia University Press, 2018).

NOTES TO PAGES 104–106

12. Alison Bashford, "Population Planning for a Global Middle Class," in *The Global Bourgeoisie: The Rise of the Middle Class in the Age of Empire*, ed. Christof Dejung, David Motadel, and Jürgen Osterhammel (Princeton, NJ: Princeton University Press, 2019), 83–101.

13. Robert Beauregard, *When America Became Suburban* (Minneapolis: University of Minnesota Press, 2006), 6. For a revisionist view, see Becky Nicolaides, *The New Suburbia: How Diversity Remade Suburban Life in Los Angeles after 1945* (Oxford: Oxford University Press, 2024).

14. Francesca Russello Ammon, *Bulldozer: Demolition and Clearance of the Postwar Landscape* (New Haven, CT: Yale University Press, 2016); Louis Hyman, *Debtor Nation: The History of America in Red Ink* (Princeton: Princeton University Press, 2012).

15. Beauregard, *When America Became Suburban*, 109–10; on the ways housing policy after World War II diverged between the United States and other nations, see Nancy H. Kwak, *A World of Homeowners: American Power and the Politics of Housing Aid* (Chicago: University of Chicago Press, 2015).

16. "Flight to the Suburbs," *Time* 63, no. 12 (March 22, 1954): 122; Lizabeth Cohen, *A Consumer's Republic: The Politics of Mass Consumption* (New York: Alfred A. Knopf, 2003), 194–296. For a historical treatment of critiques of consumer culture in this period see Daniel Horowitz, *The Anxieties of Affluence: Critiques of American Consumer Culture, 1939-1975* (Amherst: University of Massachusettes Press, 2005).

17. James Patterson, *Grand Expectations: The United States, 1945–1974* (New York: Oxford University Press, 1996), 334.

18. Self, *American Babylon*, esp. 97–98.

19. C. W. Griffin Jr., "Specialists Diagnose the Stricken American City," *Saturday Evening Post*, August 3, 1963.

20. Self, *American Babylon*, 2.

21. Patterson, *Grand Expectations*, 334–36; Jon Teaford, *Twentieth-Century American City* (Baltimore, MD: Johns Hopkins University Press, 1993).

22. Beauregard, *When America Became Suburban*; Kyle Riismandel, *Neighborhood of Fear: The Suburban Crisis in American Culture, 1975–2001* (Baltimore, MD: Johns Hopkins University Press, 2020).

23. Sarah E. Igo, *The Known Citizen: A History of Privacy in Modern America* (Cambridge, MA: Harvard University Press, 2018), x.

24. "If You're Thinking of Going There: What to Know About and Look For," *Life*, October 19, 1962, 69, 73.

25. "State of California Real Estate Bulletin," July 1963.

26. For a general overview for this period in California, see Starr, *Golden Dreams* and for a perspective on Northern California see Malcolm Harris, *Palo Alto: A History of California, Capitalism, and the World* (New York: Little, Brown, and Company, 2023).

27. Richard G. Lillard, *Eden in Jeopardy: Man's Prodigal Meddling with His Environment* (New York: Knopf, 1966), 4.

28. Kenneth T. Jackson, "Race, Ethnicity, and Real Estate Appraisal: The Home Owners Loan Corporation and the Federal Housing Administration," *Journal of Urban History* 6 (August 1980): 419–52; Richard Rothstein, *The Color of Law: A Forgotten History of How Our Government Segregated America* (New York: Liveright, 2017); LaDale C. Winling and Todd M. Michney, "The Roots of Redlining: Academic, Governmental, and Professional Networks in the Making of the New Deal Lending Regime," *Journal of American History* 108, no. 1 (June 2021): 42–69.

29. Daniel HoSang, "Race and the Mythology of California's Lost Paradise," *Boom: A Magazine of California* 1, n. 1 (Spring 2011): 37.

30. HoSang, "Race and the Mythology of California's Lost Paradise," 39.

31. "A Plan for Low Rent Housing and Neighborhood Redevelopment in Santa Barbara," 1966, SBHC Mss 1, Series 1, Subseries B, Box 9, Folder Mayor's Advising Committee on Human Relations, 1966, CDCC.

32. Housing Committee, Santa Barbara Citizens' Advisory Council, "Housing Needs in Santa Barbara, California," May 8, 1948, SBHC Mss 1, Series 1, Subseries B, Box 12, Folder Santa Barbara Citizens' Advisory Council: Report on Housing Needs in SB, 1948, CDCC.

33. William Bronson, *How to Kill a Golden State* (Garden City, NY: Doubleday, 1968), 9.

34. Lillard, *Eden in Jeopardy*, 5.

35. Bronson, *How to Kill a Golden State*, 9–11.

36. Lillard, *Eden in Jeopardy*, 13.

37. Lillard, *Eden in Jeopardy*, 18.

38. Lillard, *Eden in Jeopardy*, viii.

39. *Future Environments of North America: Being the Record of a Conference Convened by the Conservation Foundation in April 1965, at Airlie House, Warrenton, Virginia* (Garden City, NY: Natural History, 1966), 319.

40. Raymond F. Dasmann, "Man in North America," *Future Environments of North America: Transformation of a Continent*, ed. F. Fraser Darling and John P. Milton (Garden City: Natural History Press, 1966), 326–34.

41. California Department of Fish and Game, 46th Biennial Report, 1958–60.

42. "How Would You Characterize California's Environmental Problems," typewritten sheet, SBHC Mss 1, CDCC Series 1B, Box 4, Folder California Tomorrow 1970–1975.

43. Raymond Fredric Dasmann, *The Destruction of California* (New York: Macmillan, 1965), 6.

44. Dasmann, *Destruction of California*, 206–11.

45. Lillard, *Eden in Jeopardy*, 42.

46. Christopher Tunnard and Boris Pushkarev, *Man-Made America: Chaos or Control? An Inquiry into Selected Problems of Design in the Urbanized Landscape* (New Haven, CT: Yale University Press, 1963), ix.

47. Tunnard and Pushkarev, *Man-Made America*, 3.

48. Tunnard and Pushkarev, *Man-Made America*, 393.

49. "Position Paper on the Development of the South Coastal Region of Santa Barbara County," December 1970, SBHC Mss 1, Series 1, Subseries A, Allied Protection and Improvement Association, Box 1, Folder 10, CDCC.

50. "Flight to the Suburbs," *Time* 63, no. 12 (March 22, 1954): 102.

51. On intertwined shifts in urban form and consumption, see Alistair Kefford, *The Life and Death of the Shopping City: Public Planning and Private Redevelopment in Britain since 1945* (Cambridge: Cambridge University Press, 2022); and David Smiley, *Pedestrian Modern: Shopping and Modern Architecture, 1925–1956* (Minneapolis: University of Minnesota Press, 2013).

52. Robert E. Cubbedge, *The Destroyers of America* (New York: Macfadden-Bartell, 1971), 21.

53. Garrett Hardin, "The Tragedy of the Commons," *Science* 162, no. 3859 (1968): 1243–48.

54. Woodhouse, *Ecocentrists*; Thomas Robertson, *The Malthusian Moment: Global Population Growth and the Birth of American Environmentalism* (New Brunswick, NJ: Rutgers University Press, 2012).

55. For a critique of the concept, see Fabien Locher, "Cold War Pastures: Garrett Hardin and the 'Tragedy of the Commons,'" *Revue d'Histoire Moderne & Contemporaine* 60, no. 1 (January 2013): 7–36.

56. Hardin, "Tragedy of the Commons," 1248.
57. Garrett Hardin, "Living on a Lifeboat," *Bioscience* 24, no. 10 (October 1974): 561.
58. Hardin, "Living on a Lifeboat," 562.
59. Garrett Hardin, "Lifeboat Ethics: The Case against Helping the Poor," *Psychology Today* (September 1974), 38.
60. Melinda Cooper, *Counterrevolution: Extravagance and Austerity in Public Finance* (Brooklyn, NY: Zone, 2024), 319.
61. On Ehrlich and population, see Thomas Robertson, "Revisiting the Early 1970s Commoner-Ehrlich Debate about Population and Environment: Dueling Critiques of Production and Consumption in a Global Age," in *A World of Populations: Transnational Perspectives on Demography in the Twentieth Century*, ed. Heinrich Hartmann and Corinna R. Unger (New York: Berghahn, 2014), 108–25.
62. Daniel Callahan, "Doing Well by Doing Good: Garrett Hardin's 'Lifeboat Ethic,'" *Hastings Center Report* 4, no. 5 (December 1974): 3.
63. For context, see Meg Jacobs, *Pocketbook Politics: Economic Citizenship in Twentieth-Century America* (Princeton, NJ: Princeton University Press, 2007).
64. J. Frederick Dewhurst, "Tomorrow's Crystal Ball," California Recreation Conference Workshop, Planning for Tomorrow's Leisure, c. 1956, SBHC Mss 1, Series 1, Subseries B, Box 3, Folder California Parks and Recreation Society, 1953–60, CDCC.
65. Howard Brick, *Age of Contradiction: American Thought and Culture in the 1960s* (Ithaca, NY: Cornell University Press, 2000).
66. Darrell E. Napton and Christopher R. Laingen, "Expansion of Golf Courses in the United States," *Geographical Review* 98, no. 1 (January 2008): 24–41.
67. Theodore Steinberg, *American Green: The Obsessive Quest for the Perfect Lawn* (New York: W. W. Norton, 2006); Georges Teyssot, ed., *The American Lawn: Surface of Everyday Life* (New York: Princeton Architectural Press, 1999).
68. California Recreation Conference Workshop, "The Crystal Ball," 156, SBHC Mss 1, Series 1, Subseries B, Box 3, Folder California Parks and Recreation Society, 1963–60, CDCC. For another contemporary account of leisure, see also R. C. Linstromberg, "The Challenge of Leisure to the Cult of Work," *Midcontinent American Studies Journal* 8, no. 1 (Spring 1967): 20–33.
69. California Recreation Conference Workshop, "Remarks of Ellis A. Jarvis," SBHC Mss 1, Series 1, Subseries B, Box 3, Folder California Parks and Recreation Society, 1963–60, CDCC.
70. On automation, see Aaron Benanav, *Automation and the Future of Work* (New York: Verso, 2022); Jason Resnikoff, *Labor's End: How the Promise of Automation Degraded Work* (Champaign: University of Illinois Press, 2022).
71. John Atlee Kouwenhoven, *The Beer Can by the Highway: Essays on What's "American" about America* (Baltimore, MD: Johns Hopkins University Press, 1988), 16.
72. Mary Ann Gutta, "When Communities Care," *New York Times*, December 14, 1969.
73. For example, see "Planning Committee Report," August 1955, SBHC Mss 1, Series 1, Subseries B, Box 10, Folder Marin Conservation League, 1915–56, CDCC.
74. Remi A. Nadeau, *California: The New Society* (New York: D. McKay, 1963), 86.
75. Nadeau, *California*, 92–93.
76. Nadeau, *California*, 93.
77. Cubbedge, *Destroyers of America*, 9.
78. Cubbedge, *Destroyers of America*, 17.
79. Cubbedge, *Destroyers of America*, 25.

80. "Conservation Gaining Respect Due to Increase of Outdoorsmen," *Desert Sun*, August 16, 1965, 4.

81. Citizens Planning Association and Improvement Associations Minutes, September 14, 1962, SBHC Mss 1, Series 1, Subseries A, Allied Protection and Improvement Collection, Box 1, Folder 3, CDCC.

82. AIA Meeting, November 9, 1965, SBHC Mss 1, Series 1, Subseries A, Allied Protection and Improvement Association, Box 1, Folder 6, CDCC.

83. Claudia Madsen, October 18, 1974, SBHC Mss 1, Series 1, Subseries B, Box 8, Folder Foothill Preservation League, 1973–74, CDCC.

84. AIA Meeting, November 9, 1965, SBHC Mss 1, Series 1, Allied Protection and Improvement Association, Box 1, Folder 6, CDCC.

85. "Allied Improvement Association Constitution," n.d., SBHC Mss 1, Series 1, Subseries A, Allied Protection and Improvement Association, Box 1, Folder 1, CDCC.

86. "Some Current Problems and Issues," n.d., SBHC Mss 1, CDCC Series 1, Subseries A, Allied Protection and Improvement Association, Box 1, Folder 8, CDCC.

87. Minutes of Allied Protection and Improvement Meeting, November 9, 1965, SBHC Mss 1, Series 1, Subseries A, Allied Protection and Improvement Association, Box 1, Folder 6, CDCC.

88. Minutes of Allied Protection and Improvement Meeting, November 9, 1965, SBHC Mss 1, Series 1, Subseries A, Allied Protection and Improvement Association, Box 1, Folder 6, CDCC .

89. Mesa Bulletin 1, July 18, 1964, SBHC Mss 1, Series 1, Subseries B, Box 9, Folder Mesa Improvement Association, 1964–70, CDCC.

90. "Mission Canyon Association News Letter," July 1966, SBHC Mss 1 Series 1, Subseries B, Box 9, Folder Mission Canyon Association, 1930–71, CDCC.

91. Mesa Bulletin 2, September 18, 1964, SBHC Mss 1, Series 1, Subseries B, Box 9, Folder Mesa Improvement Association, 1964, 1970, CDCC.

92. Mesa Bulletin 2, September 18, 1964, SBHC Mss 1, Series 1, Subseries B, Box 9, Folder Mesa Improvement Association, 1964–70, CDCC.

93. APIA Meeting, July 19, 1963, SBHC Mss 1, Series 1, Subseries A, Allied Protection and Improvement Association, Box 1, Folder 4, CDCC.

94. APIA Press Release, February 8, 1967, SBHC Mss 1, Series 1, Subseries A, Allied Protection and Improvement Association, Box 1, Folder 8, CDCC.

95. APIA Minutes, April 19, 1963, SBHC Mss 1, Series 1, Subseries A, Allied Protection and Improvement Association, Box 1, Folder 4, CDCC.

96. APIA Press Release, February 8, 1967, SBHC Mss 1, Series 1, Subseries A, Allied Protection and Improvement Association, Box 1, Folder 8, CDCC; Montecito Protective and Improvement Association Newsletter, March 1965, SBHC Mss 34, Box 7, Folder 16, UCSB Department of Special Research Collections.

97. APIA Minutes, September 16, 1968, SBHC Mss 1, Series 1, Subseries A, Allied Protection and Improvement Association, Box 1, Folder 9, CDCC.

98. Clark Howell to City of Santa Barbara Planning Commission, October 2, 1968, SBHC Mss 1, Series 1, Subseries A, Allied Protection and Improvement Association, Box 1, Folder 9, CDCC.

99. Santa Barbara Women's Club Board of Directors to Santa Barbara Planning and City Council, October 3, 1968, SBHC Mss 1, CDCC Series 1, Subseries A, Allied Protection and Improvement Association, Box 1, Folder 9, CDCC.

100. Judith Dodge Orias to City Planning Commission, September 29, 1968, SBHC Mss 1, Series 1, Subseries A, Allied Protection and Improvement Association, Box 1, Folder 9, CDCC.

101. Citizens Planning Association of Santa Barbara to City Planning Commission, October 3, 1968, SBHC Mss 1, Series 1, Subseries A, Allied Protection and Improvement Association, Box 1, Folder 9, CDCC.

102. Resolution Opposing High Rise in El Mirasol Block, October 3, 1968, SBHC Mss 1, Series 1, Subseries A, Allied Protection and Improvement Association, Box 1, Folder 9, CDCC.

103. Memorandum to Allied Improvement Associations, January 11, 1963, SBHC Mss 1, Series 1, Subseries A, Allied Protection and Improvement Association, Box 1, Folder 4, CDCC.

104. Allied Improvement Association Minutes, February 15, 1963, SBHC Mss 1, CDCC Series 1, Subseries A, Allied Protection and Improvement Association, Box 1, Folder 4, CDCC.

105. "Beachfront Access Question Remains," *Santa Barbara News-Press*, January 15, 1959.

106. Draft Resolution of the Allied Protection and Improvement Association, October 7, 1970, SBHC Mss 1, Series 1, Subseries A, Allied Protection and Improvement Association, Box 1, Folder 10, CDCC.

107. Self, *American Babylon*, esp. chap. 3; on environmental politics directly, see Brandon M. Ward, "Suburbs against the Region: Homeowner Environmentalism in 1970s Detroit," *Journal of Planning History* 18, no. 2 (2019): 83–101.

Chapter Five

1. *Hearings before the Subcommittee on Minerals, Materials, and Fuels of the Committee on Interior and Insular Affairs*, March 13–14, 1970 (Statement of Jess Unruh, minority leader, California State Assembly), 130.

2. *Los Angeles Times*, May 6, 1969, 12.

3. Hal K. Rothman, *Saving the Planet: The American Response to the Environment in the Twentieth Century* (Chicago: Ivan R. Dee, 2000), 128.

4. *Hearing before the Subcommittee on Air and Water Pollution of the Committee on Public Works*, 91st Congress, February 24–25, 1969 (Statement of Gerald Firestone, mayor of Santa Barbara), 525–27.

5. Charles Halvorson, *Valuing Clean Air: The EPA and the Economics of Environmental Protection* (Oxford: Oxford University Press, 2021); Teresa Sabol Spezio, *Slick Policy: Environmental and Science Policy in the Aftermath of the Santa Barbara Oil Spill* (Pittsburgh, PA: University of Pittsburgh Press, 2018).

6. Paul Sabin, "Crisis and Continuity in U.S. Oil Politics," *Journal of American History* 99, no. 1 (June 2012): 181.

7. "The Ocean Is Boiling: The Complete Oral History of the 1969 Santa Barbara Oil Spill," *Pacific Standard*, https://psmag.com/news/the-ocean-is-boiling-the-complete-oral-history-of-the-1969-santa-barbara-oil-spill, accessed January 2, 2021.

8. For context, see Etienne S. Benson, *Surroundings: A History of Environments and Environmentalisms* (Chicago: University of Chicago Press, 2020); Samuel P. Hays, *Beauty, Health, and Permanence: Environmental Politics in the United States, 1965–1985* (Cambridge: Cambridge University Press, 1987); Thomas Jundt, *Greening the Red, White, and Blue: The Bomb, Big Business, and Consumer Resistance in Postwar America* (Oxford: Oxford University Press, 2014); Michael Bess, *The Light-Green Society: Ecology and Technological Modernity in France, 1960–2000* (Chicago: University of Chicago Press, 2003); Finis Dunaway, *Seeing Green: The Use and Abuse of American Environmental Images* (Chicago: University of Chicago Press, 2015); James Morton Turner, *The Promise of Wilderness: American Environmental Politics since 1964* (Seattle: University of Washington Press, 2013); Adam Rome, *The Bulldozer in the Countryside: Suburban*

Sprawl and the Rise of American Environmentalism (Oxford: Oxford University Press, 2001); Christopher C. Sellers, *Crabgrass Crucible: Suburban Nature and the Rise of Environmentalism in Twentieth-Century America* (Chapel Hill: University of North Carolina Press, 2015); Meredith Veldman, *Fantasy, the Bomb, and the Greening of Britain: Romantic Protest, 1945–1980* (Cambridge: Cambridge University Press, 1994); Frank Zelko, *Make It a Green Peace! The Rise of a Countercultural Environmentalism* (New York: Oxford University Press, 2013).

9. For environmental analysis on a more southern portion of the bight near Los Angeles, see Christina Dunbar-Hester, *Oil Beach: How Toxic Infrastructure Threatens Life in the Ports of Los Angeles and Beyond* (Chicago: University of Chicago Press, 2023).

10. John F. Curran, "Santa Barbara Channel: History of Offshore Petroleum Development," Pacific Section Society for Sedimentary Geology report, 1972.

11. Spezio, *Slick Policy*, 21.

12. Frederick deGroat Harlow, "The Oil Men and the Sea: The Future of Ocean Resource Development in Light of Santa Barbara—Some Proposals to Rectify Continuing Inadequate Federal Regulation of Offshore Leasing," *Arizona Law Review* 11 (1969): 680.

13. *United States v. California* 332 U.S. 804, 805 (1947).

14. *Hearings before the Subcommittee on Minerals, Materials, and Fuels of the Committee on Interior and Insular Affairs*, US Senate, 91st Congress, First Session on S. 1219, May 19–20, 1969, 7.

15. "Give Local Officials Public Support for Protection of Our Beaches," *Santa Barbara News-Press*, December 4, 1951; "Would You Like Some Oil Derricks Rising from the Sea off Santa Barbara?" *Santa Barbara News-Press*, November 20, 1952. For greater detail on the federal and state contestation, see Spezio, *Slick Policy*, esp. 68–89.

16. Alan V. Hager, "The Tidelands Oil Controversy: The Prize and the Responsibility," *Natural Resources & Environment* 10, no. 1 (Summer 1995): 50.

17. George A. Doumani and Nancy C. Price, "Blowout in Santa Barbara Channel: Background and Chronology," Library of Congress, LRS Report 70-201, August 10, 1970.

18. Malcolm F. Baldwin, "The Santa Barbara Oil Spill," *University of Colorado Law Review* 42, no. 33 (1970–71): 37–40.

19. Robert Easton, *Black Tide: The Santa Barbara Oil Spill and its Consequences* (New York: Delacorte Press, 1972), 35.

20. Harlow, "Oil Men and the Sea," 681.

21. Harvey Molotch, "Oil in the Velvet Playground," *Ramparts* 8 (November 1969): 44.

22. William Trombley, "Santa Barbara: Beneath the Calm a Battle Rages," *Los Angeles Times*, July 13, 1975, B1.

23. "Allied Improvement Associations" typescript, SBHC Mss 1, Series 1, Subseries B, Box 5, Folder Center for the Student of Democratic Institutions, CDCC; George Lardner Jr., "Oil Leak Fuels Conservation Dispute," *Washington Post*, February 3, 1969, A1.

24. Harry Trimborn, "Channel Drilling: Battle between Esthetics, Profits," *Los Angeles Times*, February 14, 1969.

25. Stanley M. Elliott, "Oil Key to Future," *Santa Barbara News-Press*, May 13, 1962, A1, A10; Stanley M. Elliott, "Well Dooms Sanctuary," *Santa Barbara News-Press*, May 16, 1962, A1, A5.

26. Letter to the editor, *Santa Barbara News-Press*, May 18, 1962, SBHC Mss 1, Series 1, Subseries A, Citizens Planning Association Clippings, Box 4, Folder Oil–Santa Barbara City, CDCC.

27. "Mayor's Oil Plan Praised, Rapped," *Santa Barbara News-Press*, May 16, 1962, A10.

28. Stanley M. Elliott, "Oil Revenue Tantalizing," *Santa Barbara News-Press*, May 17, 1962; Mrs. Hallock Hoffman, "Some Values above Price," *Santa Barbara News-Press*, June 5, 1962,

NOTES TO PAGES 136–140

SBHC Mss 1, Series 1, Subseries A, Citizens Planning Association Clippings, Box 4, Folder Oil–Santa Barbara City, CDCC.

29. *Hearing before the Subcommittee on Flood Control and Subcommittee on Rivers and Harbors of the Committee on Public Works* (91st Congress, First Session, February 14, 1969, Santa Barbara, California), 74.

30. Quoted in Baldwin, "Santa Barbara Oil Spill," 43.

31. Ross Macdonald, "Life with the Blob," *Sports Illustrated*, April 21, 1969, 51.

32. George A. Doumani and Nancy C. Prince, "Blowout in Santa Barbara Channel: Background and Chronology," Library of Congress, LRS Report 710-201 SP, August 10, 1970.

33. Sabin, "Crisis and Continuity," 179.

34. Robert Sollen, *An Ocean of Oil: A Century of Political Struggle over Petroleum off the California Coast* (Juneau, AK: Denali, 1998), 47.

35. Easton, *Black Tide*, 7.

36. *Hearings before the Subcommittee on Air and Water Pollution*, February 24–25, 1969, 812–13.

37. Ted Thackery Jr., "Mudslides Kill 9; Rain Damage Grows," *Los Angeles Times*, January 26, 1969, 1.

38. *Hearings before the Subcommittee on Air and Water Pollution*, February 24–25, 1969 (Statement of George Murphy, US senator for California), 470–73; Richard West, "Recovery of 3 Bodies Raises Southland Flood Toll to 100," *Los Angeles Times*, February 1, 1969, A1.

39. Robert Jensen, "How Man and Nature Caused the California Floods," *Boston Globe*, January 27, 1969, 8.

40. For more details of the blowout, see Spezio, *Slick Policy*, 121–42.

41. Easton, *Black Tide*, 8.

42. Easton, *Black Tide*, 12.

43. "Coast Oil Leak Is Plugged," *New York Times*, February 9, 1969, 1.

44. Robert H. Sollen, "Favorable Wind Keeps Oil off County Beaches," *Santa Barbara News-Press*, January 30, 1969, A1.

45. *Hearings before the Subcommittee on Air and Water Pollution of the Committee on Public Works*, February 24–25, 1969 (Statement of Lt. George H. Brown III), 800–802.

46. Ross Macdonald and Robert Easton, "Santa Barbarans Cite an 11th Commandment: Thou Shalt Not Abuse the Earth," *New York Times*, October 12, 1969; Macdonald, "Life with the Blob."

47. William M. Blair, "In the Wake of Coast Oil Slick: A Tide of Memos," *New York Times*, March 25, 1969, 30.

48. Robert H. Phelps, "Drilling Decision Blame: Udall Criticizes Own Role," *New York Times*, February 9, 1969, 1.

49. *Hearing before the Subcommittee on Flood Control and Subcommittee on Rivers and Harbors of the Committee on Public Works*, House of Representatives, 91st Congress, February 14, 1969 (Statement of George Clyde), 74.

50. *Hearings before the Subcommittee on Minerals, Materials, and Fuels of the Committee on Interior and Insular Affairs*, US Senate, March 13–14, 1970 (Statement of Alvin Weingand), 81.

51. *Hearings before the Subcommittee on Flood Control and Subcommittee on Rivers and Harbors of the Committee on Public*, February 14, 1969 (Statement of Allan Coates Jr.), 12–13.

52. "Oil Outrage against Public," *Santa Barbara News-Press*, January 31, 1969, C12.

53. "Resort Ads Can't Show Water or Beachfront, Santa Barbara Decides," *Advertising Age*, June 30, 1969, 6.

54. G. Norman Brown, "Letter to the Editor," *Santa Barbara News-Press*, July 7, 1969.
55. Easton, *Black Tide*, 23.
56. Macdonald and Easton, "Santa Barbarans Cite an 11th Commandment," 32.
57. Macdonald and Easton, "Santa Barbarans Cite an 11th Commandment," 142.
58. Hoffman, "Some Values above Price."
59. "No One Can Answer Questions for Kathy," *Santa Barbara News-Press*, February 6, 1969, Get Out! (GOO!) Collection, SBHC Mss 10, Department of Special Research Collections, UC Santa Barbara Library, University of California, Santa Barbara, Scrapbook 1 (hereafter cited as GOO!).
60. Letter to the editor from John Cushing, *Santa Barbara News-Press*, February 10, 1969.
61. Fred Eissler, "Santa Barbara's Ordeal by Oil, *Sierra Club Bulletin*, March 1969, 9.
62. Morton Mintz, "Santa Barbara 'Radicalized' by Long Oil Battle," *Santa Barbara News-Press*, July 6, 1969, C7.
63. On environmental critiques of economic growth, see Venus Bivar, "Historicizing Economic Growth: An Overview of Recent Works," *Historical Journal* 65, no. 5 (2022): 1470–89; Iris Borowy and Matthias Schmelzer, eds., *History of the Future of Economic Growth: Historical Roots of Current Debates on Sustainable Degrowth* (Oxford: Routledge, 2017); Stephen J. Macekura, *The Mismeasure of Progress: Economic Growth and Its Critics* (Chicago: University of Chicago Press 2020); Pollyanna Rhee, "Calculating Nature's Bill"; Matthias Schmelzer, "From Luddites to Limits? Towards a Systematization of Growth Critiques in Historical Perspective," *Globalizations* 20 no. 3 (2023): 447–64; Matthias Schmelzer, *The Hegemony of Growth: The OECD and the Making of the Economic Growth Paradigm* (Cambridge: Cambridge University Press, 2017).
64. Garrett Hardin, "Finding Lemonade in Santa Barbara's Oil Spill," *Saturday Review*, May 10, 1969, 19.
65. "GOO Is New Organization to 'Get Oil Out,'" clipping, January 30, 1969, Scrapbook 1, GOO!.
66. Easton, *Black Tide*, 36.
67. "The GOO Song Sheet," c. 1969, SBHC Mss 44, Box 4, Folder GOO! UCSB Department of Special Research Collections.
68. John Waugh, "That Was the Ooze That Was," *Los Angeles Times*, September 21, 1969, W11.
69. Nicholas von Hoffman, "Pouring Words on Oily Waters," *Washington Post*, February 7, 1969, B1.
70. Adam Rome, "'Give Earth a Chance': The Environmental Movement and the Sixties," *Journal of American History* 90, no. 2 (September 2003): 545.
71. Keith Makoto Woodhouse, *Ecocenrists: A History of Radical Environmentalism* (New York: Columbia University Press, 2018); Robert Gottlieb, *Forcing the Spring: The Transformation of the Environmental Movement* (Seattle: Island, 1993); Marc Mowrey and Tim Redmond, *Not in Our Backyards: The People and Events That Shaped America's Modern Environmental Movement* (New York: Morrow, 1993).
72. Bill Sluis, "Seething Citizenry," *Wall Street Journal*, August 27, 1969, 1.
73. Sluis, "Seething Citizenry," 1.
74. Molotch, "Oil in the Velvet Playground," 44.
75. Easton, *Black Tide*, ix. Introduction by Ross Macdonald.
76. Rothman, *Saving the Planet*, 127.
77. Warren Weaver Jr., "The Oil Threat to the Beaches," *New York Times*, February 9, 1969, E2.
78. "The Oil Spill Problem," First Report of the President's Panel on Oil Spills, Executive Office of the President, Office of Science and Technology, Oil Spill Information Center, SBHC

Mss 11, Box 18, Department of Special Collections, Davidson Library, University of California, Santa Barbara (hereafter cited as OSIC).

79. "The Oil Spill Problem," First Report of the President's Panel on Oil Spills, Executive Office of the President, Office of Science and Technology, UCSB, SBHC Mss 11, Box 18, OSIC.

80. "The Oil Spill Problem," First Report of the President's Panel on Oil Spills, Executive Office of the President, Office of Science and Technology (1969), 2.

81. "Offshore Mineral Resources: A Challenge and Opportunity," Second Report of the President's Panel on Oil Spills 1969, Executive Office of the President, Office of Science and Technology, SBHC Mss 11, Box 18, OSIC.

82. Richard Buffum, "A Crude Oil Policy," *Los Angeles Times*, October 8, 1969, E3.

83. Robert L. Jackson, "5 of 11 on Drilling Panel and Oil Firms' Support," *Los Angeles Times*, January 18, 1970, 10.

84. "Oil Report Secrecy Intolerable," *Santa Barbara News-Press*, July 3, 1969.

85. Frank J. Taylor and Earl M. Welty, *Black Bonanza: How an Oil Hunt Grew into the Union Oil Company of California* (New York: McGraw-Hill, 1950), 4–6.

86. "Santa Barbara Disaster," *New York Times*, February 4, 1969, 38.

87. Dick Praul, "Oil Disaster Stirs Anger in Mild Officials," *Santa Monica Times*, February 10, 1969.

88. "Environment: Tragedy in Oil," *Time* 93, no. 7 (February 14, 1969): 14.

89. Macdonald, "Life with the Blob," 51.

90. "Santa Barbara Disaster," *New York Times*, February 4, 1969, 38.

91. Timothy Cooper and Anna Green, "The Torrey Canyon Disaster, Everyday Life, and the 'Greening' of Britain," *Environmental History* 22 (2017): 101–26; Crispin Gill, Frank Booker, and Tony Soper, *The Wreck of the Torrey Canyon* (Newton Abbott: David & Charles, 1967).

92. "Santa Barbara Disaster," *New York Times*, February 4, 1969, 38.

93. Rasa Gustaitis, "The Political Education of Santa Barbara," *Los Angeles Times*, May 10, 1970, A24.

94. Gustaitis, "Political Education of Santa Barbara," A24.

95. "Many across U.S. Rap Oil Disaster," *Santa Barbara News-Press*, May 2, 1969, A6.

96. John Peterson, "Militant Citizens Step Up Fight against Channel Oil Operations," *National Observer*, January 19, 1970.

97. Max Feldman to Richard Nixon, April 14, 1969, SBHC Mss 1, Series 1, Subseries A, Santa Barbara Beautiful, Box 1, CDCC.

98. Peterson, "Militant Citizens."

99. Sluis, "Seething Citizenry," 1.

100. For more on the use of images, particularly photographs, on rising environmental awareness in the United States, see Dunaway, *Seeing Green*; Peter Galison and Caroline A. Jones, "Unknown Quantities: Peter Galison and Caroline A. Jones on Oil Spill Imaging," *ArtForum*, November 2010, 49–51; Kathryn Morse, "There Will Be Birds: Images of Oil Disasters in the Nineteenth and Twentieth Centuries," *Journal of American History* 99, no. 1 (June 2012): 124–34; Caleb Wellum, "The Ambivalent Aesthetics of Oil: Project Documerica and the Energy Crisis in 1970s America," *Environmental History* 22, no. 4 (October 2017): 723–32.

101. Richard E. Meyer, "On How to Ruin a Nice Beach," *Baltimore Sun*, November 23, 1969, K2.

102. "Slick Operators," *Berkeley Barb*, February 14–21, 1969.

103. Dennis Duggan, "Old Line Environmentalists Wake Up in Midst of Mob," *Austin Statesman*, April 9, 1971, 15.

104. Harriet Miller, "Santa Barbara's Ghastly Oil Mess," *Missoulian*, June 13, 1969.
105. Waugh, "That Was the Ooze That Was," W11.
106. Norman K. Sanders, *Stop It! A Guide to Defense of the Environment* (San Francisco: Rinehart, 1972), 3.
107. Wayne A. Phelan, "Letter to the Editor: Area Not So Desecrated," *Santa Barbara News-Press*, May 3, 1969.
108. L. K. Bangerter, "Letter to the Editor: Let's Relieve the Pressure," *Santa Barbara News-Press*, May 2, 1969.
109. Robert Carson, "Letter to the Editor," *Santa Barbara News-Press*, July 7, 1969.
110. Statement of J. Jamison Moore, "Hearings before the Subcommittee," March 13–14, 1970, 180–81.
111. Peterson, "Militant Citizens."
112. Statement of Senator Frank Moss, "Hearings," March 13–14, 1970, 10.
113. "Resort Ads Can't Show Water or Beachfront," 6.
114. Stan Whisenhunt, "Reporter Says Santa Barbara Speaks 'with Forked Tongue,'" *Santa Barbara News-Press*, June 12, 1969, D4.
115. Alvin Weingand and James Bottoms, Letter to the editor of *Los Angeles Times*, June 3, 1969, University of California, Santa Barbara, Special Collections, SBHC Mss 10, GOO Collection, Box 23.
116. John Pastier, "Conservation Group Wins Significant Legislative Battles," *Los Angeles Times*, September 28, 1969, 11.
117. "January 28 Committee Program," SBHC Mss 10, Box 23, GOO; Peterson, "Militant Citizens."
118. "The Santa Barbara Declaration of Environmental Rights," SBHC Mss 10, Box 23, GOO.
119. I am grateful to Finis Dunaway for observing this point.
120. Roderick Nash, *Wilderness and the American Mind* (New Haven: Yale University Press, 2014 [1967]), 345.
121. Nash, *Wilderness and the American Mind*, 346.
122. Macdonald and Easton, "Santa Barbarans Cite an 11th Commandment."
123. Sabin, "Crisis and Continuity," 181.
124. Peterson, "Militant Citizens."
125. "Leaders in Oil Pollution Battle Encouraged by Results of Drive," *Santa Barbara News-Press*, January 27, 1970.
126. "The Rise of Anti-Ecology," *Time*, August 3, 1970, 42. For the history of the environmental justice movement, see Eileen Maura McGurty, "From NIMBY to Civil Rights: The Origins of the Environmental Justice Movement," *Environmental History* 2, no. 3 (July 1997): 301–23; Carl Anthony, "Why African Americans Should Be Environmentalists," *Race, Poverty, and the Environment* 1, no. 1 (April 1990): 5–6; Dorceta Taylor, "Blacks and the Environment: Toward an Explanation of the Concern and Action Gap between Blacks and Whites," *Environment and Behavior* 21, no. 2 (March 1989): 175–205; Robert D. Bullard, *Dumping in Dixie: Race, Class, and Environmental Quality* (London: Routledge, 2000); Andrew Hurley, *Environmental Inequalities: Class, Race, and Industrial Pollution in Gary, Indiana, 1945–1980* (Chapel Hill: University of North Carolina Press, 1995); Ellen Griffith Spears, *Baptized in PCBs: Race, Pollution, and Justice in an All-American Town* (Chapel Hill: University of North Carolina Press, 2014); Giovanna Di Chiro, "Nature as Community: The Convergence of Environment and Social Justice," in *Uncommon Ground: Toward Reinventing Nature*, ed. William Cronon (New York: W. W. Norton, 1995); David Naguib Pellow, *Garbage Wars: The Struggle for Environmental Justice in Chicago*

(Cambridge, MA: MIT Press, 2002). On perceptions of African American support on environmentalism, see Robert Emmet Jones, "Black Concern for the Environment: Myth versus Reality," *Society and Natural Resources: An International Journal* 11, no. 3 (1998): 209–28; Robert Emmet Jones, "Blacks Just Don't Care: Unmasking Popular Stereotypes about Concern for the Environment among African-Americans," *International Journal of Public Administration* 25, nos. 2/3 (2002): 221–51.

127. "Leaders in Oil Pollution Battle Encouraged by Results of Drive," *Santa Barbara News-Press*, January 27, 1970.

128. "Leaders in Oil Pollution Battle Encouraged by Results of Drive."

129. "$9-Million Ends Suit on Oil Spill," *New York Times*, July 24, 1974, 44.

130. Council on Environmental Quality, "Environmental Quality: The First Annual Report of the Council on Environmental Quality," August 1970, 5.

Conclusion

1. Amy Larocca, "What Is It about Montecito?," *New York Times*, July 30, 2023, https://www.nytimes.com/2023/07/30/style/montecito-california.html, accessed April 12, 2024.

2. Zoe Dare Hall, "The Beautiful Discreet Enclaves Where the Super-Rich Congregate," *Financial Times*, June 13, 2014, https://www.ft.com/content/12784962-efdb-11e3-9b4c-00144feabdc0, accessed May 22, 2022.

3. Jimmy Connors, Twitter post, January 2018, 9:23 p.m., https://twitter.com/jimmyconnors/status/950931078100865024, accessed February 2, 2023.

4. Andrew Pridgen, "One of the Wealthiest Enclaves in California Is Uninsurable against Wildfires," *San Francisco Gate* (May 20, 2022), https://www.sfgate.com/centralcoast/article/Montecito-homes-uninsurable-against-fire-17184446.php?IPID=SFGate-HP-CP-Spotlight, accessed May 22, 2022; Rachel Sherman, *Uneasy Street: The Anxieties of Affluence* (Princeton, NJ: Princeton University Press, 2017).

5. Larocca, "What Is it about Montecito?"

6. Volker C. Radeloff et al., "Rapid Growth of the US Wildland–Urban Interface Raises Wildfire Risk," *PNAS* 115, no. 13 (March 27, 2018): 3314–19.

7. Damian Carrington, "The Anthropocene Epoch: Scientists Declare Dawn of Human Influenced Age," *Guardian*, August 29, 2016, https://www.theguardian.com/environment/2016/aug/29/declare-anthropocene-epoch-experts-urge-geological-congress-human-impact-earth, accessed May 23, 2022.

8. For an exploration of this critique, see Jenny Price, *Stop Saving the Planet! An Environmentalism Manifesto* (New York: W.W. Norton, 2021), 13-14.

9. Karl Jacoby, *Crimes against Nature: Squatters, Poachers, Thieves, and the Hidden History of American Conservation* (Berkeley: University of California Press, 2014 [2001]), 198.

10. Matthew L. Wald, "Automakers Use New Technology to Beef Up Muscle, Not Mileage," *New York Times*, March 30, 2006, A1, quoted in Thomas Borstelmann, *The 1970s: A New Global History from Civil Rights to Economic Inequality* (Princeton, NJ: Princeton University Press, 2013), 57.

11. Meg Jacobs, *Panic at the Pump: The Energy Crisis and the Transformation of American Politics in the 1970s* (New York: Farrar, Strauss, & Giroux, 2017), 6.

12. Sterling G. Slappey, "Heading Off an Energy Crisis," *Nation's Business*, July 1971, 26.

13. "Oil: No Need to Scrape the Bottom of the Barrel," *Nation's Business*, July 1971, 28.

14. Borstelmann, *1970s*, 156–57.

15. Caroline Petrow-Cohen, "Residents in Wealthy Montecito Are Using Boulders to Block Hikers' Parking, Bringing Warnings," *Los Angeles Times*, April 4, 2024, https://www.latimes.com/california/story/2024-04-04/residents-of-santa-barbara-county-neighborhood-montecito-using-boulders-to-block-parking, accessed April 12, 2024.

16. Haley Smith, "'Hidden' No More: Coastal Commission OKs New Public Path to Malibu Beach," *Los Angeles Times*, June 7, 2023, https://www.latimes.com/california/story/2023-06-07/coastal-commission-oks-new-public-path-to-malibu-beach, accessed April 12, 2024.

Index

aesthetics: benefits of, 11, 136; of charm, 18, 41, 50, 91; expression of, 36; features of, 32–34, 45, 47, 54, 58, 80, 131, 163; goals, 19; purposes, 31, 84, 135; quality of, 3–4, 28, 30, 40, 53, 57, 75, 162; of Santa Barbara, 4; uniform, 8, 32, 35, 53, 61, 70
air quality, 120
American Museum of Natural History, 90
architects, 20–24, 26–27, 29–34, 38, 40–41, 50, 52, 63, 65–70, 87, 93, 96–97, 99, 101
architecture, 7, 18–20, 23–25, 35, 51, 57, 70, 74, 98; Californian, 33, 41, 52; commercial, 8, 27; domestic, 4, 44, 67; Japanese, 29, 31; Mission style, 31; Spanish Colonial Revival, 3, 13, 36, 38–40, 95, 162; Western, 30
art, 23, 30, 33, 39–40, 42, 63, 75–76, 96, 128, 159; and art education, 56, 59–60, 74; and Carnegie, 59; and civic politics, 61, 67; community, 57; and Community Arts Association (CAA), 45, 56, 58–60, 74, 79, 149; language of, 67; programs, 61; and Santa Barbara, 1, 14; and science, 88; and social role, 58; social value of, 56

Better Homes Week, 10, 45, 68–71, 73, 96
Boston Transcript, 18

Carnegie Corporation, 58–60
Carnegie Foundation, 25
civics (the civic): and architecture, 8; "art feeling" of, 44; authority, 79; and belonging, 41; and beautification schemes, 8, 14, 45, 69, 74, 99, 122; civic duty, 61; civic organizations, 8, 47; spirit of, 29; and identity, 51, 56; and improvement, 67, 74, 85, 87, 150; and leaders, 3, 19–20, 28, 84, 100; pride in, 18, 94; symbolism of, 76

climate, 21, 24–25, 31, 41, 44, 47, 51–53, 65, 67, 78, 80, 83–84, 97, 134; Californian, 40, 52, 76, 93, 130; "Cytherean," 39; Mediterranean, 3; Mexican, 40; and plants, 96; subtropical, 98; temperate, 86, 104; and topography, 92; tropical, 67, 82
climate change, 11, 160–62
Community Arts Association (CAA), 45, 47, 50–51, 56–61, 65, 67–68, 70, 74
conservation, 5, 7–9, 34, 43, 79, 85, 89–90, 94, 101, 110, 117, 133–34, 141
conservationists, 84, 88, 133, 135, 142, 152, 162
construction, 13, 15, 24, 28, 30–32, 38, 51–52, 54, 61, 63, 68, 71, 79, 90, 115, 119–20, 122; and development, 138; highway, 105; housing, 104, 106–7

Darnton, Robert, 6
development, 8, 30, 69, 87, 92–93, 104–6, 111, 119, 123, 126, 137; and architecture, 38, 40, 56–58, 67; and California, 44; and Community Arts Association (CAA), 61; cultural, 86; economic, 23–24, 28, 43, 82; and environmentalism, 6, 14, 6; housing, 103, 109–10, 122, 125; national, 19; oil, 133–34, 142, 147, 158; real estate, 21; resource, 134; social, 9, 43; suburban, 105–7; urban, 9, 14–15, 44, 49–50, 53, 67, 102, 111, 138
domestic architecture, 67
domestication, 10, 15
domestic conditions, 4, 122
domestic customs, 71
domesticity, 5–6, 45, 79, 86, 161
domestic labor, 56, 73
domestic landscape, 74
domestic realm, 7, 14, 45, 47, 79, 162
domestic spaces, 9, 61, 63, 87, 98

earthquakes, 15, 17–20, 24–31, 34–36, 38, 41–42, 51, 71, 162
Easton, Robert, 141, 143, 156
economics: agenda of, 68; associations, 79; benefits added, 61, 65, 67, 134; and change, 16, 33–34, 47, 105–6, 141; conditions of, 88, 149–50, 164–65; and growth, 5, 108, 142, 152, 158; health of, 11; interests, 131, 134; and investment, 4, 19, 153; and life, 111; and opportunities, 109; progress in, 117; prosperity of, 50, 115, 144; and rights, 9; value of, 5, 57, 59, 71, 85, 92, 154
environmentalism, 8, 10, 13, 119, 126, 155, 159, 163; and activism, 163; and climate change, 11; conservationism, 8; development of, 6, 14; and Earth Day, 130; and environmentalists, 102, 104, 143, 147, 158; extreme, 164; growth of, 3–4, 7; homeowners, 5; and ideology, 109; legitimacy of, 118; ownership, 5–6, 9, 16, 131, 161–62, 165; and Santa Barbara oil spill, 4; tools of, 157
environmental quality, 4–6, 8–11, 15, 47, 78, 103–4, 117, 119, 131, 134, 139, 145, 155, 157–58, 161–65

garden clubs, 79, 98
gardening, 78, 85, 93–98, 115
gardens, 45, 60, 63, 70–71, 76, 79, 83–84, 87, 90–91, 94–97, 99; botanic, 15, 78, 85, 92–93, 100, 162; public, 118
Garden Street, 73

Hardin, Garrett, 13, 104, 112–15, 123, 142
Harding, Warren, 68
Hoffmann, Bernhard, 27, 29, 32, 35, 50–51, 53, 56
Hoffmann, Gertrude, 27
home economics, 51, 86–88
homeownership: 10, 14–15, 45, 47, 61, 63, 65, 68–69, 71, 75, 103–4, 106, 109; advocates of, 6; affluent, 3; and culture, 4; and environment, 162–63; and garden projects, 8; individual, 116; private, 74, 111
housing, 16, 52, 58, 108, 115, 117; advocates of, 6; affordable, 102, 106–7; authority, 107; conditions, 54, 67, 69; construction, 104; developments, 103, 109–10, 119, 125; multifamily, 104, 121, 123; programs, 68; quality, 52, 63, 68, 73; and segregation, 106; shortages, 70; suburban, 109; units, 105
Hutchins, Maynard Robert, 101, 103

international environmentalism, 3

landscape, 3, 42, 74, 91–92, 98, 103–5, 109, 111, 117, 120, 135, 162; beauty of, 23; burned, 12; designers, 87; domestic, 74; and gardens, 70; modern, 13; racialized, 15; technological, 116; urban, 4; Western, 23
landscape architects, 70, 93, 96–97, 99

national, the: boundaries, 85; characteristics, 24, 30; disasters, 155; histories, 20; and nationalism, 15; movements, 14; and organizations, 45; national parks, 89, 108; national suffrage, 56; and power, 6; and territorial expansion, 8, 38, 45
natural, the: 6, 9–10, 13–14, 24, 38, 113, 131, 162; disasters, 18, 41, 161; and the environment, 3, 19, 23, 34, 47, 51, 79, 96–97, 116, 119, 134, 152; landscapes, 92, 134; natural beauty, 1, 4, 50, 57, 61, 84–85, 96–97, 104, 107, 113, 131, 135–37, 141–43, 146, 150–51; natural selection, 89, 91; and resources, 5, 44, 84, 94, 104, 127, 133, 137, 144–47, 152, 158; surroundings, 3–4, 8, 15, 19, 28, 44, 47, 49, 57, 95, 108, 111, 118, 123

"plantation negro," 90
plant cultivation, 4, 63, 69–71, 76, 78, 84–86, 95–96
plant migration, 91
plants, 15, 76–80, 82–83, 88, 90–94, 97, 99, 162, 165
politics and the political: authority, 10; culture, 4, 47–48; leaders, 4, 68, 151; power, 57, 120, 144, 150; rights, 9
pollution, 6–8, 11, 59, 87, 99, 113, 117, 131, 142, 145, 149, 154, 156–57; oil, 130, 144, 150, 152
public, the: accessibility of, 125; environments, 87; interest, 117, 146; life, 56, 92; officials, 53, 99; the public good, 53, 60, 104, 131, 135, 162; and public opinion, 94, 97; public relations, 120, 142, 154; regulations, 47; services, 121; spaces, 125; structures, 3, 63, 67, 69; values, 99

quality of life, 4, 8, 49, 63, 110, 113, 115, 121, 130, 137, 142, 150–51, 158, 164–65

racial hierarchy, 40, 44, 79–80
racial identity, 30
racial inequality, 9, 15
racial segregation, 8, 54, 106, 110
reconstruction, 19–20, 28–29, 35–36, 38, 162
Republican Party, 16, 103, 137, 140, 143–44, 149
republican values, 56

Santa Barbara (CA), 14, 21, 25, 29, 51, 61, 67, 74, 84, 92, 99–100, 106, 110, 130, 163; and Architects Advisory Council, 32; and architecture, 27, 44, 56; and Asian population, 35; beautification of, 59; and Black residents, 71, 73; and boosters, 38; Botanic Garden, 93; building program, 65; and celebrities, 12; Channel, 1, 128, 132–37, 140, 142–43, 146–47, 153–54, 157–58; and Chinatown, 36; and Chumash, 21; and citizenship, 83; City Schools, 98; civic leaders, 20; College, 106; and conservation, 94; County, 12, 138, 148; development, 23, 38, 49–50, 102; downtown,

65, 70; and earthquakes, 29, 34, 41; and the environment, 3, 10–11, 47, 102, 117–18, 122, 136, 141; and environmentalism, 5, 13, 102, 139, 155–56; evolution of, 14; Garden Club, 94–96; Harbor, 139; homeowners, 111, 119, 126; and immigrants, 76; and landscape, 3; Mexican community, 71; Mission, 118; and Montecito, 97, 160; and Roderick Nash, 9; and norms, 8; and Herbert Nunn, 17; oil spill, 1, 4, 144, 151–52, 159; and poverty, 106; and Republican Party, 16; residents of, 1, 13, 120, 126, 131, 150, 161–62; and Santa Ynez, 36; and segregation, 73; and Spain, 8–9, 20, 24, 31; and Thomas Aquinas College, 11; and urbanism, 53, 104; and white residents, 45, 75; Women's Club, 71, 123
Santa Barbara Botanic Garden, 93
Santa Barbara Daily News, 27
Santa Barbara Garden Club, 94–96
Santa Barbara Morning Press, 54

Santa Barbara News-Press, 34, 53, 122, 125–26, 137, 147, 153
Sierra Club Bulletin, 1, 141
soil quality, 82
Sollen, Robert, 137
suburban growth, 126
suburban housing, 109, 112
suburbanization, 6, 9, 48, 104, 111, 126
suburban sprawl, 4

urban, the: beauty of, 28, 40; community, 10; conditions, 19, 45, 54, 104; design, 4, 15, 19, 45, 51, 58, 87; economy, 48; environments, 34, 119; landscape, 4; planning, 50, 110; reconstruction, 28; settlements, 13–14, 50, 105; space, 58; uniformity, 65
urban-built environment, 3
urbanism, 53, 59
urbanization, 47–48, 70, 73, 84, 88, 92, 141